LGBTQ VOICES IN EDUCATION

LGBTQ Voices in Education: Changing the Culture of Schooling addresses the ways in which teachers can meet the needs of LGBTQ students and improve the culture surrounding gender, sexuality, and identity issues in formal learning environments. Written by experts from a variety of backgrounds including educational foundations, leadership, cultural studies, literacy, criminology, theology, media assessment, and more, these chapters are designed to help educators find the inspiration and support they need to become allies and advocates of queer students, whose safety, well-being, and academic performance are regularly and often systemically threatened. Emphasizing socially just curricula, supportive school climates, and transformative educational practices, this innovative book is applicable to K–12, college-level, and graduate settings, and beyond.

Veronica E. Bloomfield is Adjunct Faculty in the College of Educational Studies at Chapman University, USA.

Marni E. Fisher is Adjunct Faculty in the College of Educational Studies at Chapman University, USA.

LGBTQ VOICES IN EDUCATION

Changing the Culture of Schooling

Edited by Veronica E. Bloomfield and Marni E. Fisher

Routledge
Taylor & Francis Group

NEW YORK AND LONDON

First published 2016
by Routledge
711 Third Avenue, New York, NY 10017

and by Routledge
2 Park Square, Milton Park, Abingdon, Oxon, OX14 4RN

Routledge is an imprint of the Taylor & Francis Group, an informa business

© 2016 Taylor & Francis

Library of Congress Cataloging in Publication Data
Names: Bloomfield, Veronica E., editor. | Fisher, Marni E., editor.
Title: LGBTQ voices in education : changing the culture of schooling / edited by Veronica E. Bloomfield and Marni E. Fisher.
Description: New York, NY : Routledge, 2016. | Includes bibliographical references and index.
Identifiers: LCCN 2015037576| ISBN 9781138187085 (hardback) | ISBN 9781138187092 (pbk.) | ISBN 9781315643403 (ebook)
Subjects: LCSH: Lesbian students. | Gay students. | Bisexual students. | Transgender youth--Education | Sexual minorities--Education. | Homosexuality and education.
Classification: LCC LC2575 .L53 2016 | DDC 370.86/64--dc23
LC record available at http://lccn.loc.gov/2015037576

ISBN: 978-1-138-18708-5 (hbk)
ISBN: 978-1-138-18709-2 (pbk)
ISBN: 978-1-315-64340-3 (ebk)

Paperback cover image: © Eric Nava
Typeset in Bembo
by Saxon Graphics Ltd, Derby

Printed and bound in the United States of America by Publishers Graphics, LLC on sustainably sourced paper.

CONTENTS

DEDICATION

We appreciate the contributions each author has made to this volume and are confident the reader will find a wealth of information, resources, and insights in the chapters that follow. We also want to honor this book's origin and the mentor who gave us the opportunity to serve as co-editors.

This book is the result of the hard work, dedication, and commitment of Dr. Anna V. Wilson. We met her as graduate students at Chapman University where Anna taught for the College of Educational Studies. Anna holds doctorates in criminology and education, taught over 35 years, wrote over 100 scholarly articles, made numerous conference presentations, and contributed to university life in a variety of ways. Along her academic journey, she underwent a personal transformation when she came out as a lesbian. This affected her scholarship, her theorizing, and the courses she both taught and developed along the way. She has long been established as an LGBTQ activist and scholar.

Issues of justice, equity, and diversity have been ever-present threads throughout Anna's career and scholarship. She had a long history of involvement and participation in the civil rights movement and the women's movements of the 1960s. More recently, she was involved in the movement for marriage equality. Based on her experience as a lesbian scholar, she wanted to develop a book that addressed issues of LGBTQ students and teaching from a variety of perspectives. Drawing upon her large network of colleagues and associates, she made the call for contributors, and received so many responses she developed an outline for a second volume. At this time, Veronica was her graduate assistant, and Anna invited her to be co-editor on the book. This invitation epitomized Anna's approach to teaching and learning pedagogy embodying openness, innovation, and inclusion.

Issues of marginalization were a significant part of Anna's tenure, as for many years she was the only "out" professor on campus. Though serving as a beacon of hope and providing safe space for both colleagues and students who were LGBTQ (and their allies), she experienced social shunning, critique, and felt her personal and academic safety threatened at times.

As this book traveled toward final editing, Anna brought Marni, her last graduate assistant, on board to the project. When Anna retired, she was committed to the completion of the book, and it was more important that the book be published than it bear her name.

We honor Anna for her strengths, her scholarship, and her courage. Having benefited from her guidance and mentoring, we are proud to carry on her legacy.

FOREWORD

Kris De Pedro

One prominent narrative pervading our media and public policy is that schools are failing children. The emergence of the standards movement and federal accountability policies aimed to raise the academic excellence of all children, especially the most vulnerable students. Unfortunately, policy makers utilize standards and accountability policies to punish schools for not meeting externally imposed standards of academic achievement. There are scholars and educators, such as myself, who have made it their life's work to engage in a different dialogue, which identifies schools as community-based institutions. These institutions can support and affirm the most marginalized, oppressed, and traumatized youth in our society.

Schools were my sanctuary. As a questioning student in high school, and, later on, a queer student in college and graduate school, schools were places I could be my authentic self. This was especially true in high school. I attended an all-male Jesuit high school in Los Angeles in the mid-1990s. At the time, being gay, queer, or transgender was still evolving in the mainstream culture, as seen in television shows (e.g. *Ellen, Will & Grace*) and music (all of Madonna's catalog). A queer culture was also emerging in my own high school. We didn't have a gay–straight alliance (GSA) or any physical space officially devoted to queer youth, and I went through four years of college-prep level high school coursework with no mention of anything queer. The sanctuary I speak of did not exist in our campus chapel. Instead, it existed in informal spaces and grew organically. In my sophomore year, I joined the yearbook committee and had many friends in theater. In yearbook, neither my friends nor I self-identified as queer (though half of us are now); however, our talk was queer and, I would add, filled with joy. In the presence of Ms. Y, our faculty advisor, my yearbook friends and I had a daily ritual—lip syncing to Brandy and Monica's "The Boy is Mine" and/or anything by Lauryn Hill in a "Paris is Burning" meets Downtown Los Angeles Catholic school boy kind of way. We also "read" and/or "threw shade" at one another on a daily basis—in a similar way to what we now see among queer men and heterosexual women on *The Real Housewives of Atlanta* and *Fashion Queens* on Bravo. Ms. Y would laugh with us each time, making it safe to be ourselves.

My theater friends self-identified as gay and were very out. Before every first Friday Mass, we drove to the Old Pantry Café in Downtown Los Angeles for breakfast. Though I didn't know the words, I marveled at their beautiful voices as they sang musical numbers from *Rent*. One clear morning, I noticed their attractive faces adorned with eyeliner they had purchased at Claire's in the Beverly Center, and I couldn't stop cracking up when they yelled and hollered, "Oh My God, he's so hot!" at the Calvin Klein model on a large billboard around the corner from our high school campus. Apparently, they marveled at beautiful men in magazines all the time in their CLC—their Christian Life Community—moderated by Ms. T, our high school's LGBTQ-ally. In these spaces, I felt a true sense of belonging. Those were my GSAs. The freedom to enact my gender expression and fluid sexual identity was there, if I wanted to.

Fast forward almost two decades—college degrees, life in New York City, failures and successes—I am now a professor about an hour away from my beloved high school, in a serious same-gender relationship, coping with homophobia with a biological family I love, and navigating personal and work life. Recently, I've started to mentor youth, passing forward the acceptance I'd gained from my high school friends in yearbook and theater. A friend introduced my partner and I to "Jay," a 16-year-old boy from a rural town 90 miles east of Los Angeles. Unlike my high school sanctuary, Jay does not have the freedom to enact his emerging gender expression and sexual identity. When he came out, both parents called him a "faggot," a "fudgepacker," and other homophobic slurs. In secret, Jay wears heels, dresses, indulges in makeup, and can do the choreography of Beyonce's "7/11" better than anyone else. Also, one of our favorite activities is talking about boys he likes and "hot" male celebrities like Justin Bieber. We offer him verbal affirmation and encouragement, telling him that his existence is a gift. With his parents and at school, he is forced to wear hypermasculine clothing. I am reminded from time to time that he is still a child who deserves the right to be free and explore his gender expression, yet, because he is in a homophobic family and school environment, he is encountering one of the trappings of adulthood—the need to "fit in."

Jay's current struggle reminds me of the basic human right of feeling affirmed and loved unconditionally. There are queer youth throughout the country, who are rejected by family and friends, and have no sanctuaries to be their authentic selves.

Jay's current challenge is why this volume is so critical to the lives of LGBTQ youth. We must remind ourselves in this celebratory stage of the LGBTQ civil rights movement (i.e. SCOTUS and marriage) that throughout the country there are queer youth who have minimal family support, have experienced the trauma of rejection from parents and religious communities, have no outlets to freely express their authentic selves, and have few to no opportunities to interact with other LGBTQ youth in a safe space. As rejected young adults, they may seek affirmation and support in toxic relationships, high-risk sexual encounters, abusive partners, drug use, and addiction. Schools are critical to the lives of queer youth. With supportive and affirming teachers, schools have the potential to be spaces of healing and recovery from LGBTQ-related trauma and oppression.

Fortunately, students like Jay have teachers who create safe spaces for them, so they can be inspired to live out their dreams and develop into their authentic selves. A national movement to make all schools safe and inclusive for LGBTQ youth has been underway for the past decade, and teachers play a critical role. There are teachers who cite research from the Gay, Lesbian, and Straight Education Network (GLSEN) and literature in education and psychology. This research has identified four evidence-based strategies for LGBTQ inclusive schools. These include enumerated anti-bullying and discrimination policies, LGBTQ-inclusive curriculum, and the presence of a student-led gay-straight alliance can make schools protective and safe spaces for LGBTQ youth. When these components are in place, students like Jay, in theory, can experience being affirmed and accepted.

As scholars and practitioners in education know, translating research to practice on a large scale is challenging to say the least, especially when we enact reform for marginalized student populations. A quick review of the educational reform literature would attribute this failure to a lack of organizational capacity, the dearth of financial resources, the need for identification systems, a lack of accountability, and so forth. However, in my own work with teachers and principals, I have found that two critical barriers to change are fatigue and lack of knowledge. The experience of many educators, including myself, is one of being overworked and overwhelmed—test preparation, Common Core standards, maintaining relationships with students' parents, daily assessments, and the list goes on. Principals navigate district priorities, bureaucratic processes, and the unique challenges facing their school communities. All too often, teachers and principals have the intention to support LGBTQ youth, but lack both capacity and knowledge of concrete strategies to integrate into their daily practices. Where do educators find the time, energy, and knowledge to make schools safe for LGBTQ students?

In my own work with LGBTQ youth, I need constant inspiration and constant learning to continue my advocacy work and scholarship for LGBTQ youth. Collectively, the chapters in this volume provide educators with inspiration and knowledge. Educators and scholar-practitioners throughout the country have written pieces on how educators can make concrete changes to their own practices, policies, and school cultures. These chapters will instill a sense of urgency among educators to start GSAs in their schools, to include

LGBTQ issues in daily conversations and curricula, and mentor queer youth, as they encounter homophobia and/or transphobia from peers and teachers. As a result of these daily changes to practice and awareness, youth in situations like Jay's will have consistent safe spaces, where they have the freedom to be their authentic selves.

PREFACE

Entering the Conversation:
Dancing with Dragons

Veronica E. Bloomfield and Marni E. Fisher

In this book, most chapters address, acknowledge, and intentionally incorporate issues pertaining to LGBTQ identities in schools. The authors break silences and social taboos, not only by specifically addressing LGBTQ issues, but also by speaking of gender, sexuality, and sexual orientation candidly and openly in educational settings. Although focused on LGBTQ issues, this book is written for any educator who seeks support and understanding in creating safe and thought-provoking learning environments. It is a book for LGBTQ students and teachers, as well as their colleagues, families, allies, and friends. We hope many people will read these chapters and be inspired to teach a lesson, start a club, or host an event that would otherwise have seemed intimidating or unattainable. We hope readers realize being an ally for LGBTQ youth does not have to be a lonely or scary venture. Our students count on us to make schools a safe place. This is true for students with cultural and linguistic diversity, from a variety of socioeconomic backgrounds, with differing abilities, from non-traditional family structures, and LGBTQ students who face the highest rate of bullying, harassment, and threats of violence on campus. Given the current hostile contexts for queer youth, your presence and practices inspired by this book could prove life-saving.

We chose the imagery of dancing with dragons because it evokes a number of images. "The phrase 'here there be dragons' [commonly] refers to the spaces beyond the edges of the map, the unknown, and the uncharted waters" (Fisher 2013, 18), which anything pertaining to LGBTQ is all too often in education: considered to be off the map, unknown or unknowable, ignored, suppressed, and deliberately uncharted. Dragons can also:

> represent the deep structure of education. Yes, dragons can represent strength, but they can also represent ruthlessness, oppression, and

destruction. Even if we slay the dragon, his[1] bones remain embedded in our educational system. A way must be found to tame him, lure him to sleep, and/or transcend him.

(18)

Paired with these deep structures are the hegemonic patterns of heteronormativity, trapping us within a dragon bone maze of binary and arborescent[2] roles and behaviors. The dragon may represent our fears: fears of educators about challenging and changing the status quo, of LGBTQ students and teachers who feel they *must* hide and/or suppress a vital part of who they are, of everyone who fears difference and change; "[we] can see him there, one eye slit open, watching me lazily to see what [we] will do" (18). The dragon can also be within us: that inner voice, strength, and power to create change.

The term "queer" also has a number of connotations, ranging from derogatory referents to positive affirmations. As described by Danné Davis in Chapter 8:

often among progressive thinkers and radical individuals, queer is an affirming referent ... In academic contexts, "queer" is used to trouble taken-for-granted epistemologies and customaries (Kumashiro 2002, Mayo 2010) pushing for new understandings and intersections of being and identity critical to education (Meyer 2007).

(117)

Thus, our queer dragons challenge us to explore the unknown, trouble the established, and discover new understandings. We dare you to join us on this journey: chart the uncharted, create spaces for the silenced to speak, challenge the educational dragon bones, and find your inner dragon so you, too, might dance with queer dragons.

Key Terms for the Conversation

There are a number of terms specific to discussions revolving around LGBTQ issues used throughout the book. Entering the conversation about LGBTQ issues in educational settings, we offer the following definitions for major LGBTQ and social justice terms.

LGBTQ Terms

For many years, the acronym LGB was used to signify the Lesbian, Gay, and Bisexual community. However, just as the world is not divided into two simple definitions of "male" and female," neither is it divided into a simple definition of "gay" or "straight." As expansions in the area of sexuality and gender identity have been understood, additional letters have been added to incorporate a wider variety of categories. For example, LGBTQ, which we commonly use throughout this book, might stand for Lesbian, Gay, Bisexual, Transgender or Transsexual, and Queer or Questioning. Other acronyms might be GLBT, LGBT, LGBTQIA, LGBTTIQQ, LGBTTIQQ2SA with the letters standing for Lesbian, Gay, Bisexual, Transsexual, Transgender, Intersex, Queer, Questioning, 2-Spirited, Asexual, and Allies. Here are some of the common definitions:

Lesbian	A lesbian is "a female-identified person who is attracted romantically, physically, or emotionally to another female-identified person" (TSA 2011, para. 1).
Gay	While TSA identifies "gay" as "a male-identified person who is attracted romantically, physically, or emotionally to another male-identified person" (para. 2), the *Oxford Dictionary* (2014b) notes under usage, that the term "gay in its modern sense typically refers to men ... but in some contexts it can be used of both men and women."
Bisexual	Someone who is bisexual is "a person who is attracted romantically, physically, or emotionally to both men and women" (TSA 2011, para. 3).
Transgender	"Transgender" is a term "for people whose gender identity, expression or behavior is different from those typically associated with their assigned sex at birth." Transgender is a broad term and is good for non-transgender people to use. "Trans" is shorthand for "transgender." (Note: Transgender is correctly used as an adjective, not a noun, thus "transgender people" is appropriate but "transgenders" is often viewed as disrespectful) (NCTE 2014, para. 1).
Transsexual	Transsexual is considered "an older term for people whose gender identity is different from their assigned sex at birth who seek to transition from male to female or female to male. Many do not prefer this term because it is thought to sound overly clinical" (NCTE 2014, para. 5). As an option, "trans★," with an asterisk, has also been used by Sam Killerman (2014), as "an umbrella term that refers to all of the identities within the gender identity spectrum ... the asterisk makes special note in an effort to include all non-cisgender gender identities, including transgender, transsexual, transvestite, genderqueer, genderfluid, non-binary ... genderless, agender, non-gendered, third gender, two-spirit, bigender, and trans man and trans woman" (para. 1).
Two Spirited	"A Two Spirit person is a male-bodied or female-bodied person with a masculine or feminine essence. Two Spirits can cross social gender roles, gender expression, and sexual orientation" (NativeOUT 2014, para. 5). Although indigenous

	groups have names for two-spirit individuals on their own languages, this term was adopted to acknowledge the place of honor and purpose that LGBTQ persons have held historically in tribal communities.
Queer	Queer is "an umbrella term which embraces a variety of sexual preferences, orientations, and habits of those who do not adhere to the heterosexual and cisgender majority. The term queer includes, but is not exclusive to lesbians, gay men, bisexuals, transpeople, and intersex persons. Traditionally, this term is derogatory and hurtful, however, many people who do not adhere to sexual and/or gender norms use it to self-identify in a positive way" (TSA 2011, para. 4). The term "queer" might be used by "anyone who a) wants to identify as queer and b) who feels somehow outside of the societal norms in regards to gender or sexuality" (PFLAG 2014, para. 3).
Questioning	This term makes space for individuals who are exploring aspects of their gender and sexuality and have not settled on a particular category of identification. It is an intentionally undefined and ambiguous term.
Intersex	The Tahoe Safe Alliance (TSA) (2011) defines someone who is "intersex" as having "physical sex characteristics [that] are not categorized as exclusively male or exclusively female" (para. 6). The National Center for Transgender Equality (NCTE) (2014) defines "intersex" as "a term used for people who are born with a reproductive or sexual anatomy and/or chromosome pattern that does not seem to fit typical definitions of male or female. Intersex conditions are also known as differences of sex development (DSD)" (para. 18).
Asexual	Someone who is "asexual" is "a person who is not attracted to anyone, or a person who does not have a sexual orientation" (TSA 2011, para. 7).
Agender	"Agender" might also be used either independently, or within the "trans" umbrella; "'Agender' by definition means 'someone without gender' … a person who identifies as agender doesn't feel as if they belong anywhere on the gender spectrum at all" (Stiffler 2014, paras. 5–6). There is a distinction between "asexual" and "agender," however. While someone who is "asexual" lacks sexual attraction to anyone, someone who is "agender" is a person "with the same complex set of desires and attractions as anyone else" (para. 9), they just do not identify with a specific *gender*.
Ally	An "ally" is "a person who does not identify as LGBTQIA, but supports the rights and safety of those who do" (TSA 2011, para. 8).[3]

Clearly, the conversation about what the acronym "LGBTQ" represents can, and should be, complex. For the sake of consistency, this book uses "LGBTQ" throughout to represent all variations of the acronym.

While these terms are current norms, as the multiplicity of acronyms imply, none of these are complete definitions, nor do people who identify as LGBTQ fall easily into one category. One particularly useful explanation of this is Killerman's (2015) Genderbread Person from ItsPronouncedMETROsexual. com, which illustrates how each person might fall on a continuum within the various attributes that define gender. Killerman defines these as: (1) gender identity, which is "how you, in your head, define your gender, based on how much you align (or don't align) with what you understand to be the options for gender"; (2) gender expressions, which is "the way you present gender, through your actions, dress, and demeanor, and how those presentations are interpreted based on your gender norms"; (3) biological sex, which is "the physical sex characteristics you're born with and develop, including genitalia, body shape, voice pitch, body hair, hormones, chromosomes, etc."; (4) sexual attraction; and (5) romantic attraction (see Figure 0.1).

There are a number of other common terms throughout the book outside the definitions of the LGBTQ acronym. Some of the discussions revolve around gender, various "hetero" terms referring to heterosexuality, and homophobia.

Gender is a complicated term. The common understanding is that there are two genders, but the scientific reality is as broad as the color spectrum (Stiffler

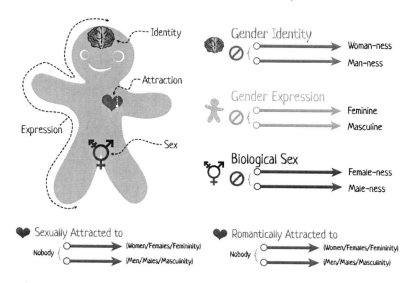

FIGURE 0.1 The Genderbread Person

2014). According to the World Health Organization, "'Sex' refers to the biological and physiological characteristics that define men and women. 'Gender' refers to the socially constructed roles, behaviors, activities, and attributes that a given society considers appropriate for men and women" (Stiffler 2014, para. 1).

Some "hetero" terms include the definition of **heteronormativity**, "a world view that promotes heterosexuality as the normal or preferred sexual orientation" (*Oxford Dictionaries* 2014c); heterosexuality as a given instead of being one of many possibilities, and heterosexist/heterosexism, which are a system of attitudes, bias, and discrimination in favor of opposite-sex sexuality and relationships. It can include the presumption that other people are heterosexual or that opposite-sex attractions and relationships are the only norm and therefore superior. Another term used is "cisgender": "Denoting or relating to a person whose self-identity conforms with the gender that corresponds to their biological sex; not transgender" (*Oxford Dictionaries* 2014a).

Homophobia is a fear of or bias against homosexuality and homosexuals and can also refer to social stigmas against homosexuality. Homophobia can manifest as negative feelings and attitudes toward non-heterosexual behavior, identities, and relationships. Examples include jokes, physical attacks, workplace discrimination, and negative media images.

Social Justice Terms

Social justice is based on a vision of equitable distribution of wealth, opportunities, resources, and privileges within given society. Under these conditions, people are able to fully realize their potential, have agency in the direction of their lives, and not be dependent upon external sources for personal fulfillment. This term is widely used in a myriad of fields from theology to sociology. Here it is discussed in terms of its relevance to the field of education. Social justice, being concerned with diversity, which "generally includes topics such as age, disability, gender, sexual orientation, gender orientation, social class, spirituality and religion, lifestyle, health status, vulnerability, and other personality features" (Smith, Ng, and Brinson 2008, citing Hays 1996), is relevant when discussing issues pertaining to LGBTQ teachers and student in schools, and especially when it comes to the topic of curriculum. Related terms such as critical pedagogy, critical literacy, democratic classrooms, and transgressive teaching emerge throughout the book.

Critical pedagogy is the inclusion and application of social justice and the application of praxis, as described by Freire (1970/2005), which is the practical application of theory (*Merriam-Webster* 2013), and the integration of reflection and action required to transform the world and change oppression (Freire 1970/2005). "The role of critical pedagogy is not to extinguish tensions. The prime role … is to lead students to recognize various tensions and enable them to deal effectively with them" (Freire and Macedo 2009, 355). According to Kellner

(2000), "Critical pedagogy considers how education can provide individuals with the tools to better themselves and strengthen democracy, to create a more egalitarian and just society, and thus to deploy education in a process of progressive social change" (197).

Critical literacy "encourages readers to question, explore, or challenge the power relationships that exist between authors and readers. It examines issues of power and promotes reflection, transformative change, and action" (Norris, Lucas, and Prudhoe 2012, 59). According to Coffey (2014):

> Critical literacy is the ability to read texts in an active, reflective manner in order to better understand power, inequality, and injustice in human relationships … The development of critical literacy skills enables people to interpret messages in the modern world through a critical lens and challenge the power relations within those messages. Teachers who facilitate the development of critical literacy encourage students to interrogate societal issues and institutions like family, poverty, education, equity, and equality in order to critique the structures that serve as norms.
>
> (paras 1–2)

Through this, critical literacy also demonstrates how these "norms" do *not* represent the experiences for all members of society.

A **democratic classroom** is one that models democratic values and processes, respects individuals, and gives students a voice in decision making. Democratic classrooms recognize that students bring a wealth of background, history, and culture to the classroom and build upon this, "supporting and affirming students' identities *while at the same time* encouraging students to become members of the larger community" (Nieto 2003, 39). As a form of "associated living" (Dewey 1916), democracy considers the good of the community (Sehr 1997), "making the classroom a democratic setting where everyone feels a responsibility to contribute is a central goal of transformative pedagogy" (hooks 1994, 39). This entails developing classroom community (Apple and Beane 1995) and student relationships (Bishop and Berryman 2006) while ensuring students have a space where their voices may be heard. By being given freedom with power balanced with responsibility, students are given a chance to develop intrinsic motivation, which "counts the most because what students do when they can do what they want to do is what really matters" (Eisner 2002, 581).

While a transgression involves a violation of accepted or imposed boundaries, especially those of a social accepted nature, **teaching transgressively** means that teacher and student intentionally cross socially constructed boundaries to engage in critically conscious dialogue about the status quo (hooks 1994). This can include acknowledging the "hidden curriculum" of schools, teacher bias and life experience, incorporating student interest and inquiry, and "talking back to" formally sanctioned curricula. Teaching for social justice is considered transgressive because it is predicated upon acknowledging that inequity exists in structural and systematic ways. Critical pedagogy, critical literacy, and democratic classroom practices are also transgressive as they view students as agents of knowledge making and promote student empowerment in affecting oppressive and unjust social conditions.

A Little Bit of Historical Background

Table 0.1 offers a timeline of the historical background on LGBTQ issues in the United States compiled from Infoplease.com (2013), Leitsinger (2013) and PBS (2014).

TABLE 0.1 LGBTQ Timeline

1924	The Society for Human Rights in Chicago becomes the country's earliest known gay-rights organization.
1948	In *Sexual Behavior in the Human Male*, Alfred Kinsey reveals to the public that based on his research, homosexuality is far more widespread than was commonly believed.
1951	The first national gay rights organization, the Mattachine Society, was formed by Harry Hay, whom many consider to be the founder of the gay-rights movement.
1953	President Dwight Eisenhower signs Executive Order 10450, banning homosexuals from working for the federal government or any of its private contractors.
1955	The Daughters of the Bilitis, the first lesbian rights organization in the United States, is established in San Francisco.
1956	American psychologist Evelyn Hooker shares her research which concluded that homosexuality is not a clinical entity and that heterosexuals and homosexuals do not differ significantly. Her work becomes very influential in changing clinical perceptions of homosexuality.
1958	In One, Inc. *v.* Olson, the United States Supreme Court ruled in favor of the First Amendment rights of the lesbian, gay, bisexual, and transgender magazine *One: The Homosexual Magazine*. This marked the first time the United States Supreme Court ruled in favor of homosexuals.
1966	The world's first transgender organization, The National Transsexual Counseling Unit, established in San Francisco. Members of the Mattachine Society stage a "sip in" at the Julius Bar in Greenwich Village, where New York Authority Liquor prohibited the serving of gay patrons and bars on the basis that homosexuals are disorderly. The Mattachine Society later sues the New York Liquor Authority and though no laws were overturned, the New York City commission on human rights declared that homosexuals have the right to be served.
1969	June 28—Stonewall Riots: police raid the Stonewall Inn, Greenwich Village, New York City. Riots were incited by police harassment of gays and lasted several days. Many consider this event the start of the gay rights movement.
1970	June 27 and 28—On the one-year anniversary of the Stonewall Riots, gay pride parades are held in New York City, Chicago, San Francisco, and Los Angeles.

1973   The American Psychological Association removes homosexuality from its diagnostic manual of mental disorders.

1974   Kathy Kozachenko wins a seat on the Ann Arbor, Michigan City Council and becomes the first openly gay American elected to public office.

1978   November 27—Harvey Milk, the first openly gay person elected to a public office in a large city, is assassinated. He was a member of the San Francisco Board of Supervisors.

1979   National March on Washington for lesbian and gay rights is held in Washington, DC.

1980   At the Democratic National Convention in August, Democrats become the first political party to endorse a homosexual rights platform, with the Democratic Rules Committee stating that it will not discriminate against homosexuals.

1981   July 3—*New York Times* prints the first story of a rare pneumonia and skin cancer found in 41 gay men in New York and California. The Centers for Disease Control initially refers to this disease as GRID, Gay Related Immune Deficiency Disorder. When symptoms are found outside the gay community, Bruce Voeller, biologist and founder of the National Gay Task Force, successfully lobbies to change the name of the disease to AIDS, Auto Immune Deficiency Syndrome. Gay advocacy groups form to deal with the AIDS crisis.

1982   Wisconsin becomes the first state to outlaw discrimination on the basis of sexual orientation.

1987   May 30—Rep. Barney Frank becomes the first openly gay member of Congress. He served 16 terms as a Democratic representative from the state of Massachusetts.

   October 11—Hundreds of thousands of activists attended the National March on Washington to demand that President Ronald Reagan address the AIDS crisis. Although reported since 1981, it was not until the end of his presidency that Reagan began to speak publicly about the epidemic.

1988   May and June—the Centers for Disease Control mails a brochure, *Understanding AIDS*, to every household in the United States. Approximately 107,000,000 brochures were mailed.

1990   August 18—President George Bush signs a federally funded program for people living with AIDS called the Ryan White Care Act. Ryan White was a teenager from Indiana who contracted the AIDS virus in 1984 through a blood transfusion. After being barred from attending school because of his HIV-positive status, White became a well-known activist for AIDS research and antidiscrimination.

1991   Created by New York-based organization "Visual AIDS," the red ribbon is adopted as a symbol of awareness and compassion for those living with HIV and AIDS.

1993   President Bill Clinton enacts "Don't Ask, Don't Tell" preventing gays from openly serving in the military.

1996   Congress passes the Defense of Marriage Act (DOMA), which barred recognition of same-sex marriage.

   Coretta Scott King, widow of civil rights leader Martin Luther King Jr., receives criticism from members of the black civil rights movement for calling upon the civil rights community to join the struggle against homophobia.

1997   April 30—Ellen DeGeneres comes out on her prime time TV show *Ellen*. Many other LGBTQ celebrities have followed suit.

1998   Matthew Shepard, a 21-year-old college student, dies after being beaten and tied to a split rail fence outside of Laramie, Wyoming.

2000   The Boy Scouts of America officially bar gay scouts and leaders from membership.

         The Laramie Project, a play by the Tectonic Theater, debuts to combat homophobia and raise awareness about hate crimes.

         Vermont becomes the first state to allow same-sex civil unions.

2004   May 17—Massachusetts becomes the first state to legalize same-sex marriage.

2005   Civil unions become legal in Connecticut in October.

2006   Civil unions become legal in New Jersey in December.

2007   In November, a bill ensuring equal rights in the workplace for gay men, lesbians, and bisexuals is approved by the House of Representatives.

2008   In February, a New York State Appeals Court unanimously votes that valid same-sex marriages performed in other states must be recognized by employers in New York, which grants same-sex couples the same rights as other couples.

         The state of Oregon passes a law allowing same-sex couples to register as domestic partners, which allows them some spousal rights of married couples.

         On October 10, the Supreme Court of Connecticut rules that same-sex couples have the right to marry. This makes Connecticut the second state to legalize civil marriage for same-sex couples.

         In California Proposition 8, a constitutional amendment that bans same-sex marriage, is voted into law.

2009   President Obama signs the Matthew Shepard and James Byrd Junior Hate Crime Prevention Act.

         April 3—the Iowa Supreme Court unanimously rejects the state law banning same-sex marriage.

         On May 6, the governor of Maine legalizes same-sex marriage, but the law is overturned when Maine citizens vote in November.

         June 3—New Hampshire becomes the sixth state in the nation to allow same-sex marriage.

         June 17—President Obama signs a referendum allowing the same-sex partners of federal employees to receive benefits.

         August 12—President Obama posthumously awards Harvey Milk the presidential medal of freedom.

2010   March 3—same-sex marriage is legalized in the District of Columbia.

         August 4—it is determined that Proposition 8 violates the 14th amendment's equal protection clause and is overturned in California.

         December 18—"Don't Ask, Don't Tell" is repealed by President Barack Obama.

2011   New York becomes the largest state to allow gay and lesbian couples to marry.

2012   February 13—Washington becomes the seventh state to legalize gay marriage.

         March 1—Maryland becomes the eighth state to legalize gay marriage.

         May 2—Rhode Island legalizes same-sex marriage.

         May 7—Delaware legalizes same-sex marriage.

May 9—President Obama becomes the first sitting president to support same-sex marriage.

May 13—Minnesota State Senate votes 37 to 30 in favor of legalizing same-sex marriage.

October 21—New Jersey becomes the 14th state to recognize same-sex marriages.

November 5—Illinois becomes the 15th state to recognize same-sex marriages.

November 6—Tammy Baldwin, a seven-term Democratic congresswoman from Wisconsin, becomes the first openly gay politician elected to Senate.

November 12—Hawaii becomes the 16th state to recognize same-sex marriage.

2013 February 27—Over 100 Republicans back a legal brief asking the Supreme Court to rule that same-sex marriage is a constitutional right.

March—California's Proposition 8 is ruled unconstitutional by the Supreme Court and overturned.

April 29—Jason Collins of the NBA's Washington Wizards announces in an essay in *Sports Illustrated* that he is gay. "I'm a 34-year-old NBA center. I'm black and I'm gay." Collins is the first active athlete in the NBA, NFL, NHL, or MLB to make the announcement.

May—The Boy Scouts of America lift their ban on gay scouts, but their ban of gay leaders remains.

June—The Supreme Court of the United States declares the Defense of Marriage Act (DOMA) to be unconstitutional.

The United States Supreme Court blocks any further same-sex marriage in Utah while state officials appeal the decision that was made by Judge Shelly in December 2013.

2014 January 10—the Obama administration announces that the federal government will recognize the marriages of the 1,300 same-sex couples in Utah, even though the state government has decided not to do so.

May 19—same-sex marriage becomes legal in Oregon when a U.S. federal district judge rules that the state's 2004 constitutional amendment banning same-sex marriage is in violation of the equal protection clause of the U.S. Constitution.

May 20—a judge strikes down the same-sex marriage ban in Pennsylvania, making this state the 18th to legalize gay marriage.

2015 June 27–U.S. Supreme Court rules state prohibitions on same-sex marriage as unconstitutional.

Note: Timeline compiled from Infoplease.com 2013; Leitsinger 2013; and PBS 2014.

Acknowledging and Appreciating Family Diversity

Recognizing and addressing LGBTQ moves beyond the question of sexuality; it becomes a matter of family diversity. Just as multicultural education recognizes that children enter the classroom with a multitude of cultural, ethnic, and familial backgrounds (Nieto 2002, Nieto and Bode 2012), and education should use this rich background to build upon and share diversity (Darder, Baltodano, and Torres

2009, Dewey 1916), there needs to be a recognition that "family" carries definitions outside the nuclear roles of mother, father, and 2.4 children. Family diversity includes children living with grandparents, divorced/re-married parents and blended families, extended families living together, adopted children with both birth parents and adopted parents, families where members have (dis)abilities, and families with two mothers or two fathers instead of the traditional mother/father role. Family diversity may include patterns outside those we have named. The need to acknowledge and embrace the non-traditional familial forms moves beyond any question of sexuality or heteronormativity and into recognition that "family" can come in a variety of formats, and the core meaning of what it is to *be family*—to love and care for one another—does not change with the familial form. Furthermore, failure to recognize the multiple familial forms and accept the many family structures sets up any child whose family structure is "different," regardless of how that difference manifests, for ostracizing and bullying (Reichman 2012).

Being an Ally

According to the Ally Campaign, "an ally acts when people face discrimination and supports the rights of marginalized people" (Mount Sinai Hospital 2015). The three steps of being an ally are to be self-aware; identify the privilege you have, using it to create change; and speak up and take action. When being an ally for LGBTQ colleagues and students, the first (ongoing) step is to be aware of the ways our own histories influence how we view our own and others' sexualities, sexual orientations, gender identities and expressions, biologies, and attractions. We have to be aware of how our views of students, their communities, and their identities can positively or negatively affect their educational experiences. We do not become self-aware in a vacuum. As allies, we are aware because we open ourselves up to being empathetic to and learning from people with life experiences very different from our own. Being an ally means being willing to be corrected, being willing to be educated by others, being willing to be wrong, to make a mistake, and to keep moving forward. Being an ally means the cause is more important than our ego.

In This Book

There are three major sections to this book. In the first section, "Raising Awareness: Troubling the Waters," the chapters examine how we can begin to address the needs and rights of students and develop a more socially just curriculum within all education, whether K–12, college level, graduate, or beyond. Moving from the first section to the second, the first interlude by Stacy Schupmann offers the voice of a lesbian woman interwoven with her performance poetry as she lives with the effects of external forces, such as others' perceptions, religious perspectives, and law on her rights and marriage.

The second section, "Climate and Culture: Fostering Positive Identities," examines how LGBTQ issues affect school climate and culture, and continues the discussion of how educators can support students. In the second interlude, which moves us from the second to the third sections, Anna Wilson examines her role in higher education through a mosaic of scholarship, reflection, expression, and identity.

The third section, "Transformative Practices," examines and offers socially just educational approaches for transforming apathy, resistance, and persecution through innovative and engaging educational practices. The book finishes with a reflective *dénouement* re-examining ideas of gender and identity.

Conclusion

We hope reading this book will provide you with strategies, ideas, and further resources; that it will help you either find your own ways to speak up and continue discussions around gender identity, gender expression, and sexual orientation, or in becoming an ally for LGBTQ students, colleagues, friends, and family members. May this be one step among many in our collective journeys of solidarity with one another, for our students, and for the world.

Notes

1   As large portions of educational history, politics, and policy have been in the hands of men, despite women's dominant roles as teachers, I have made the dragon of my educational metaphor that has emerged from these male-centric areas male as well. There are, of course, women who have added to these structures. Oddly enough, in fiction, male dragons are more likely to show up as hoarders and destroyers, while female dragons are often (but not always) either queens, or carry other helpful or nurturing traits.

2   Arborescence, based on Deleuze and Guattari's (1987) concepts of duplicating the root-tree and root-book, notes that most thinking merely replicates itself in a hierarchical manner. Original thought requires mapping (as opposed to tracing) and rhizomatic deterritorialization, using "successive singularities" (11) to develop expanding circles of convergence outside expected limits or directions.

3   Further information can be found at tahoesafealliance.org, nativeout.com, transsexual. org, pflag.org, and glsen.org.

References

Apple, Michael W., and James A. Beane. 1995. *Democratic Schools*. Alexandria, VA: Association for Supervision and Curriculum Development.

Bishop, Russell, and Mere Berryman. 2006. *Culture Speaks: Cultural Relationships and Classroom Learning*. Wellington, NZ: Huia Publishers.

Coffey, Heather. 2014. *Critical Literacy*. Learn NC; University of North Carolina (UNC) School of Education 2014 [cited July 16 2014]. Available from http://www.learnnc. org/lp/pages/4437.

Darder, Antonia, Marta Baltodano, and Rudolpho D. Torres. 2009. *The Critical Pedagogy Reader*. 2nd ed. New York: Routledge.

Deleuze, Gilles, and Feliz Guattari. 1987. *A Thousand Plateaus: Capitalism and Schizophrenia*. Minneapolis, MN: University of Minnesota Press.

Dewey, John. 1916. *Democracy and Education: An Introduction to the Philosophy of Education, Text-Book Series in Education*. New York: The Macmillan Company.

Eisner, Elliot W. 2002. "The Kind of Schools We Need." *Phi Delta Kappan* no. 83 (8): 576–584.

Fisher, M. E. 2013. *Here There be Dragons: The Initial Defining of Prism Theory and Prismatic Inquiry*. Dissertation, College of Educational Studies, Champan University, Orange, CA.

Freire, Paulo. 1970/2005. *Pedagogy of the Oppressed*. Translated by M. B. Ramos. 30th Anniversary ed. New York: Continuum. Original edition, 1970. Reprint, 30th Aniversary.

Freire, Paulo, and Donaldo Macedo. 2009. "Rethinking Literacy: A Dialogue." In *The Critical Pedagogy Reader*, edited by Antonia Darder, Marta Baltodano and Rudolpho D. Torres, 354–364. New York: Routledge.

hooks, bell. 1994. *Teaching to Transgress: Education as the Practice of Freedom*. New York: Routledge.

Infoplease.com. 2013. "The American Gay Rights Movement: A Timeline." In *Information Please® Database; Society and Culture; Gender Issues*. New York: Pearson Education, Inc.

Kellner, Douglas. 2000. "Multiple Literacies and Critical Pedagogies." In *Revolutionary Pedagogies: Cultural Politics, Instituting Education, and the Discourse of Theory*, edited by Peter Pericles Trifonas, 196–221. New York: Routledge.

Killerman, Sam. 2014. *What Does the Asterisk in "Trans*" Stand For?* It's Prounounced METROsexual 2014 [cited July 12 2014]. Available from http://itspronounced metrosexual.com/2012/05/what-does-the-asterisk-in-trans-stand-for/.

Killerman, Sam. 2015. *The Genderbread Person v.3.0 [Web log post and edughraphic]* 2015 [cited July 26 2015]. Available from http://itspronouncedmetrosexual.com/2015/03/ the-genderbread-person-v3/.

Kumashiro, Kevin K. 2002. *Troubling Education: Queer Activism and Anti-oppressive Education*. New York: RoutledgeFalmer.

Leitsinger, Miranda. 2013. "Gay Rights Timeline: Key Dates in the Fight for Equality." *NBC News*, March 23, 2013.

Mayo, Cris. 2010. "Queer Lessons: Sexual and Gender Minorities in Multicultural Education." In *Multicultural Education: Issues and Perspectives*, edited by J. A. Banks and C. A. M. Banks, 209–227. Hoboken, NJ: Wiley.

Merriam-Webster. 2013. "Praxis." Springfield, MA: Merriam-Webster.

Meyer, Elizabeth J. 2007. "'But I'm Not Gay': What Straight Teachers Need to Know about Queer Theory." In *Queering Straight Teachers: Discourse and Identity in Education*, edited by Nelson M. Rodriguez and William F. Pinar, 15–32. New York, NY: Peter Lang.

Mount Sinai Hospital. 2015. *How Can I Be an Ally?* Mount Sinai Hospital 2015 [cited June 12 2015]. Available from http://www.mountsinai.on.ca/about_us/human-rights/ally/ally-tools/how-can-i-be-an-ally.

NativeOUT. 2014. *Two Spirit 101* 2014 [cited June 30 2014]. Available from http://nativeout.com/twospirit-rc/two-spirit-101/.

NCTE. 2014. Transgender Terminology. http://transequality.org/Resources/Trans Terminology_2014.pdf.

Nieto, Sonia. 2002. *Language, Culture, and Teaching: Critical Perspectives for a New Century*, *Language, Culture, and Teaching*. Mahwah, NJ: Erlbaum.

Nieto, Sonia. 2003. *What Keeps Teachers Going?* New York: Teachers College Press.

Nieto, Sonia, and Patty Bode. 2012. *Affirming Diversity: The Sociopolitical Context of Multicultural Education*. 6th ed. Boston, MA: Pearson Education.

Norris, Katherine, Lisa Lucas, and Catherine Prudhoe. 2012. "Examining Critical Literacy: Preparing Preservice Teachers to Use Critical Literacy in the Early Childhood Classroom." *Multicultural Education* no. 19 (2): 59–62.

Oxford Dictionaries. 2014a. "Cisgender." Edited by J. Pearsall. Oxford: Oxford University Press.

Oxford Dictionaries. 2014b. "Gay." Edited by J. Pearsall. Oxford: Oxford University Press.

Oxford Dictionaries. 2014c. "Heteronormativity." Edited by J. Pearsall. Oxford: Oxford University Press.

PBS. 2014. *Timeline: Milestones in the American Gay Rights Movement*. PBS 1995–2014 [cited July 5 2014]. Available from http://www.pbs.org/wgbh/americanexperience/features/timeline/stonewall/.

PFLAG. 2014. *A Definition of "Queer."* Parents, Families and Friends of Lesbians and Gays (PFLAG) 2014 [cited June 30 2014]. Available from http://community.pflag.org/abouttheq.

Reichman, Henry. 2012. "Censorship dateline." *Newsletter on Intellectual Freedom* no. 61 (5): 201–227.

Sehr, David T. 1997. *Education for Public Democracy*. New York: State University of New York.

Smith, Shannon D., Kok-Mun Ng, and Jesse Brinson. 2008. "Multiculturalism, Diversity, and Social Advocacy: A 17 year Content Analysis of *Counselor Education and Supervision*." *Counselor Education and Supervision* no. 47: 249–263.

Stiffler, A. 2014. 5 Things You Should Know About Your Agender Acquaintance. *Everyday Feminism Magazine*, http://everydayfeminism.com/2014/07/5-things-about-agender/.

TSA. 2011. *What Does LGBTQIA Mean?* Tahoe Safe Alliance, November 10, 2011 [cited June 30 2014]. Available from http://tahoesafealliance.org/for-lgbqtia/what-does-lgbtqia-mean/.

SECTION I

Raising Awareness
Troubling the Waters

Veronica E. Bloomfield and Marni E. Fisher

Schools are not often sites of support, affirmation, or safety for LGBTQ students and teachers. Educators who attempt to incorporate elements of gender and sexual identities are often met with resistance. Sometimes those educators are the queer dragons, creating change in resistant systems, and sometimes the dragons they dance with include curriculum and standards, administration, school boards, community members, and religious or political groups. Sexuality is a hot-button issue; people are passionate about it for many reasons. There are LGBTQ allies and advocates whose passion ignites fear and resistance in others. In turn, there are proponents of intolerance and outright hate who inadvertently bolster compassion for LGBTQ youth and adults from unlikely sources.

The sensitivity to and about this topic can make beginning the conversation a difficult task. Each of the four chapters in the section addresses the needs and rights of children in unique ways and seeks a more just and inclusive curriculum in K–12 education, graduate education, and life.

Michael Sadowski's work examines the notion of what each child has the "right to" in educational settings. He addresses the steps teachers can take in putting these rights into practice, specifically how to incorporate LGBTQ history, contributions, and life experiences into the curriculum.

Lynda Wiest, Cynthia Brock, and Julie Pennington call attention to the fact that LGBTQ issues receive minimal attention in Teacher Education programs and how to counter this minimization with awareness and advocacy. Addressing both homophobia and heteronormativity in group discussion, they seek an end to all forms of bullying around these topics.

Veronica Bloomfield's chapter anecdotally describes the challenges of teaching and parenting through issues of gender and sexuality. She provides developmentally appropriate resources for home and school that foster a curriculum of acceptance and inclusion, honoring the experiences of the "whole child."

The final chapter of this section, by Marni Fisher and Kevin Stockbridge, examines the need to create safe spaces for student voices. Coming from religious education systems, they examine how, even in a conservative environment, difference and diversity can be shared within safe spaces created for student voice.

As each chapter indicates, there is no one right way or one easy way to do this work. The process of having conversations and offering counter-narratives are learning experiences in and of themselves, even if the outcomes are not always the desired end. In this way, the authors offer their own frustrations and self-critiques in order to push the conversation forward, showing how to make adjustments along the way, not as a sign of failure but as simply what is needed.

We hope you will feel more comfortable in troubling the waters wherever you may be, once you read these accounts. Raising awareness is a process we each must be courageously committed to in order for the needs of LGBTQ students and teachers to have both visibility and merit.

1

HOW OLD IDEAS CAN HELP NEW TEACHERS

Support for LGBTQ Students as a Core Value

Michael Sadowski

Whenever I introduce a new group of teacher education students or other preservice educators to research about LGBTQ youth and schooling-related issues, I first ask them to reflect silently as emerging educators on their core values that led them toward a teaching career in the first place. Although these values vary from person to person, themes that commonly emerge include social justice, a commitment to equity, a passion for learning, and the desire to share what they cherish about their teaching disciplines (e.g., history, literature, mathematics) with young people.

With these deeply held beliefs tapped, I ask students to complete this sentence: "I believe every student in a public school has a right to ..." Students write privately for a few minutes, after which I ask them to share some of their ideas aloud while I collect them on the board. Since in many cases I have asked students to complete some reading about LGBTQ issues before the class, some of the rights they identify are those one might expect to hear directly after students have read this material: "a safe learning environment"; "freedom from bullying and harassment"; "acceptance and respect at school." Often, however, students are able to think beyond the content of the reading and come up with a broad spectrum of things to which they believe all students are entitled and that drive their most fundamental motivations to pursue careers in education: "opportunities to develop their own unique talents and skills"; "adequate resources to help them learn"; "supportive, encouraging teachers." Some students even say things like "proper nutrition."

This list of rights serves as a backdrop for a presentation and discussion of current data about the school experiences of LGBTQ students and the risks these youth face both in and out of school. If my classroom is equipped with a projection screen, I use the screen both to conceal the list of rights students have generated and to display slides highlighting key data from two sources. We begin with the most recent data from the Gay, Lesbian and Straight Education Network (GLSEN) School Climate Survey (Kosciw et al. 2014). Although numerous articles about school-related risks affecting LGBTQ youth have appeared in peer-reviewed journals (Chesir-Teran and Hughes 2009, D'Augelli, Pilkington, and Hershberger 2002), none of these approaches the breadth of issues that the GLSEN survey addresses: anti-LGBTQ language, verbal harassment, physical attacks, the responses of teachers to anti-LGBTQ language and harassment, LGBTQ representation (or lack thereof) in school curricula, the relationship between victimization and school performance, and the specific experiences of lesbian and bisexual girls, transgender youth, and LGBTQ youth of color. Moreover, the consistency of GLSEN's findings over multiple, biennial administrations of the School Climate Survey lends credibility to its data, which—though not based on random sampling—represent the perceptions of more than 7,800 students in grades 6 through 12 (mostly LGBT-identifying) from across the country.

Data from the GLSEN School Climate Survey

Findings from the GLSEN survey about anti-LGBTQ language and harassment include:

- Nearly three-quarters (71.4%) hear the word "gay" used in a derogatory way (e.g., "that's gay") either "frequently" or "often" at school.
- Over 60 percent hear other homophobic language (e.g., faggot, dyke, homo) either "frequently" or "often" at school.
- Ninety percent were "bothered or distressed" to some degree by anti-LGBTQ language heard at school.
- Seventy-four percent have been verbally harassed at school either "frequently," "often," or "sometimes" in the past year, and 36 percent have been physically harassed.
- Nearly half (49 percent) have been cyberbullied by peers—harassed online, over email, and/or in text messages (Kosciw et al. 2014).

Another central focus of our discussion involves the responses of teachers to homophobic language, harassment, and violence. Although some of GLSEN's findings point to the positive difference supportive teachers and other school staff make in the lives of many LGBTQ students, data from the survey also suggests some teachers fail to provide a safe learning environment and may even contribute to LGBTQ students' victimization:

- Over 40 percent of the students said teachers never intervene when they hear students use homophobic language, and another 39 percent said teachers intervene only "some of the time."

- About 4 percent "frequently" or "often" hear teachers and other school staff make homophobic remarks, and another 14 percent "sometimes" hear this language from school adults.
- Among students who had been harassed, 57 percent never reported it to school staff, and the most frequently cited reason was they believed reporting would be ineffective (Kosciw et al. 2014).[1]

Finally, our slide-based discussion focuses on some of the risks, both academic and otherwise, LGBTQ youth face as a result of victimization or hostile school climates. I end with data from the most recent Massachusetts Youth Risk Behavior Survey (MYRBS), which is based on questionnaire responses from more than 2,700 students in randomly selected high schools across the state. Even though the teacher education program in which I am currently working is based in New York, I use MYRBS data because Massachusetts is one of the few states that includes questions about self-identified sexual orientation and/ or same-sex sexual activity on its Youth Risk Behavior Survey and has been disaggregating youth risk data by sexual orientation for nearly two decades. Consistently, students are shocked by the MYRBS statistics showing roughly one-quarter of gay, lesbian, and bisexual youth have attempted suicide, a rate more than five times that of their heterosexual peers (24.4% vs. 4.2%). The students also are surprised by data showing that lesbian, gay, and bisexual students (the survey does not include any items to determine transgender identity) are more than five times as likely as their heterosexual peers (15.3% vs. 2.9%) to skip school because they feel unsafe (Massachusetts Department of Elementary and Secondary Education 2015).[2]

At this point in the discussion, my students and I turn off the slides, raise the screen, and reveal again the list we generated at the beginning of the class. As one might predict, students are immediately struck by the mismatch between the rights they identified as belonging to all students—based on what they consider their core values as educators—and the experiences of LGBTQ youth in U.S. schools, as depicted in the GLSEN survey results and the MYRBS data.

Our discussion continues: Which of the rights we articulated as belonging to all students are violated or compromised for LGBTQ students, assuming that the GLSEN and MYRBS data accurately reflect their experiences? Here, the connections (or, perhaps more accurately, disconnections) students identify between their list and the data usually begin with such rights as feeling safe at school and attending school free from harassment and bullying. Probing more deeply, however, students often note how a broader spectrum of generally agreed upon student rights are violated on a regular basis based on the GLSEN and/or MYRBS data. These insights vary from class to class, but in recent sessions participants have focused on such issues as the rights of students to:

- *develop their own unique skills as learners*, a right that is compromised if LGBTQ students skip classes or school because they feel unsafe, or if they feel silenced in classes where central aspects of their identities are not represented;
- *be supported and encouraged by teachers*, some of whom, the data show, fail to address the needs of LGBTQ youth adequately and, in some cases, may even harbor and enact homophobic attitudes themselves;
- *participate in extracurricular activities that expand their horizons*, since some LGBTQ students may believe they would not be welcome in certain school athletic or extracurricular activities, and many schools still do not have gay–straight alliances;
- even *receive adequate nutrition*, a right some of my students have convincingly argued could be jeopardized if LGBTQ students feel unsafe in the school cafeteria, which, along with hallways, are among the most common locations for anti-LGBTQ harassment to occur (Bochenek and Brown 2001).

Without a doubt, the preservice teachers in future sections of my courses will have a heightened awareness of bullying and harassment, LGBTQ youth suicide, and possible links among them following a wave of incidents related to these issues that have made national news. In the most highly publicized of these cases, Rutgers University freshman Tyler Clementi jumped off the George Washington Bridge after his roommate reportedly recorded an intimate encounter between him and another man and posted accounts of it online. Although we can never presume to know, many speculated the "cyberbullying" that Clementi experienced played a significant role in his emotional distress and perhaps even his decision to take his own life.

Clementi's death and reports of other LGBTQ youth suicides have prompted a national focus on bullying, several anti-bullying initiatives in the public and private sectors, and the online "It Gets Better" campaign in which celebrities, political figures, and others provide video-recorded messages of hope to LGBTQ youth struggling with harassment, bullying, and isolation. As the GLSEN and MYRBS data show, neither the harassment of LGBTQ youth nor their heightened risk for suicidal behaviors are new phenomena, but the raised national consciousness about these issues, should it last, are likely to have an effect both on the future cohorts of preservice teachers and on the schools and administrators with whom they work.

The Two Graduate School Contexts

Undoubtedly, the contexts in which I have taught preservice educators about LGBTQ issues have been factors affecting the extent that they have been receptive to these issues being addressed openly in K–12 schools. My first experiences in teaching this material primarily to preservice educators took place at the Harvard Graduate School of Education between 2003 and 2006. In the school's Teacher

Education and School Leadership Programs, I taught stand-alone sessions for several years, the first half of which followed a format similar to the one I describe in the previous section, and the second half focused on case studies where students worked in small groups to problem solve a situation related to homophobia in a school context. These case studies, some drawn from the work of educator Michael Kozuch, involve such issues as opposition to efforts to start a gay–straight alliance, a teacher being targeted with homophobic language, and homophobia in a school sports context. With the slide presentation in the background, students were called to discuss how they would address the case as educators, and how they might use arguments grounded in core values to defend their solution to potential opponents.

Since these groups at Harvard were relatively large (as many as 100 students) when I first started conducting the workshops, I expected to encounter at least a few participants in each session with objections to addressing LGBTQ issues openly in a K–12 context. Yet, in all these sessions, which involved upwards of 400 students over several years, no student ever raised such objections. If students with objections were in any of the sessions, they were most likely in the minority at Harvard's Graduate School of Education and may therefore have felt unsafe voicing these opinions to their peers. I would also like to think, however, that the framing of the issue around core values and widely agreed upon student rights led at least some students to rethink their stances when the alarming data on issues affecting LGBTQ youth were presented in this way.

Since 2005, I have been a faculty member in the Master of Arts in Teaching Program at Bard College (another secondary teacher education program that likely attracts a disproportionately liberal student body). At Bard, I use my lesson juxtaposing core values and universal student rights with the GLSEN and MYRBS data in the context of a course entitled "Identity, Culture, and the Classroom." This course has afforded me an even broader framework to discuss the rights of all students and the responsibilities of teachers concerning LGBTQ youth. The course begins with foundational theories about identity development in adolescence, particularly those of Erik Erikson (1968) who, despite what some might characterize as homophobia in some of his writing, was undeniably a pioneer in the field of child and adolescent psychology. Working from Erikson's theories about adolescence representing a particular time of "crisis" (or turning point) for the development of identity, we discuss how adolescents grapple, primarily unconsciously, with questions of self-definition and their place in the world. We also discuss the responsibility of teachers to serve as deliverers of course content and as what Nakkula and Toshalis (2006) called "applied developmentalists": adults entrusted with ensuring young people follow positive developmental trajectories that allow them to learn and achieve to their fullest potential.

This groundwork-setting conversation about identity theory provides an additional backdrop for the discussion of LGBTQ issues, which takes place several weeks later in the context of discussions about other identity-related issues associated with race, gender, ethnicity, social class, ability/disability, and language. Many of the readings come from my edited book *Adolescents at School: Perspectives on Youth, Identity, and Education* (Sadowski 2008a) and authors such as Ferguson (2000), Fordham and Ogbu (1986), Gilligan (1996), Tatum (1997), among others. The exploration of LGBTQ issues in classrooms and schools thus takes place amid a larger conversation about how schools provide or fail to provide opportunities for students from historically marginalized groups to develop positive identities as learners.[3]

Students' Responses to Studying LGBTQ Issues

As a final project for "Identity, Culture, and the Classroom," students are called upon to draft a "plan of practice" articulating how they envision themselves working to create learning environments, both within their classrooms and in their larger school communities, that support the positive development of students both as learners and as people. Students are required to draw on at least three "literatures" for these final projects (e.g., research and/or theory about ethnicity, gender, and race) and how these inform the ways they conceive of their responsibilities as teachers.

Over the years, many students have chosen to cite the GLSEN and/or MYRBS data in their final projects and to argue for the rights of all students to a supportive learning environment. Other class participants have drawn on broader theories of identity to illustrate why focused work around LGBTQ issues will be an essential aspect of their practice as professional educators.[4] In the following excerpts, two students, one certified to teach history and the other preparing to teach mathematics, discuss their plans to incorporate LGBTQ issues into their course curricula based on these core principles:

> Along with black history and women's history, I feel it is especially important (due to the highly common neglect of this subject) to include the history of lesbian, gay, bisexual, and transgender people into my curriculum ... Students of varying sexual orientations are often completely neglected from history courses, which may make them feel even more marginalized and outside the school community than they already feel. I plan on studying the Stonewall riots in my classroom and possibly using excerpts from a book titled *Gay New York* by Chauncey [1994] to demonstrate the impact that gay culture and movements have had on our society. There is also a lot of gay history that dates back to ancient Greek and Roman times, which is often neglected as well. I want all of my students, regardless of race, sexual orientation, and gender, to understand that the group(s) they identify with did have a place in history, and they shouldn't ever feel like they are alone or unimportant.

From the [GLSEN] School Climate Survey, we see a marked difference between schools with and without inclusive curricula … Considering my subject area is math, how can I incorporate LGBTQ themes into the classroom? If we talk about Turing machines in computer science, we will undoubtedly discuss British mathematician Alan Turing, a gay man whose code-breaking helped the British immeasurably in WWII. Also, in story problems, rather than using the nuclear definition of family, I can refer to the many different kinds of families there are in reality.

Other students have discussed the need for teachers not only to create inclusive curricula, but also to ensure that LGBTQ students are represented and supported in the larger school community:

As an educator, our responsibilities extend beyond simply teaching our discipline. In all areas it is crucial that we are open to developing caring, trusting relationships with our students. As evidenced earlier in discussing the lack of staff support for LGBT students, it is abundantly clear that these relationships are missing … If the school does not already have a gay-straight student alliance (GSA), it would be my first priority to speak to the principal about beginning one.

Students in my classes who are LGBTQ themselves have sometimes focused on the role they might play as role models and mentors, drawing both on the research we read about the lack of representation of openly LGBTQ people in schools (Bochenek and Brown 2001, Sadowski 2008b) and on the value of mentoring for students in supporting positive development and orientation toward the future (Rhodes et al. 2007):

The value of mentor relationships can positively influence all students struggling with identity issues, especially LGBTQ students … LGBTQ students who are struggling with their identity, unfortunately, cannot always rely on support from the home, since many people harbor very opinionated beliefs against the queer community … As an "out" queer teacher, I have the ability to provide my students with a resource that many of my future colleagues cannot. This support can come in the form of displaying a "Safe Space" sticker, incorporating LGBT issues into my curriculum, actively addressing homophobic language in the hallways, advising the school's GSA, or providing students with an adult mentor with whom they feel comfortable discussing issues of identity.

Attempts to address LGBTQ issues in middle and high schools can often be met with opposition from administrators, school boards, and community members on religious and/or political grounds. Thus, I add a component to the "plan of practice" assignment asking students to consider potential obstacles they might encounter putting their ideas into effect in a real-world school context and articulating how they might argue in the face of opposition. As one student recently explained in her "plan of practice":

> Some parents or other groups may resist including LGBTQ issues into the curriculum. But if educators ignore certain students and certain issues because celebrating their interests, needs, or backgrounds is too controversial or too difficult, then school would never become a place for social reform. Teachers can never help make their students well-rounded, caring people if they don't do everything in their power to demonstrate that they themselves are caring and compassionate enough to embrace the backgrounds of all their students, even if it is challenged by others.

Some Caveats

I believe the "plans of practice" students articulate in their final papers for "Identity, Culture, and the Classroom" represent their sincere intentions to creative inclusive classrooms, curricula, and school communities. I recognize, however, that the extent to which these intentions are realized once students are working in the real world of K–12 schooling—with its competing political agendas and where school boards and administrators often discourage teachers from raising controversial issues—quite likely varies from graduate to graduate. Based on admittedly anecdotal evidence, I can state that at least some teachers who completed the teacher education programs at Harvard and at Bard are indeed applying principles they articulated as graduate students. Since I have begun teaching about LGBTQ issues, I have heard from numerous former students, sometimes years later, who were seeking additional advice on starting a gay–straight alliance or incorporating LGBTQ issues into their curricula. I would like to think our lesson framed around core values has helped numerous graduates of my class who have started GSAs or have successfully created space for LGBTQ voices in their classrooms.

In my future work, I intend to investigate the extent to which the framing of LGBTQ issues within the context of larger concepts, such as core values, student rights, and identity development, influences how in-service teachers implement and/or argue for positive change. School mission statements, often seen prominently displayed in lobbies or hallways, drive many schools. These statements commonly refer to core values, student rights, and overarching goals: the school's mission to provide a safe and challenging learning environment; the right of all students to a high-quality education; the school's objective to develop the unique skills and talents of every learner. All of these are "old ideas" that virtually any administrator or school board member would agree are central to the purposes of public schooling—based on the deeply held beliefs that got *them* involved in education in the first place. Moreover, the renewed national focus on bullying has led to many school- and district-based initiatives that, in most cases, are not considered controversial but are based on principles of safety on which members of the local community agree. Of course, some educators will encounter resistance where conservative religious groups or right-wing political organizations might brand them as "pro-gay." In such cases, teachers should seek help from national organizations such as GLSEN or the California-based GSA Network (www.gsanetwork.org), or whatever organizations might exist in their states or communities, to learn about their own and their students' rights and to consider various strategies for countering this opposition successfully.

LGBTQ students have the same rights as other students, plus a few specific to their needs: the right to be "out" at school if they so choose, the right to have LGBTQ identities represented in curricula, the right to be free from harassment based on their sexual or gender identities. Teachers empowered with strong arguments about the needs of LGBTQ students, framed in the language of these larger ideals, are best prepared to articulate to their colleagues why the inclusion of LGBTQ issues, despite any possible controversy, is within their fundamental obligation as educators and is in keeping with the broader mission of any school community.

Notes

1   The most recent GLSEN National School Climate Survey report and numerous state level reports are available at http://www.glsen.org/article/2013-national-school-climate-survey.

2   In this context, I emphasize that many LGBTQ youth are resilient and thriving, and 76 percent surveyed for the MYRBS did not report a suicide attempt.

3   Drawing primarily on readings in psychology, ethnography, and education research the course places emphasis on how identity is shaped by power dynamics in American society in terms of race, gender, sexual orientation, ethnicity, class, ability, language, and other factors. A course syllabus may be requested by writing to the author: msadowsk@bard.edu.

4   Quotations from student papers written for "Identity, Culture, and the Classroom" are cited anonymously with permission of the authors.

References

Bochenek, Michael, and A. Widney Brown. 2001. *Hatred in the Hallways: Violence and Discrimination against Lesbian, Gay, Bisexual, and Transgender Students in U.S. Schools.* New York, NY: Human Rights Watch.

Chauncey, George. 1994. *Gay New York: Gender, Urban Culture, and the Making of the Gay Male World, 1890-1940.* New York: Basic Books.

Chesir-Teran, Daniel, and Diane Hughes. 2009. "Heterosexism in High School and Victimization Among Lesbian, Gay, Bisexual, and Questioning Students." *Journal of Youth and Adolescence* no. 38 (7): 963–975. doi: 10.1007/s10964-008-9364-x.

D'Augelli, A., N. Pilkington, and S. Hershberger. 2002. "Incidence and Mental Health Impact of Sexual Orientation Victimization of Lesbian, Gay, and Bisexual Youths in High School." *School Psychology Quarterly* no. 17 (2): 148–167.

Erikson, Erik H. 1968. *Identity: Youth and Crisis*. New York: W. W. Norton.

Ferguson, Ann Arnett. 2000. *Bad Boys: Public Schools in the Making of Black Masculinity*. Ann Arbor: University of Michigan Press.

Fordham, Signithia, and John U. Ogbu. 1986. "Black Students' School Success: Coping with the Burden of 'Acting White'." *Urban Review* no. 18 (2): 176–206. doi: 10.1007/ BF01112192.

Gilligan, Carol. 1996. "The Centrality of Relationship in Human Development: A Puzzle, Some Evidence, and a Theory." In *Development and Vulnerability in Close Relationships*, edited by G. G. Noam and K. W. Fischer, 237–262. Mahwah, NJ: Lawrence Erlbaum Associates.

Kosciw, Joseph G., Emily A. Greytak, Neal A. Palmer, and Madelyn J. Boesen. 2014. *The 2013 National School Climate Survey: The Experiences of Lesbian, Gay, Bisexual and Transgender Youth in Our Nation's Schools*. New York: Gay, Lesbian and Straight Education Network (GLSEN).

Massachusetts Department of Elementary and Secondary Education. 2015. *Massachusetts High School Students and Sexual Orientation: Results of the 2013 Youth Risk Behavior Survey*. Malden: Massachusetts Department of Elementary and Secondary Education.

Nakkula, Michael J., and Eric Toshalis. 2006. *Understanding Youth: Adolescent Development for Educators*. Cambridge, MA: Harvard Education Press.

Rhodes, J. E., A. A. Davis, L. R. Prescott, and R. Spencer. 2007. "Caring Connections: Mentoring Relationships in the Lives of Urban Girls." In *Urban Girls Revisited: Buidling Strengths*, edited by B. J. R. Leadbeater and N. Way. New York: New York University Press.

Sadowski, M. 2008a. *Adolescents at School: Perspectives on Youth, Identity, and Education*. 2nd ed. Cambridge, MA: Harvard Education Press.

Sadowski, M. 2008b. "Still in the Shadows? Lesbian, Gay, Bisexual, and Transgender Students in U. S. Schools." In *Adolescents at School: Perspectives on Youth, Identity, and Education*, edited by M. Sadowski, 115–133. Cambridge, MA: Harvard Education Press.

Tatum, B. D. 1997. *"Why Are All the Black Kids Sitting Together in the Cafeteria?" and Other Conversations about Race*. New York: Basic Books.

2

EXPLORING LGBTQ ISSUES IN K–12 EDUCATION

A Dialogue with Graduate Students

Lynda R. Wiest, Cynthia H. Brock, and Julie L. Pennington

Gay, lesbian, bisexual, and transgender (LGBTQ) topics are largely ignored in K–12 schooling (Russo 2006). Unfortunately, they also receive minimal attention in teacher education. There are many reasons why educators must attend to LGBTQ issues. For example, Gruber and Fineran's (2008) study on bullying and harassment in secondary schools found that almost half of the students had been bullied. Overwhelmingly, these students were gay, lesbian, or bisexual. In addition to facing greater harassment than their non-LGBTQ peers, LGBTQ students have higher suicide rates, diminished academic achievement and aspirations, greater runaway and homelessness rates, and other forms of mistreatment including self-harm (Biegel and Kuehl 2010). Further, few public schools have clear and effective policies for dealing with harassment and bullying, particularly in relation to LGBTQ issues (Meyer 2009).

We present this chapter as a dialogue between Lynda, the first author, and a small, all-female class of graduate students in education who were mostly teachers. The dialogue shared is part of a two-hour class session addressing LGBTQ issues in schools, which Lynda conducted as a guest speaker in Cindy and Julie's class. The workshop excerpts offer ideas for possible teacher-education approaches to this topic. After introducing Lynda and some of her foundational ideas, we address the following topics from among those Lynda discussed with the class during the two-hour session: LGBTQ-related terms and misconceptions, contextual information about being gay in school and society, and approaches for addressing LGBTQ issues in school. We conclude with summary comments and suggestions.

Some Foundational Ideas

Lynda first provided the workshop agenda and a professional background on herself. She then asked students to brainstorm the meaning of educational equity before continuing with the following dialogue.

LYNDA One topic that falls under educational equity is gay, lesbian, bisexual, and transgender (LGBTQ) issues in K–12 schools. It is an overlooked topic. I will tell you now that I am gay so you don't have to wonder the whole time. I'm often reluctant to say I'm gay at the beginning of a conversation because I don't want to shut down honest conversation (Ferfolja 2007).

I believe that if change is to occur, it must start where we are (Erchick and Kos 2003). So, if you believe being gay is a bad thing or a topic that should not be addressed in school, I want you to feel free to say that. I don't want you to hold back because of who I am. Before I knew I was gay, which was in my later twenties, I was heterosexist, perhaps even homophobic, and I still consider myself heterosexist to some degree. Here is what I mean. I might see people and initially presume them to be straight (Allen 2005). That is a heterosexist thing to do, and we do it because we've been socialized that way (Rimm 2005). How often do we see billboards that show two men or two women kissing? We don't, and yet we see that with heterosexual couples all the time. If we had grown up seeing these things regularly as part of our society, it would not be a big deal and we would not make heterosexist assumptions.

LGBTQ-Related Terms and Misconceptions

LYNDA Homophobia versus heterosexism. Can anyone define these terms and explain the difference between the two?

JENNY I would say homophobia is probably more of an active phobia of gay and lesbian folk and heterosexism is something many people take for granted. Like you said, heterosexual people just assume other people are heterosexual because it is the "accepted norm" in society. I would just assume adults are married to people of the opposite sex without questioning my assumption.

LYNDA Thank you. Does anyone else want to try to distinguish between homophobia and heterosexism?

SANDRA Wouldn't phobia be more along the lines of a fear?

NINA Heterosexism. Wouldn't that be more like thoughts and presumptions and prejudgments, but not necessarily fearing?

LYNDA Heterosexism involves an assumption that male–female relationships are the norm and people are heterosexual. A heterosexist way of looking at the world can, and often does, result in prejudice (Rimm 2005). People may be unaware they are being heterosexist. Homophobia, on the other hand, is more active; it is a fear of and distaste for homosexuals (Lipkin 2004). Here are sample items from a "heterosexual questionnaire" (Kimmel and Messner 2001, 407). Consider how heterosexuals might respond to being asked these questions, which are similar to those often posed to homosexuals:

1. What do you think caused your heterosexuality?
2. A disproportionate majority of child molesters are heterosexual. Do you consider it safe to expose children to heterosexual teachers?
3. With all the societal support marriage receives, the divorce rate is spiraling. Why are there so few stable relationships among heterosexuals?
4. To whom have you disclosed your heterosexual tendencies? How did they react?

Questions like those help show what it might feel like if you have to constantly expend energy defending and explaining yourself. That is what the world is typically like for gay people.

Here is an example that helps illustrate a heterosexist view of the world. My partner and I split up earlier this summer. One day I was speaking with a straight friend, and I was telling her about my break-up. At one point, she said, "Well, have you thought about dating men?" I didn't get angry because I know a lot of people don't understand what it is like to be gay. Also, I welcome the opportunity for people to be honest with me so we can talk about issues. But I doubt my friend would say to a straight woman who just had a break-up, "Hey, have you thought about dating women?" (*laughter*)

I'd also like to address use of the term "sexual preference" which implies sexual orientation is something one prefers. It is not something you can control or change; it is an orientation (Lugg 2003). Most gay people prefer the term sexual orientation. People get mistaken ideas because gay people "come out" at different times in their lives. Early in my life, I dated men because I did not realize I was gay. I couldn't understand why dating men did not "fit" for me, and I did not realize I was gay until my later twenties. I didn't *change* from heterosexual to gay at that point. Rather, I found where I really belonged.

Another misconception is that gay people do not like people of the other sex. I have lots of male friends and brothers and nephews, and I love them all. My being gay has nothing to do with ill feelings towards the other sex or bad experiences with men. People sometimes ask or wonder why I am gay. They may assume I was sexually abused. I was not. Sexually abused people can be gay or straight, of course.

Still another misconception is that gay people are attracted to all members of the same sex. For example, some people believe that just because someone is female, I am interested in them. Sorry, I do not mean to burst your bubble here (*laughter*), but the women I am attracted to are few and far between.

Think about yourself. If you are a heterosexual woman, are you attracted to every male you encounter? (*laughter*) Of course not. Attraction is much more complex than that—for both gay and straight people. In short, just like heterosexuals do not have to justify themselves and their sexuality, gay people would prefer not to have to explain and justify their sexual orientation.

Being Gay in School and Society

LYNDA You may have heard reports that 5–10 percent of the population is gay. This is likely a conservative estimate. Remember, many people "come out" later in life or never come out or perhaps don't even fully recognize their own orientation. Even those who do consider themselves gay may not disclose this information on a survey. It's important to realize some heterosexual students have gay, lesbian, bisexual, or transgender family members. LGBTQ issues impact quite a few students (Russo 2006).

Bullying is one of the most troublesome school-related issues for children who are gay or thought to be gay (Tomsho 2003). Table 2.1 provides the results of a 2002 National Mental Health Association survey of 760 students ages 12 to 17 asked about bullying at school. The students reported that youth who are gay or thought to be gay is the largest category of bullying, and the percent is twice that of the next highest category. Note that students are also bullied just because they are thought to be gay. Unfortunately, gay-related bullying is not being addressed effectively in schools (Russo 2006), even though young people's safety and well-being is at stake (Pollock 2006).

Here is an example of a gay put-down. Earlier this summer, my partner's four-year-old son was invited to a birthday party across the street. The children at the party were ages 3 through 5. The father hosting the party announced, "Now we're going to play 'Smear the Queer' [a game of bravado where children, typically boys, tackle and pile up on the person possessing a ball or other object that makes them 'it' until they toss it away or have it taken from them]." We later spoke with the father privately to tell him we

TABLE 2.1 School Bullying by Category

Targets of School Bullying	
Latino youth	2%
Asian youth	3%
White youth	3%
Black youth	4%
Fat youth	11%
Youth who dress differently	12%
Youth who are gay or thought to be gay	24%

found this derogatory. The father contended that there was nothing wrong with playing "Smear the Queer." Later, he said he canvassed his friends, and they all felt this was an acceptable game. I asked if he thought it would be okay to play a game called "Smear the Black Person" or "Smear the Christian." Unfortunately, he did not get my point, even though he was a devout Christian. Somehow, many think a game called "Smear the Queer" is okay. It is similarly offensive when people use the term, "That's so gay," which is clearly intended as a criticism.

ALICE If you look at the top three categories for bullying on the table [being overweight, dressing differently, and being gay], you could argue two of those three categories do involve personal choice [being overweight and dressing differently]. Most people probably do not understand that being gay is not a choice like what we choose to wear or how much and what we choose to eat.

LYNDA Misunderstanding and negative stereotyping of gays is a problem in general (Mayberry 2006). For example, associating being gay with deviant sexual practices is a serious concern. Deviant sexual practices, such as pedophilia, are as likely—or rather, in the case of pedophilia, more likely— to occur in the straight community as in the gay community. As another example, promiscuity can be an issue in the gay community, but guess what? From what I've heard, it is also an issue in the straight community! (*laughter*) Shocking I know, but it's true! (*laughter*) We are the same. We have the same slice of people as straight people. This includes people who are monogamous and treat sex as something that belongs only within a loving relationship and those who are sexually promiscuous.

In general, LGBTQ students are at a greater risk of physical and psychological danger, physical violence, sexual harassment, verbal harassment, name-calling, insults, taunting, and invisibility at school than their non-gay peers (Mayberry 2006, Pollock 2006). Many gays lack validation, the acknowledgment that we exist. When I was a doctoral student at Indiana University, one of my professors described a successful mathematician who committed suicide in his thirties. The professor then said what a shame it was that this man couldn't accept his sexuality. This single comment was validating to me and gave me a sense of support from this professor.

The stress of trying to hide as a gay person can be overwhelming. If you are heterosexual, imagine what it might be like to avoid letting others know you are heterosexual. You might, for example, avoid mentioning your husband or boyfriend and, if you do, you might just speak of him as a friend.

In school, there are many negative consequences of the stress associated with being gay. Gay students are three to five times more likely to have decreased academic performance than straight students (Cooper and White 2004). This often results in lower GPAs and lower college aspirations. Of course, some gay people overcompensate and become overachievers.

However, this is not the norm. Gay students in school have a higher rate of school absenteeism—often due to an unsafe climate at school—and gay children are more likely to be kicked out of their homes, run away from home, attempt suicide, drop out of school, and abuse drugs and alcohol (Sadowski 2003).

There are commonalities in the ways people from marginalized groups are mistreated (McCready 2004). For example, as Table 2.1 shows, people from marginalized groups are often bullied. However, there are differences between LGBTQ students and other marginalized groups. Gay children are likely to have straight parents, often leading to rejection and friction. Gay children may hide the fact that they are gay from their family. Sometimes gay children are even kicked out of their homes because of their sexual orientation. Gay children may go through stressful situations, and may not have parents who can say, "I understand. I've been there too. Let me tell you what I went through and how I handled it."

It can be difficult for gay people to identify other gay people. One of my friends said, "I wish we [gays] were all born purple so people would know how many of us are out there and we could find each another." Gay people are faced with the dilemma of "coming out" every day to people who may presume they are straight. Sometimes I wish I could just go on national TV like Ellen DeGeneres and tell everyone, "I am gay!" (*laughter*) Seriously, school should be a safe place for all students, and for gay students in particular, because their homes might not even be safe places (Cooper and White 2004, Lipkin 2004, Mayberry 2006).

The Need to Address LGBTQ Issues in Our Schools and Communities

LYNDA I'd like to pose a question. Do you think we are adequately addressing LGBTQ issues in our schools and communities?

SANDRA I would say, "No." I am substituting in many schools this year, and I have never seen LGBTQ issues brought up in any of the schools. Also, I was raised in a very tiny town, and no one brought up this issue in my community. In fact, when I saw you at the farmer's market this past summer; I could only assume that your partner was with you?

LYNDA Yes.

SANDRA I suspected that, and I was fine with that, but my cousin (who is younger than me) was with me when we saw you and your partner. My cousin was raised in the same small town as me. She said, "Did you know her?" I said, "Yeah, and she is awesome. She taught me a lot. I actually like math because of her." My cousin said, "That's cool, but don't you think she is gay?" I said, "Maybe, but I don't really care. I just see her as an awesome person." My cousin was totally taken aback that I would accept—and even like and respect—a gay person. Because I grew up in the same community, I know my cousin had never addressed LGBTQ issues in our school or our community. If she had, she would likely have been more accepting of gay people.

LYNDA I appreciate it when an opportunity like that comes up and people respond the way you did. That is exactly what we need. We need conversation that is more honest. We need more education. Education is crucial, and it happens both formally and informally. I have another question: How many of you have seen LGBTQ issues addressed in any significant way in school?

KELLY I have not seen LGBTQ issues addressed broadly in school, but I addressed gay issues once in a classroom of second graders. I was teaching in an African American community, and I heard some second graders making derogatory comments about homosexuals. I said, "Well, do you know what a homosexual is? You explain to me what a homosexual is and then we'll talk about the comments you are making about homosexuals." Needless to say, the children did not understand the term homosexual. I actually got some children's books about prejudice and homosexuality. However, there was some backlash from parents in the community when I introduced the books.

BETH We are talking about the rights and needs of gay students, but what about gay teachers? I think it is tragic that gay teachers must hide their sexual orientation because they could talk with and relate to gay children in schools.

LYNDA You are right that there are issues in schools that pertain to gay teachers as well as gay students (King 2004). I have found that LGBTQ issues are often feared in schools. For example, when I taught in a middle school after I realized I was gay, it terrified me to think about the possible repercussions of being a gay middle school teacher. I never lied about my sexual orientation, but I certainly hid it.

There is not much being done in schools for gay students and teachers (Biegel and Kuehl 2010, Cooper and White 2004). Certainly, LGBTQ issues are very sensitive and thus difficult to address. I admire people with the courage to do so. I think we need to teach children in a gentle way. This means helping others critically examine their perspectives and practices and the potential consequences in a non-threatening manner. Just telling someone to stop their behavior often isn't the best way to reach others.

NINA This is the first time in my whole life LGBTQ issues have ever been discussed in a classroom setting (Lipkin 2004). I have talked with my family about topics such as drugs and sex, but never LGBTQ issues. In school, I have talked about racism, sexism, poverty, and everything else; LGBTQ issues have been "off limits" in school and at home.

LYNDA The silence about LGBTQ issues is staggering. The more we do to create a better society, the more we all benefit. We need straight allies! That is, people need to stand up for important issues even if they do not directly affect them.

Here are some more questions: If you think we should address LGBTQ issues in school, when and how should we do so? Is there a particular grade level you would recommend? How should we address the topic?

NINA I don't think there is a time when children are too young to start learning about LGBTQ issues. I think a lot of psychological damage can happen to people and their families when LGBTQ issues are kept silent. Here is an example. My mother-in-law is a lesbian. She has four children, and she was married for 25 years. My husband is the only one out of her four children to accept her. I tell her I'm fine with her and that she is my mom. We call her partner Aunt Dee, and we love Aunt Dee. However, her other children turn their backs toward her. I think that is because they lack education and understanding about LGBTQ issues.

LYNDA Sometimes if we accept people who are gay, we may feel like a lone voice. But that is where change starts—with a few people who care and are willing to speak up (Bennett 2004). So, it sounds like you are saying it is important to start teaching about acceptance of gay people at a very young age.

RHONDA Well, I think the "how" to address gay-related issues is a good question. Two years ago, I had a student in my classroom with two dads. In my classroom, my students write letters home each Friday to tell their parents what they did and what they learned that week. As we talked about how to write the greeting for the letter, I told my students that they could write: "Dear Mom and Dad, or Dear Dad and Dad." I further told my children that families are different, and that is normal. We talked about LGBTQ issues from the perspective of family structure. I am not sure if I handled the situation right, but I was not sure what else to do.

LYNDA Even small things like what you did are big! It may seem small to explain different ways to write a greeting to a letter, but your action was not small. Positively and publicly acknowledging that there are different kinds of families benefited not only the child who had two dads, but it undoubtedly helped expand the thinking of the other children in your class. So, in reality, the "simple" thing you did is actually quite monumental. Some teachers are afraid to even say something like that at school, fearing they may get in trouble. I don't see how you could get in trouble for stating a fact. It is pure fact that there are a lot of same-sex parented families in the United States (Lugg 2003).

ALICE The reason I don't even say small things about gay-related issues at school is that I am never sure where conversations with the children will go. Children can start asking lots of questions. I wonder things like, "How much should I talk about?" and "What might happen if I discuss gay-related issues at school?"

LYNDA I think the best we can do is to not beat ourselves up for not responding perfectly and to keep educating ourselves to develop more knowledge and better skills (Ohlander, Batalova, and Treas 2005). One way we, as teachers, often develop better skills is to reflect on situations we do not feel we handled in the best manner (Birden 2005). When we look back, we can explore what happened, how we handled the situation, and how we might handle it differently the next time.

ALICE Students in my classroom have told me they have family members who are gay. They have also described some of the pain they have watched family members experience. For that reason, I think we need to address LGBTQ issues. When I was raising my four children, I tried to take a "normal" approach with them. When I discussed dating with my children, I told my daughters they may have girlfriends, and I told my sons they might have boyfriends. That was my way of letting them know that dating people of the same sex is normal. The beauty of my approach with my children was that when they went off to college and encountered gay people, they were advocates for gays because being gay seemed normal to them. I think it is important to talk about LGBTQ issues as normal and acceptable.

LYNDA If we talk about issues positively and inclusively, we normalize them. I appreciate it when I hear someone use the terminology "spouse or partner" or when I fill out a form that says this. We help children when we let them know from an early age that being gay is okay (Rofes 2005).

Specific Strategies for Addressing LGBTQ Issues in School

LYNDA Parents play a crucial role in children's education at home and at school. If you are going to address LGBTQ issues in your classroom, do you think you should send home permission slips to let parents know in advance? Should parents have the right to opt their children out of LGBTQ-related discussions?

KELLY Well, another approach might be to talk with your principal before addressing LGBTQ issues in your classroom. If you have heard your students making anti-gay comments, you may want to talk with your principal about addressing this kind of talk in your room.

ALICE Addressing LGBTQ name-calling in our classrooms is a normal thing to do (Ohlander, Batalova and Treas 2005). It is in the same category of name-calling because someone is fat. Name-calling for any reason is not appropriate, and we have a responsibility to address that in our classrooms. I believe we have a responsibility to address gay-related name-calling in our classrooms. If a parent raised this as an issue, I'd defend my decision to address gay name-calling as fitting in the general category of not tolerating name-calling. Would I need a permission slip to address name-calling in my classroom? No. If parents raised my addressing of anti-gay name-calling as an issue, I'd say, "If your child is getting teased because of having brown hair, do you want me to send home a permission slip to say that I'm going to address the issue in my classroom that children can't tease brown-haired kids?" Of course not. That's silly.

BETH I think that we should not need to send home permission slips to address concerns about marginalized groups or stereotypes. If I were addressing marginalized groups in my classroom, I would consider gays one of the marginalized groups. I do not believe that I need parent permission slips to address this issue.

ALICE While I do see a lot of validity to what you all are saying, I am torn. I think parents have a right to know what their kids are learning in school. If I were a parent, I would want to know: What are you going to tell my child about homosexuality? I just do not know if we should send a note home.

JENNIE Well, then, if you are worried about addressing LGBTQ issues in your classroom, maybe you could just send a note home mentioning all of the topics you are going to cover in your class and inviting the parents of your children to come sit in your classroom any time they would like to do so. This would not allow parents to opt their children out of instruction. Rather, it would invite them to join you.

RHONDA At the beginning of the [school] year, I send a letter home to parents saying they will be receiving a letter from me each month outlining what topics we will address. So, if—for example—I say at the beginning of the school year we will be addressing families the first month of school, I mention that we will address such topics as the type of families that we have, family relationships, and what it means to be part of a family. I always put at the bottom of my letters that parents are invited to join the children and me in our classroom for the lessons related to these topics.

KELLY I think we should send letters to parents letting them know what we are addressing in our classrooms. Then, the ball is in their court. We, as teachers, should not try to hide what we are addressing in our classrooms. However, we also should not make it easy for parents to opt their children out of the topics/issues we address in class.

LYNDA Yes, and as some of you have said, LGBTQ issues fit naturally within topics that pertain to types of families, name-calling, bullying, biases, and stereotypes.

CHERIE Well, many people argue that the schools and teachers are not going to tell them what their child should know and learn. While I do see that side of the argument, I believe we are discussing the teaching of respect. We are not discussing teaching about sex. In my classroom, I have a responsibility to teach about respect, and I believe that is something parents have to accept.

NINA Yes, but doesn't the teaching of respect fall under the issue of moral education? Is that appropriate to address in our classrooms?

CHERIE See, I think parents have the right to opt their kid out of anything they want. They can opt them out of long division if they want to.

NINA But the children will not be promoted to the next grade then.

CHERIE I just think parents get to decide about their own child.

ALICE Well, I agree with sending home a letter letting parents know what topics we will address in class. However, sometimes LGBTQ issues come up outside of lessons, like the name-calling situations we have already discussed. When sensitive issues come up in my classroom, I tell my children they should go home and discuss these issues with their parents so their parents know what we have been discussing in school.

LYNDA I do want to share my personal perspective about some of the issues you have been raising. I do not think we can let parents opt their children out of lessons we believe are important to the curriculum. Why? Because where would this end? If, for example, we want to teach about famous African Americans during Black History month, what if we have racist parents who object? Some parents may believe sex education is a different matter. However, sexual orientation does not fall under that category (Lugg 2003, Morris 2005). I believe we need to normalize gay issues as much as possible (Ohlander, Batalova and Treas 2005). Consequently, anything we, as teachers, might do that would take gay issues out of the curriculum would bother me. If we sent a permission slip home for that separately from other things we teach, we would make it seem abnormal. I would not want us to send home a school newsletter saying something like: "We will address homosexuality in class next week. Come and see me if you have any concerns." Yes, information and communication with parents is important, but I believe that when we raise LGBTQ issues with parents, we do not want to make addressing gay issues abnormal in any way.

I would like to end this conversation by discussing some strategies, approaches, and ideas we, as teachers, may want to use to normalize gay issues and include them in our classrooms.

- Show support of gays in subtle ways (e.g., display a rainbow flag or a pink triangle as a demonstration of LGBTQ support).
- Teach about gay-related issues. For example, where did the rainbow flag come from? What about the pink triangle?
- Use inclusive language. Say, for example, "your two parents" rather than "your mother and father."
- Object to the use of inappropriate gay-related language, jokes, or humor.
- Be aware of gay-related resources to share with children and their parents.
- Introduce historical or contemporary LGBTQ people into class material.
- Include gay-related children's books in school/classroom libraries (e.g., *Zack's Story*, *Daddy's Roommate*, and *Heather Has Two Mommies*), and read these books to students.
- Invite gay guest speakers into the classroom.

These are some of many ways you can address LGBTQ issues in school. I hope you will try one or more of these ideas in your classroom.

Implications for Teacher Education

After Lynda left, Cindy and Julie facilitated discussion of Lynda's session. The discussion was intended to stimulate thinking about possible ways to address LGBTQ issues in pre-service and in-service teacher education classrooms by sharing information (relevant statistics and research findings) and engaging in semi-structured discussion where students were encouraged to be open and honest in sharing their thinking. This format allowed students to gain factual information, process ideas, and share strategies. However, an ideal scenario would allow more time, preferably involving more than one class period, to explore topics in greater depth and breadth.

Lynda initially addressed general gay-related content to develop context before focusing specifically on the school setting, generating insight into issues and concerns that affect LGBTQ students before discussing classroom approaches to addressing LGBTQ issues. The "resilience" of LGBTQ students might also be addressed; some LGBTQ students use their experiences to develop strength and strategies for moving through the world.

Techniques Lynda used included giving specific (sometimes personal) examples, using humor, and facilitating discussion that allowed students to comment on presented material and respond to teaching-related questions. These techniques helped students connect with the material, feel "safe" and reflect on and offer ideas related to classroom issues they may face. It is important to carefully plan key information and discussion questions in advance.

Prospective and practicing teachers often generate good strategies for addressing LGBTQ issues in schools. It is useful to structure and encourage this collective brainstorming. However, teacher educators should also play a key role in providing "hard evidence" and suggested instructional approaches. We conclude by suggesting the following strategies for teacher educators:

- Establish a safe climate where students may be open and honest, taken seriously, and treated with respect regardless of their views.
- Include factual information, such as data on the percent of students who are LGBTQ or have LGBTQ family members, LGBTQ students' school performance and experiences (attendance, achievement, behavior, interactions with others, etc.), and attention schools devote to LGBTQ matters (e.g., school policies and teacher interventions or lack thereof).
- Use specific examples and personal stories, preferably from varied sources.
- Pose carefully planned questions related to what students may face as future or present teachers, such as those asking students to consider in which grade levels it is appropriate to address these issues and in what manner, as well as

how they will communicate with school principals and parents proactively and reactively on this topic.

- Help students understand that sexual minorities cannot be lumped into one group. Take time to learn about the differing experiences and needs of youth who are gay, lesbian, bisexual, transgender, intersex, and so forth, in addition to understanding the role of gender identity and gender expression.
- Use varied instructional approaches, such as hearing/viewing presented data, reading and discussing articles or stories, watching films, listening to guest speakers, role playing, and engaging in small- and whole-group discussions.
- Provide students with resources for furthering their own knowledge and consulting for teaching purposes (e.g., helpful websites and youth literature booklists).
- Research practical ideas to provide strategies for incorporating LGBTQ material into curriculum, supporting and encouraging LGBTQ individuals (students and colleagues), and interacting with parents and principals (see "Selected Resources" below).

Selected Resources

The Gay, Lesbian and Straight Education Network (GLSEN): http://www.glsen.org/.
Meyer, Elizabeth J. *Gender and Sexual Diversity in Schools*. New York: Springer, 2010.
Safe Schools Coalition: http://www.safeschoolscoalition.org/safe.html.

References

Allen, Louisa. 2005. "Concrete and Classrooms: How Schools Shape Educational Research." *British Journal of Sociology of Education* no. 26 (4): 491–504.

Bennett, Lisa. 2004. "Break the Silence." *Teaching Tolerance* no. 26: 36–39.

Biegel, Stuart, and Sheila James Kuehl. 2010. *Safe at School: Addressing the School Environment and LGBT Safety Through Policy and Legislation*. Boulder, CO: National Education Policy Center.

Birden, Susan. 2005. *Rethinking Sexual Identity in Education*. Lanham, MD: Rowman and Littlefield.

Cooper, Karyn, and Robert E. White. 2004. *Burning Issues: Foundations of Education*. Lanham, MD: Scarecrow Education.

Erchick, Diana B., and Raylene Kos. 2003. "Emergent Voices: Confronting Sociopolitical Elements in Preservice Education." *Pedagogy, Culture & Society* no. 11: 189–200.

Ferfolja, Tania. 2007. "Teacher Negotiations of Sexual Subjectivities." *Gender & Education* no. 19 (5): 569–586. doi: 10.1080/09540250701535584.

Gruber, James E., and Susan Fineran. 2008. "Comparing the Impact of Bullying and Sexual Harassment Victimization on the Mental and Physical Health of Adolescents." *Sex Roles* no. 59 (1/2): 1–13. doi: 10.1007/s11199-008-9431-5.

Kimmel, Michael S., and Michael A. Messner. 2001. *Men's Lives*. Boston: Allyn and Bacon.

King, James R. 2004. "The (Im)possibility of Gay Teachers for Young Children." *Theory Into Practice* no. 43 (2): 122–127.

Lipkin, Arthur. 2004. *Beyond Diversity Day: A Q & A on Gay and Lesbian Issues in Schools.* Lanham, MD: Rowman and Littlefield.

Lugg, Catherine A. 2003. "Sissies, Faggots, Lezzies, and Dykes: Gender, Sexual Orientation, and a New Politics of Education?" *Educational Administration Quarterly* no. 39 (1): 95–134. doi: 10.1177/0013161x02239762.

Mayberry, Maralee. 2006. "School Reform Efforts for Lesbian, Gay, Bisexual, and Transgendered Students." *The Clearing House: A Journal of Educational Strategies, Issues and Ideas* no. 79 (6): 262–264. doi: 10.3200/TCHS.79.6.262-264.

McCready, Lance T. 2004. "Understanding the Marginalization of Gay and Gender Non-Conforming Black Male Students." *Theory Into Practice* no. 43 (2): 136–143.

Meyer, Elizabeth J. 2009. *Gender, Bullying and Harassment: Strategies to End Sexism and Homophobia in Schools.* New York: Teachers College Press.

Morris, Marla. 2005. "Queer Life and School Culture: Troubling Genders." *Multicultural Education* no. 12 (3): 8–13.

Ohlander, Julianne, Jeanne Batalova, and Judith Treas. 2005. "Explaining Educational Influences on Attitudes toward Homosexual Relations." *Social Science Research* no. 34 (4): 781–799. doi: 10.1016/j.ssresearch.2004.12.004.

Pollock, Sandra L. 2006. "Counselor Roles in Dealing with Bullies and Their LGBT Victims." *Middle School Journal* no. 38 (2): 29–36.

Rimm, Sylvia. 2005. *Growing Up Too Fast: The Rimm Report on the Secret World of America's Middle Schoolers.* Emmaus, PA: Rodale Press.

Rofes, Eric E. 2005. *A Radical Rethinking of Sexuality and Schooling: Status Quo or Status Queer?* Lanham, MD: Rowman and Littlefield.

Russo, Ronald G. 2006. "The Extent of Public Education Nondiscrimination Policy Protections for Lesbian, Gay, Bisexual, and Transgender Students: A National Study." *Urban Education* no. 41 (2): 115–150. doi: 10.1177/0042085905284957.

Sadowski, Michael. 2003. "Growing up in the Shadows: School and the Identity Development of Sexual Minority Youth." In *Adolescents at School: Perspectives on Youth, Identity, and Education*, edited by Michael Sadowski, 85–101. Cambridge, MA: Harvard Education.

Tomsho, Robert. 2003. "School's Efforts to Protect Gays Face Opposition." *The Wall Street Journal*, February 20.

3

SPEAKING OF SEXUALITY

Teaching, Learning, and Mothering through the Questions

Veronica E. Bloomfield

For José

It took me years to feel comfortable speaking about sexuality. Moving beyond childhood and teen experiences to becoming a teacher and a mother caused me to gain competency in unexpected ways. Yet, my willingness to meet the questions as they arose provided me opportunities for both personal and academic growth.

Speaking of (My) Sexuality

As a straight, white, middle-class woman, I have few memories where LGBTQ issues were specifically addressed or acknowledged in my K–12 education. Growing up, I was fortunate to have parents who allowed me to ask questions, and who answered them from an educational standpoint. As an elementary student, I knew where and how babies came from, about menstruating, and that one of my parents' best friends was gay. I understood changes would happen to my body during adolescence, but I did not comprehend how profoundly my feelings would affect my sexuality, or vice versa.

I think it is common to associate sexuality with adolescence or adulthood, but as Covington (1991) observed, our sexualities are with us the whole of our lives. Our sexualities grow and change and are not necessarily fixed parts of our identity. When I consider sexuality as a thread running throughout my life, my earliest memory takes place in pre-school. I recall my friend Michelle and I running through the sand box, being chased by two boys from our class. We would scream, giggle, and run away from them. Then we would make our way back to them in the sandbox, converse a little, bait them, and be chased all over again. This was the pre-school version of flirting. We had feelings about what was happening. We had feelings toward and about our friend-boys. They may not have been sexual feelings, per se, but they were related to our gender and sexualities. I was not self-conscious of these feelings, perhaps had no words for them. I did not consciously register them, and thus did not speak of them.

The next related memory I have was in third grade. I was "liked" by a boy whom I did not like back. He bugged me about it daily, saying, "You like me; you like me." I answered back, "No, I do not like you," to which he smugly replied, "I know you don't *like* me, you *love* me." I was mortified. I felt voiceless. I ran away and hid in a far corner of the playground.

This situation caused unexpected feelings in the pit of my stomach. I felt nervous, uncomfortable, and exposed. I did not want to be liked *or* teased this way. I was embarrassed by the situation, but spoke of it to no one. I did not know I could or should talk about these feelings, and, even if I had known, my embarrassment would have kept me silent. These instances could be considered extensions of what Eisner (1979/2002) calls the "null" curriculum. These early experiences shaped how I did (and did not) perceive my gender and sexuality.

When I was a teen, the ideal female body was "the waif," incarnate in the small frame of Kate Moss. At 17, I was a size 12 and curvier than many of my peers. I was aware my body did not resemble theirs, and I harbored self-hate and body shame. When looking in a full-length mirror, I frequently wished I could cut the flesh off my hips, belly, stomach, and thighs. I did not look like those women in magazines, on billboards, television advertisements, in movies, and other media where they were explicitly sexualized and objectified, but wished I did. At the same time, I did not want to be seen like that—as a thing. I wanted to be a person with sexuality; I didn't want my sexuality to determine my personhood. In addition, fear was closely linked with my sexuality. Movies, teen novels, after-school specials, and even high school guest speakers warned of the dangers of physical attack and rape. Some of this information was helpful and practical, but some was detrimental, inferring that I was a target, but not one of my own making. Threats to my physical safety became linked to my sexualized, female body.

As an adolescent I did not relate to the images of women I saw in movies, magazines, and television shows. Most women in my family did not look, dress, or behave in flirtatious or overtly sexualized ways. I inferred at a young age that there was more than one way to "be a woman," when I compared the beauty routines of my next door neighbor's mother to my own. I had never before seen the eyelash curler, hot rollers, mascara, or lip wax she used. Although the womanly ways of my mother and grandmother did not match the glossy photographs and images I ingested regularly, I internalized these external messages and believed I needed to be other than how (or what) I was in order to be socially acceptable. I needed to be thinner, blonder, taller. I needed to be flawless, hairless, big eyed, and buxom. I needed to be less like myself and more like those images. Years later, I still wage a constant inner battle between self-acceptance and self-loathing. As a feminist, I know better. However, I can't keep myself from the compulsion. I am not alone in this. A wealth of research discusses the media's effect on the self-esteem and body image of young women and girls (APA 2014, Kilbourne 1979/1987, Meyers and Biocca 1992, Tiggeman and Lynch 2001).

When I was a freshman in high school, I received a valentine from a male classmate. It was third grade all over again, except this time it was in sexually explicit writing. On this valentine, a classmate I barely knew detailed in writing what he wanted to do with me sexually. I got a sinking feeling in my stomach. The noise and activity of homeroom blurred around me as I prayed no one else could see what I was reading. I got up from my desk in a haze and threw it away. I could not even finish reading it. I wanted to run away and hide, as I had done on the playground in third grade. I was embarrassed, humiliated, and spoke of it to no one.

For the next four years, and beyond, I wore baggy clothes: long-sleeved shirts and blouses, turtlenecks, long skirts, and dresses. I hid my body. I did not want to be acknowledged or judged for my physicality. I wanted to be seen for me, not for my "blossoming" adolescent frame. Wanting to hide from unwanted sexual advances meant I also hid myself from any potential suitors, and disconnected from the part of me that could have taken initiative in seeking out pleasure and connection on my own terms.

Hiding myself to avoid unwanted attention meant I was also hidden from and felt overlooked by individuals I found attractive. It was a peculiar dance, the dance of my adolescent sexuality: wishing to be simultaneously seen yet overlooked, wanting attention from some, while wishing to be invisible to others; wishing to be noticed yet not harmed.

Each of these anecdotes took place in school settings. School was not only a place of formalized learning, but of socialization, anxiety, excitement, and fear. Lessons and class discussions about how our social experiences with one another affected both our self-image and educational experiences were absent. I did not learn to critique advertisements, movies, and other media portrayals until I was well into college where I realized how strategies like media literacy and critical analysis not only fostered academic abilities, but also can make a difference in how children and youth view themselves and the world, contributing significantly to how they can affect change and assert their own agency.

Speaking of (Student) Sexualities

This prior knowledge accompanied me into the classroom as a fifth grade teacher. Despite my own struggles with food and body image, I was shocked to see 10-year-old girls skipping food in the lunch lines because "they were fat." I was surprised to hear them talk about movies they had seen, quoting risqué innuendos. Even though they did not fully understand what was said, these portrayals affected their self-perceptions and generalizations about gender, sexuality, and romantic relationships.

I was responsible for "the talk," given annually to students with signed permission slips. For one week, anatomy, biology, and sexuality were included in the official school curriculum. Over time, I realized gender and sexuality were present in the classroom every day of the entire year, even when unspoken and unrecognized. It was present when students developed crushes on one another and waited for each other by the bathrooms at recess, when 10- and 11-year-old girls began menstruating, when someone's older sister or mother got pregnant and/or had a baby, when someone repeated sexual references from a song or movie, and when students used the word "gay" as an insult. My students experienced changes in their bodies, felt new feelings, and developed new questions such as when, during a fractions lesson, one student raised her hand and said, "What's a virgin?" I wasn't expecting that. With 28 pairs of eyes fixed upon me I looked right at her and said, "That's a good question! We will talk about that a little bit later." She wasn't embarrassed and neither was I. My credentialing program had provided preservice teachers with tools to be allies and advocates for a diverse student body, but no one prepared me for moments like these. I relied on my own common sense and judgment, knowing my reactions to student questions were a direct reflection of how comfortable I felt in dealing with these topics in my own life.

One of the greatest queries of children and adolescents is, "Am I normal?" (Rosenzweig 2012). Children who grow up with the privilege of fitting into a heteronormative society have mixed feelings about growing up, belonging, and accepting themselves. These feelings compound exponentially for LGBTQ students. As educators, we have a responsibility to treat all of our students with dignity and respect. Oftentimes it is our own life experiences, family values and upbringing, and our relationship to our own genders and sexualities that can make us hesitant to address these issues, especially in academic settings.

Over the years, I relied on several strategies to address gender and sexuality in age-appropriate ways. Classroom libraries, acknowledging and appreciating diversity, questioning stereotypical gender roles, class discussions, classroom practice, and discussing the power of words all offer starting points for educators and parents interested in expanding their repertoire to include gender and sexuality.

Classroom Libraries

The types of books we have available (or absent) in our classrooms are part of the hidden curriculum, part of unspoken messages we unknowingly communicate to students. If you are not comfortable overtly discussing issues regarding sexuality and gender identity as part of your classroom practice, you can begin by sending affirming and inclusive non-verbal messages through the medium of your classroom library. (If there is not a library space or extra bookshelf in your room, you can use the whiteboard rail as a display shelf.) Displaying books, and having other age-appropriate resources available is one way you can begin to act as an ally. Many age-appropriate picture books, chapter books, novels, and educational materials can normalize the experience of LGBTQ students while educating the rest of the student body. An online search using keywords "gay," "lesbian," and "children's books" resulted in several comprehensive lists that include titles such as *Donovan's Big Day* (Newman and Dutton 2011), *How it Feels to Have a Gay or Lesbian Parent* (Snow 2004), *The Different Dragon* (Bryan 2006), *And Tango Makes Three* (Richardson, Parnell, and Cole 2012). Chapter books for older children and youth, which feature gay and lesbian characters or themes, include *Box Girl* (Withrow 2001), *Totally Joe* (Howe 2011), *The Boy in the Dress* (Walliams and Blake 2010), and *The Popularity Papers* (Ignatow 2010). The Rainbow List is another resource for educators, family members, and the greater community. Developed by the American Library Association, the Rainbow List is a bibliography of books with significant gay, lesbian, bisexual, or transgender content, and which are aimed at youth, birth through age 18 (Rainbow Books 2014, http://glbtrt.ala.org/rainbowbooks/archives/1103). The Gay, Lesbian, and Straight Education Network (GLSEN.org) has many educational resources available, such as educator guides, LGBTQ inclusive curriculum, and lesson plans on bullying, bias, and diversity (GLSEN 2015). The Centers for Disease Control and Prevention (CDC) offer online resources for youth, such as bullying information, questions and answers for LGBTQ youth, the "It Gets Better" project, and help for suicide prevention (2015, http://www.cdc.gov/lgbthealth/youth-resources.htm). Teaching Tolerance provides information and resources on creating an inclusive LGBTQ school climate, bullying and LGBTQ students, and suggestions for how to ally yourself with LGBTQ youth (2015, www.tolerance.org). Of course, it would be wonderful to read excerpts from any of these books or resources aloud and to be able to discuss them as a learning community, but merely making them visible and available may be a first step to incorporating these topics into your teaching practice.

Acknowledging and Appreciating Family Diversity

One way to talk about issues pertaining to sexuality and diversity is to let students talk about their own life experiences. If you do not feel comfortable discussing these issues with confidence, you can create a space where students can share and educate one another. Our students come to us with a wide range of life experiences and family backgrounds. Part of honoring diversity and promoting inclusiveness can include celebrating family diversity. Giving students an opportunity to talk about their lives and the people they spend time with outside of school can enrich the curriculum and deepen conversations about equity and social justice. Value judgments do not need to be assigned. There is more than one way to be a family, and they all reflect the many ways to be human and to be in relationship with one another. Many of the children's books mentioned previously can connect to the topic of family diversity, and films such as *That's a Family* (Chasnoff 2009), available at newday.org, include portrayals of same-sex families alongside adoptive, legal guardian, divorced, grandparent-led, and heterosexual families. The Family Acceptance Project provides resources for family members to support their LGBTQ children. Their videos are used to educate and support diverse families with LGBTQ children, and to help the families decrease rejecting behaviors. The short documentary *Always My Son* (Kleiman and Ryan 2010) chronicles one family's experience of coming to accept the sexuality of their child (familyproject.sfsu.edu/family-videos).

Questioning Stereotypical Gender Roles

In the 1990s, Dr. William Pollack (1999) introduced the concept of "the boy code," along with the notion of a "gender straitjacket" for boys. Pollack noticed that despite the positive impact the feminist movement and initiatives, such as Title IX, had on the educational experiences of girls, not much progress had been made regarding the emotional lives of boys. According to Pollack, the "boy code" is a set of cultural norms and expectations that relegate boys to appear unfeeling, unfazed, and independent. The "gender straitjacket" rewards young men for conforming to traditional expectations and performances of masculinity, while punishing, shunning, and shaming young boys and men for showing emotion, vulnerability, and empathy. Although this book is based on meeting the needs of LGBTQ students, we cannot forget to advocate for the affirmation of the full emotional spectrum of all children as part of creating inclusive environments. As educators, this means we do not shame, embarrass, or shun any child for expressing vulnerability, emotion and/or empathy, and intentionally affirm those who do. According to Pollack, the gender straitjacket lays a foundation for a masking of emotions, which can lead to anger, depression, and violence of one form or another. If we want heterosexual males, who often occupy positions of power in our society, to become allies for oppressed and marginalized groups, we must also become their allies in allowing and encouraging them to feel and express the full range of human emotions.

Pollack (1999) suggests the starting place is becoming sensitive to the early signs of masking feelings. The second step is learning a new way to talk to boys so that they don't feel afraid or ashamed to share their true feelings. Thirdly, he suggests accepting a boy's own emotional schedule, which means learning how to give the boy the time he needs before he is ready to talk. The fourth step involves connection through action, meaning that rather than having a formal talk about "feelings," an adult can join in a preferred activity. The idea is that by participating in an activity, a connection will be established that will allow the child to open up. Finally, Pollack suggests sharing our own experiences. By discussing times that were challenging and how we dealt with them, children (and in this case, especially boys) will hopefully begin to feel less ashamed of their own vulnerable feelings.

Another resource was developed by Dr. Poppy Moon. An eight-week, small group guidance program for boys in third through fifth grade (Moon and

Bowman 2009), *Operation Breaking the Boy Code* is designed as an art therapy group which gives elementary-age boys an opportunity to experience and celebrate different areas of masculinity. Through this program, boys work their way through seven lessons that examine the definition of masculinity and meaning of brotherhood in a variety of cultures.

Despite the influence of the feminist movement and Title IX on educational policy and practice, young women and girls also experience the negative and restricting effects of a gender straitjacket. Though it may be socially acceptable for females to be more "in touch" with their emotions, their physicalities are policed and repressed by the proliferation of one kind of "perfect" body image, the beauty myth, and the objectification of the female body. Julia Taylor (2014) developed *The Body Image Workbook for Teens: Activities to Help Girls Develop a Healthy Body Image in an Image-Obsessed World* to provide practical exercises and tips that address the most common factors that can lead to negative body image. Melissa Atkins Wardy (2014) wrote *Redefining Girly: How Parents Can Fight the Stereotyping and Sexualizing of Girlhood, from Birth to Tween* and is the founder of "Pigtail Pals and Ballcap Buddies," an online marketplace, blog, and advocacy group. *The Sexualization of Girls and Girlhood: Causes, Consequences, and Resistance* (Zurbriggen and Roberts 2012) and *The Lolita Effect: The Media Sexualization of Young Girls and What We Can Do About It* (Durham 2008) are additional resources on this topic. The American Psychological Association formed a task force to examine and summarize the best psychological theory, research, and clinical experience addressing the sexualization of girls via media and other cultural messages. The Report of the APA Taskforce on the Sexualization of Girls documents the sexualization of girls, negative consequences, as well as positive alternatives and approaches to counteracting the influence of sexualization on girls (Zurbriggen et al. 2007). These included media literacy, athletics, extracurricular activities, comprehensive sexuality education, activism by parents and families, alternative media, and empowerment groups. Further research and resources are available through the American Psychological Association's website (APA 2014, http://www.apa.org/pi/women/programs/girls/).

Building empathy with our students and encouraging the development of empathy between students is a key element of releasing the gender straitjacket, and creating safe and inclusive learning environments. Many other lesson plans and curriculum resources regarding empathy and creating safe learning communities are available online. For example, Teaching Tolerance (2015, www.tolerance.org) has created resources for developing empathy with age-appropriate lessons grouped by grade span from kindergarten through twelfth grade.

Styles of communication also have an impact on the way students relate to one another. Despite cultural backgrounds and personal preferences, students can learn respectful and effective ways to communicate with one another both in and outside of school. Again, there are a number of online resources available, on topics such as non-violent communication (CNVC 2016, www.cnvc.org), and restorative justice (Alfred 2015, http://www.rjtica.org, Restorative Justice Center 2015, rjcenterberkeley.org), which are also helpful strategies to use in academic settings.

Class Discussions

For those educators who are hesitant to discuss issues of sexuality, oftentimes the topic of gender can be a starting point in promoting critical thinking and acceptance of individual diversity. Subjects as wide ranging as science, mathematics, music, art, or history provide opportunities to discuss the implications of gender as it pertains to each subject matter. Why were there so few female biologists or mathematicians in past eras? Who are the leading female physicists, biologists, and historians at this time in history? How were women and men portrayed in a certain piece of literature, film, or artwork? How does the time period in which the work was produced reflect the cultural values and assumptions of the author or artist? How can we both honor and problematize these portrayals to be more accurate, affirming, and inclusive? Educators and students alike come to the classroom with their own stereotypes and biases. Creating a classroom environment where both teachers and students can interact and expand their awareness is beneficial for everyone. It is exciting for students to see teachers learning and growing along with them; this also positions teachers as role models for lifelong learning.

In elementary-age classrooms, discussions can be based on teachable moments when comments, teasing, or jokes arise as well as from opportunities provided by the curriculum. Conversations about gender roles and stereotypes can easily originate when discussing current events. Elements of pop culture such as magazine ads, song lyrics, music videos, or movie clips provide rich opportunities to observe, identify, analyze, and challenge the ways genders are portrayed, especially for upper elementary-age children. For example, the Buck Institute for Education showcases a middle school project on gender roles (BIE 2009, http://bie.org/object/video/middle_school_project_gender_roles). This project-based learning experience chronicles middle school students at a charter school in New Jersey working on an interdisciplinary project combining the subjects of Language, Arts, History, Biology, and Media Literacy. This is one example of the powerful learning that can take place around these issues that also connect to rigorous, standards-based learning outcomes.

The organization Read Write Think provides a complete lesson plan for a middle school activity called "He Said/She Said: Analyzing Gender Roles through Dialogue" on their website (Podolski 2014; readwritethink.org). Author Jacqueline Podolski has created four complete lesson plans, through which teachers guide students as they examine stereotypes of what it means to be a man or woman in a particular society. Throughout the activities, students compare the dialogue of male and female characters as they relate to or disrupt gender stereotypes. This activity can be modified to be more age-appropriate for primary grades, and the contents can be altered for a given subject matter.

Gendered Fictions (Martino and Mellor 2000) was written for high school students in order to help them explore how fiction and non-fiction texts construct gender. Students are encouraged to take up "gendered" reading positions that support or challenge particular versions of masculinity and femininity. The authors provide excerpts from 13 texts for analysis to help students develop critical competence in "reading" gender. Whatever format you use, beginning the conversations regarding gender, stereotypes, and identity can be beneficial in providing accurate representations of sexuality.

Classroom Practice

While it is important to question stereotypical gender roles as part of discussion and analysis, it is also important for educators to consider the way our behaviors may unintentionally reinforce gender stereotypes. For example, when I examined the list of classroom jobs, I realized most physically active jobs, such as "desk arrangers" or "trash monitors," were assigned to male students, whereas "sink monitor" or "paper monitor" were assigned to girls. Even though these positions rotated throughout the school year, I noticed my tendency to assign physical jobs to male students and passive or stereotypically domestic roles to female students. I had to break this unconscious habit, so class jobs were no longer assigned according to gender. In addition, one year I noticed a lunchtime soccer league had been organized. When I examined the list of names on the wall, I saw all of the soccer players were upper grade boys, and all of the cheerleaders were upper grade girls. Not only was this a violation of Title IX, but it also conflicted with the concepts of equality and inclusion I promoted during class discussions. In short, I recognized my students were receiving mixed messages. I met informally with the principal and noon duty aides, and both player and cheerleader lists become co-ed. Two days later, a star soccer athlete in my room took *her* place on the field.

Being a critical educator is a lifelong process. There were times I experienced great success, as well as challenging circumstances. Yet, these challenges or disappointments cannot prevent us from engaging in the continuous process of creating equitable and inclusive learning environments for students.

Discussing the Power of Words

Establishing norms or shared community values can be a useful teaching tool in creating positive classroom settings. When is the last time you heard a student say, "You throw like a girl," "That's lame," "You're so ghetto," "That's gay!" or another comment that is an insult disguised as a value judgment based on someone's perceived gender, ability, social economic status, or sexuality? This happens all too often. When students use demeaning language toward one another, we can ignore the comments, which non-verbally communicates our complicity with what was said, or we can directly and compassionately intervene. Children may use inappropriate language without knowing the full meaning or ramification of the words. These are teachable moments. We can talk about the meaning, the history, and/or the implications of language. We can talk about who these words hurt, how they hurt, and why. We can explain why the use of these words harms our learning community and how, out of respect for one another, we need to be thoughtful about the words that we use. Having done this, we can hold them accountable for choosing *other* words with which to express themselves. In addition, if we ask students to refrain from using a specific term, it is helpful to provide them with alternative options. Although students might laugh or giggle, role-playing different situations in class and having them practice substituting one word for another can make the transition easy, even enjoyable.

There may be instances where students say something or interactions occur quickly, surprising us or leaving us unsure how to proceed. Despite the fact that quality teaching incorporates teachable moments, in a world where scripted teaching has been pushed (Ede 2006), some teachers might feel an immediate reaction or spontaneous teachable moment would interrupt the flow of the lesson and/or be handled too hurriedly. In these instances, teachers may want to reflect and revisit the instance on a different day. Returning to a topic and touching on something that recently happened also models the reflecting and revisiting process for students.

It is important to note that our conversations occur within a larger educational context, one predicated upon structural oppression. Having reflective and informative conversations with students can have a significant impact on your classroom community, and can raise awareness about the structural inequality inherent in our educational system. According to Winter and Leighton (2001), structural violence is almost always invisible, embedded in social structures, and normalized by stable institutions and regular experience. "Structural violence occurs whenever people are disadvantaged by political, legal, economic, or cultural traditions. Because they are longstanding, structural inequities usually seem ordinary—the way things are and always have been" (99). Structural violence is manifest in unequal access to resources, political power, education, health care, or legal standing. Discussions and lessons that pertain to gender and sexuality connect to affecting change within a system that has historically marginalized many student groups, LGBTQ being one among several.

Along these same lines, it may be helpful to expose older students to the concept of intersectionality, as it relates to not only a plurality of personal signifiers, but to the interlocking web of oppressions, and how all forms of oppression are related (Crenshaw 1991). This is an important teaching point for students, as being lesbian, gay, or transgender is not an identity that exists in isolation; rather, it interacts with one's culture, class, ability, religious perspective, among many other facets of life.

Speaking of (Childhood) Sexuality

If teaching was a wake-up call for me about gender and sexuality, motherhood has been a sounding alarm. Parenting classes, talk shows, magazine articles, and books provided background information about safety precautions, childhood illnesses, sleep aids, nutrition, conflict resolution, and discipline. None of them prepared me for the ways in which gender and sexuality would be a part of my mothering experience and my child's growth and development from a very early age.

I had been a classroom teacher for eight years when my son was born. Pregnancy and impending parenthood became an arena for discussion, debate, and creativity. Knowing that gender was a social construction and the different ways we perform/resist our own genders, as parents, our basic premise was this: *I want my child to be happy. I will not deter or direct his interests based on preconceived notions of gender. I will encourage his development by following his lead, his own personality, and try to mitigate the gender stereotypes and sexism of our culture as much as possible.* A first attempt at this was not telling anyone the gender of the baby in utero because gender knowledge dramatically alters the kinds of gifts, clothing, and toys given. As a result, the gifts received leaned toward yellow and green blankets, onesies, and a variety of toys. There were items necessary for baby care, but the decision not to reveal the baby's gender successfully avoided the princess vs. bulldozer dichotomy.

Despite attempts at socially conscious parenting, as early as pre-school my son would come home and say things like, "Boys are stronger than girls" or "Only girls wear tights." I tried to provide counter-narratives. In response to the first comment, his father would talk about female athletes and refer to my natural childbirth. Concerning the second comment, I showed him an online video of Baryshnikov dancing. He was duly impressed. We talked about how different people in different places do things differently. He knows that men in our family wear pants and shorts but not dresses; yet, he has been to the Highland Games and seen plenty of men in kilts. Conversely, he has been known to wander around the house and say things like, "Pink is for everybody."

When he was a toddler, he would put on one of my t-shirts and call it a "dress," which was appropriate, as the t-shirt fell below his knees. "I want to wear a dress," he would say and go into my closet. On days I wore jewelry to work, he would put on my bracelets and clomp around the house in my shoes. None of this behavior was discouraged. (Although one day when his father came home from work, we were watching *The Sound of Music*, wearing "dresses" and my jewelry. Upon seeing us and hearing the soundtrack, his father wandered into the kitchen muttering, "I am secure in my sexuality!") Similarly, if I wore clips or barrettes in my hair, my son would ask to wear them. I know homosexuality is a biological reality. I knew wearing my jewelry would not "make" my child gay, anymore than playing sports would "make" him straight. He is who he is and should be able to experience the full range of human expression, whatever that means to him.

So, he helps me bake in the kitchen wearing his grandma's aprons. And, he plays sports outside in the backyard. He has a baby doll he cares for and loves tremendously, but he also plays with dinosaur toys, trucks, and action figures. He likes to sing and dance, wrestle and pounce, visit museums, and go on hikes. I think the same is true for most children, as all of these activities are fun, engaging, and interesting. One holiday he wore his pajamas with one of my grandmother's aprons on top. While the cookies were baking, he played with his Transformer toys. I thought YES! This is what wholeness looks like: he can be a complete self, with the various desires and interests of his heart, and not have pieces of him cut off or buried because he has been forced into a constricting gender performance.

As my son has grown into his elementary years, he has asked questions in innocence and curiosity that have given me pause. "Do kids ever have sex?" "Can teenagers have babies?" "Since I am not supposed to kiss girls until I grow up, should I kiss boys instead to see what it's like?" "My penis feels tingly. What does that mean?" "What is sexy?" "What does it mean when someone says a girl or woman is 'hot?'" I grappled with how to answer his questions, knowing there is often no one "right" answer. Each person would answer based on their own values and beliefs and each of my answers connected to other important topics. For example, the question about kids having sex related to appropriate behavior, child safety, and sexual abuse. Books related to these topics that I found helpful were: *Your Body Belongs to You* (Spelman and Weidner 1997), *It's My Body* (Freeman and Deach 1982), *The Bare Naked Book* (Stinson and Collins 2006), all of which were written for children; and *The Sex-Wise Parent: The Parents' Guide to Protecting Your Child, Strengthening Your Family, and Talking to Kids about Sex, Abuse, and Bullying* was an outstanding adult read (Rosenzweig 2012). Regarding teenagers, sex, kissing, and growing up, I deferred to books such as *It's Perfectly Normal* (Harris and Emberley 2009), *Where Do Babies Come From?* (Sheffield and Bewley 1984), and *What's Happening to my Body?* (Madaras, Madaras, and Sullivan 1983/2007a, b). Each of these books normalizes bodies, human sexuality, and adolescence, while depicting the context of sex as being one between two consenting adults.

Each of these situations reflected questions and experiences my child was having, and, yet, I had my own reactions. Watching my child develop, being witness to his gender and sexuality reminded me of my own experiences. How does this make me feel? What do I say? How do I respond? We live in a very sexualized society. Driving on the freeway before my child could read, he saw billboards for strip clubs, scantily clad female models advertising cars, appliances, restaurants, and clothing (to name a few). He heard snippets of songs on the radio, dialogue on prime time television shows, and adult conversations between family members. In the made-for-children media, he saw predominantly heterosexual relationships, love portrayed by physical activities such as kissing and embrace, the inevitability of romance and coupling.

Why wouldn't children have questions as they try to process this information? As they try to make meaning of their own bodies and bodily experiences? I expected to talk with my child about growth, development, and sexuality, but I assumed it would begin around the same time as it did for my fifth grade students. I did not expect it to start when he was a toddler. I did not expect it to cause me hope, anxiety, self-doubt, and awe. Parents and educators alike struggle when it comes to speaking about gender and sexuality, even as we raise and teach children who live in a culture that simultaneously sexualizes everything while treating the topic of sexuality as deviant and taboo. Pornography and Puritan values collide in the mainstream landscape of American popular culture.

I have learned to speak of sexuality as a life-giving force, and to recognize its presence in my own life. I have seen how my reactions to my child's queries has the potential to shame or affirm, to ridicule or normalize, thusly affecting his self-image, gender identity, and self-esteem. In pondering the questions that children have asked me over the years, I revisit those moments from my own development. Perhaps some of the things I say are also to comfort my own childhood and adolescent self. These conversations and instances are moments of liberation—small and quiet—where I speak my own body, identity, and belief. Now I welcome the questions. There is so much to learn, and we can do it together.

References

Alfred, Rita Renjitham. 2015. *Restorative Justice Training Institute.* Restorative Justice Training Institute 2015 [cited July 29 2015]. Available from http://www.rjtica.org.

APA. 2014. *Sexualization of Girls.* American Psychological Association [cited June 29 2014]. Available from http://www.apa.org/pi/women/programs/girls/.

BIE. 2009. Middle School Project: Gender Roles. YouTube: Buck Institute for Education.

Bryan, Jennifer. 2006. *The Different Dragon.* Illustrated by Danamarie Hosler. Ridley Park, PA: Two Lives Publishing.

CDC. 2015. *LGBT Youth Resources.* Centers for Disease Control and Prevention, Nov. 12, 2014 [cited Aug. 1 2015]. Available from http://www.cdc.gov/lgbthealth/youth-resources.htm).

Chasnoff, Debra. 2009. *That's a Family!* Groundspark, Women's Educational Media.

CNVC. 2016. *Center for Nonviolent Communication: An International Organization.* The Center for Nonviolent Communication 2016 [cited 2016]. Available from http://www.cnvc.org.

Covington, Stephanie. 1991. *Awakening Your Sexuality: A Guide for Recovering Women.* Center City, MN: Hazelden.

Crenshaw, Kimberle. 1991. "Mapping the Margins: Intersectionality, Identity Politics, and Violence against Women of Color." *Stanford Law Review* (6): 1241. doi: 10.2307/1229039.

Durham, Meenakshi Gigi. 2008. *The Lolita Effect: The Media Sexualization of Young Girls and What We Can Do About It.* Woodstock, NY: Overlook Press.

Ede, Anita. 2006. "Scripted Curriculum: Is It a Prescription for Success?" *Childhood Education* no. 83 (1): 29–33.

Eisner, Elliot W. 1979/2002. *The Educational Imagination: On the Design and Evaluation of School Programs.* 3rd ed. Upper Saddle River, NJ: Prentice Hall.

Freeman, L., and C. Deach. 1982. *It's My Body.* Seattle, WA: Parenting Press.

GLSEN. 2015. Gay, Lesbian, and Straight Education Network (GLSEN) 2003–2015 [cited June 23 2015]. Available from http://glsen.customer.def6.com/participate/gsa/about-gsas.

Harris, Robbie H., and Michael Emberley. 2009. *It's Perfectly Normal: A Book about Changing Bodies, Growing Up, Sex and Sexual Health.* Sommerville, MS: Candlewick Press.

Howe, J. 2011. *Totally Joe.* New York: Atheneum Books for Young Readers.

Ignatow, Amy. 2010. *The Popularity Papers: Research for the Social Improvement and General Betterment of Lydia Goldblatt & Julie Graham-Chang.* New York: Amulet Books.

Kilbourne, J. 1979/1984. *Killing Us Softly: Advertising's Image of Women.* Available from www.jeankilbourne.com.

Kleiman, Vivian, and Caitlin Ryan. 2010. *Always My Son.* United States: The Family Acceptance Project.

Madaras, Linda, Area Madaras, and Simon Sullivan. 1983/2007a. *What's Happening to My Body? Book for Boys.* Revised ed. New York: HarperCollins.

Madaras, Linda, Area Madaras, and Simon Sullivan. 1983/2007b. *What's Happening to My Body? Book for Girls.* Revised ed. New York: HarperCollins.

Martino, W., and B. Mellor. 2000. *Gendered Fictions.* Urbana, IL: National Council of Teachers of English.

Meyers, P. and Biocca, F. 1992. "The Elastic Body Image: The Effect of Television Advertising and Programming on Body Image Distortions in Young Women." *Journal of Communication,* 42(3): 108–33.

Moon, P., and S. Bowman. 2009. *Operation Breaking the Boy Code: 8 Week Guidance Program for Boys (Grades 3–5).* Chapin, SC: YouthLight.

Newman, L., and M. Dutton. 2011. *Donovan's Big Day.* New York: Tricycle Press.

Podolski, J. 2014. *He Said/She Said: Analyzing Gender Roles through Dialogue.* National Council of Teachers of English. Available from http://www.readwritethink.org/classroom-resources/lesson-plans/said-said-analyzing-gender-287.html.

Pollack, William S. 1999. *Real Boys: Rescuing Our Sons from the Myths of Boyhood.* New York: Henry Holt & Company.

Rainbow Books. 2014. *Rainbow Project Reading List 2014.* Gay, Lesbian, Bisexual, and Transgender and Social Responsibilities Round Tables of the American Library Association (ALA) 2014 [cited June 6 2014]. Available from http://glbtrt.ala.org/rainbowbooks/archives/1103.

Restorative Justice Center. 2015. *Restorative Justice Center, UC Berkeley.* UC Berkeley [cited July 29 2015]. Available from rjcenterberkeley.org.

Richardson, Justin, Peter Parnell, and Henry Cole. 2012. *And Tango Makes Three.* New York: Simon & Schuster.

Rosenzweig, J. 2012. *The Sex-Wise Parent: The Parents' Guide to Protecting Your Child, Strengthening Your Family, and Talking to Kids about Sex, Abuse, and Bullying.* New York: Skyhorse Publishing.

Sheffield, Margaret, and Shiela Bewley. 1984. *Where Do Babies Come From?* Illustrated ed. Cape May, NJ: Cape.

Snow, Judith E. 2004. *How it Feels to Have a Gay or Lesbian Parent: A Book by Kids for Kids of All Ages, Haworth Gay and Lesbian Studies*. New York: Harrington Park Press.

Spelman, Cornelia M., and Terri Weidner. 1997. *Your Body Belongs to You*. Morton Grove, IL: Albert Whitman.

Stinson, Kathy, and Heather Collins. 2006. *The Bare Naked Book*. Toronto, ON: Annick Press, Limited.

Taylor, J.V. 2014. *The Body Image Workbook for Teens: Activities to Help Girls Develop a Healthy Body Image in an Image-Obsessed World*. Oakland, CA: New Harbinger Publications.

Teaching Tolerance. 2015. *Classroom Resources*. Teaching Tolerance [cited July 12 2015]. Available from http://www.tolerance.org.

Tiggeman, M. and Lynch, J. 2001. "Body Image Across the Life Span in Adult Women: The Role of Self Objectification." *Developmental Psychology*, 37(2): 243–53.

Walliams, D., and Q. Blake. 2010. *The Boy in the Dress*. New York: HarperCollins.

Wardy, Melissa Atkins. 2014. *Redefining Girly: How Parents Can Fight the Stereotyping and Sexualizing of Girlhood, From Birth to Tween*. Chicago, IL: Chicago Review Press.

Winter, Deborah Du Nann, and Dana C. Leighton. 2001. "Structural Violence." In *Peace, Conflict, and Violence: Peace Psychology for the 21st Century*, edited by D. J. Christie, R. V. Wagner and D. A. Winter, 99–101. Upper Saddle River, NJ: Prentice Hall.

Withrow, S. 2001. *Box Girl*. Ontario, Canada: Groundwood Books.

Zurbriggen, Eileen L., Rebecca L. Collins, Sharon Lamb, Tomi-Ann Roberts, Deborah L. Tolman, L. Monique Ward, and Jeanne Blake. 2007. *Report of the APA Task Force on the Sexualization of Girls: Executive Summary*. Washington, DC: American Psychological Association.

Zurbriggen, E., and T. Roberts. 2012. *The Sexualization of Girls and Girlhood: Causes, Consequences, and Resistance*. Oxford: Oxford University Press.

4

BREAKING THE CONSPIRACY OF SILENCE

Creating Spaces at the Intersection of Diversity and Controversy

Marni E. Fisher and Kevin Stockbridge

Taking the exploration of diversity and controversy coupled with LGBTQ issues and concerns into what Deleuze and Guattari (1987) describe as "mapping" through "rhizomatic circles" in order to deterritorialize previous established boundaries and find points of convergence offers a place where liminality crosses with the ideas of thresholds and crossroads. Within this place, diversity and controversy meet: whether we are discussing diversity in terms of race, culture, (dis)ability, religion, or gender and sexuality, points of controversy also emerge due to the clash between the dominant and non-dominant cultures, particularly when coupled with LGBTQ issues (Meem, Gibson, and Alexander 2010).

Framed by our experiences as students and teachers in private or religious educational settings that enforce silence outside dominant heteronormative and conservative viewpoints, we examine the need to accept diversity and apply social justice to education.

The question of literacy and the purpose of story emerges too often as an area for exclusion (Freire 1970/2005, Freire and Macedo 2003, Macedo, Dendrinos, and Gounari 2003) and controversy (ALAOIF 2010, Best 2010), but also offers potential connection across points of diversity (Brown and Stephens 1998, Corliss 1998, Short, Lynch-Brown, and Tomlinson 2005/2014). We need to go into our schools and classrooms not only with the tools for students to see themselves and find their voices, but also with the ability to see those students who are little pools of silence hidden among the rest. Answering this need, we offer two ways to begin: (1) by providing creative spaces for expression, and (2) by creating places for the safe discussion of all types of diversity.

Subjectivity

Like so many things, the inherent subjectivity of the researcher reflects the perspectives, bias, and various inside/outside roles (Janke 2004). This determines what we examine, what we write about, and our choice of topic.

Mapping Silence

Marni. My experiences as a student and an educator have predominantly been in private religious education. The creative, gifted child in a system that leans toward traditional forms, I was usually the outsider, deeply grateful when I ran across a non-traditional teacher with whom I could connect. Upon becoming a teacher, I leaned toward intrinsic student ownership of learning (Bishop and Berryman 2006); democratic, student-centered (Apple and Beane 1995, Dewey 1916, Sehr 1997), and creative learning (Ackerman 2003, Dewey 1916, Eisner 2002, hooks 1994); meaningful relationships with and between students (Ackerman 2003, Apple and Beane 1995, Dewey 1916, Eisner 2002, Nieto 2002), connecting them to the class (Bishop and Berryman 2006), and creating a place for student voice (hooks 1994, Nieto 2005); engaged, multimodal (Gardner 2011), diverse (Guisbond et al. 2006, Nieto 2002, Shaffer 2001), and differentiated pedagogy (Tomlinson et al. 2003); requiring higher level thinking skills (Bloom 1956), and active learning (Dewey 1916).

I know what it means to not fit within the norm, and to not know how to find my voice. I know what it is to live in silence. What I always had, though, was the ability to see myself in the stories I read.

Something I grew increasingly aware of over time was the absolute silence of anything outside normed gender roles and heteronormativity. When private schools offered professional development on social justice, then culture, (dis) ability, religious affiliation (outside that of the school community), and LGBTQ were not addressed. It was often up to the individual teacher to at least embed, or not, multiculturalism into classroom environments. Worse, I found that teaching empathy for others (SooHoo 2006) could be considered unacceptable within the private, religious school system under the wrong principal (Fisher 2013a).

Any whisper of LGBTQ issues (much less LGBTQ acceptance), however, was completely non-existent. We, the teachers, were warned we could lose our jobs if we taught anything outside of the tenants of the religion, or even if the administration found out we were living outside those tenants.

How difficult would it be for a child to find a voice and self-acceptance outside of these established gender and relationship roles? There is always a need to de-center the dominant spaces.

> We not only have to decolonize existing spaces but create non-hierarchical spaces of knowing. We cannot ask hegemonic/dominant spaces to simply

make room for other knowledges to co-exist. The politics of de-centering spaces and dominant knowledge requires that we rethink new ways of creating spaces that allow for centricity of multiple knowledge systems to contend with the asymmetrical power relations that currently exist in educational settings.

(Dei 2005, 3)

Since my area of research is the development of prism theory,[1] I am concerned with the unseen, unheard, unspoken, difficult to measure, and intuitive leaps of thoughts, intuition, genius, "the difficult to grasp or not easily quantified or measured" and the messy spaces "in between" (Fisher 2013b, 190). Using Deleuze and Guatarri's (1987) concept of mapping and rhizomatic inquiry and Jipson and Paley's (1997) method of exploring "issues of multiplicity, elasticity, ambiguity, and asignifying practice in the process of meaning-making" (8), I began reading and writing in rhizomatic circles (Deleuze and Guattari 1987) while looking at the *need* to hear the silenced student outside the gender or heteronormative norms or whose family does not reflect the heteronormative patterns.

I realized I needed more perspective; knowing silencing was not enough. Fortunately, I knew a fellow scholar with a similar background in the silences of private religious education, but with a better perspective in terms of LGBTQ experience.

A Queer Silence

Kevin. Born and raised in the American South as a Catholic school student in the Bible-belt, I always knew this world was far more nuanced than many would have us believe. Identity and power in the cultural sphere were very much connected to the hermeneutic by which one chose to analyze the world and, more importantly, the Bible. There was more than one paradigm at work in my education, and somehow, a child learns to make sense of the many divergent voices proclaiming themselves to be Truth. Indeed, I became increasingly aware of the beauty only a diversity of thought could bring. Yet, I was also keenly, and silently, aware other voices existed in my school that were straining to be heard. Not everyone was given the right to speak. Today, as an educator, I am ever more aware of the limitations placed on some voices, opinions, identities, and expressions in private institutions.

How clearly I remember the day in our religion class when Sister taught us about the "sin of homosexuality." Glibly she reminded us we could remember the intent of the Creator for marital love by the phrase: *God made Adam and Eve, not Adam and Steve.* The class laughed along with her and, with that, my developing queer voice was taught to remain silent. In realizing I was not welcome to speak about my insights on the world from the perspective of my sexuality, I was listening intently to the "hidden curriculum" (hooks 1994,

McLaren 2009) of heteronormativity. This curriculum was present throughout my entire education, from kindergarten through two Master's degrees. Indeed, not only had I been taught this part of me had no rightful place in the classroom, but also that I must be the one who enforces my own silence.

I let the story-line of these educators play out in my life. Unfit for married life in the Church, I became a priest. My passion for social justice and spiritual education were expressed in this vocation, but I ultimately found myself unhappy and estranged from my own heart. I pursued, multiple times, the elimination of my "disordered" sexual attractions, seeking spiritual and pseudo-psychological gurus to lead me into the world of "being normal." Eventually, I broke away from predominant worldview; I can proudly identify myself today as a queer man, educator and scholar.

I approach these reflections as a man acquainted with the power of silence in the oppression of entire populations in our schools. I am a teacher and community service coordinator for a Catholic high school. In my position, I continually dance the fine line between authentic education *welcoming* diversity and carefully selecting my words to avoid termination for publically acknowledging my sexual orientation. Around the country, teachers in private religious schools have found themselves suddenly jobless for being lesbian, queer, bisexual, or gay (see, for example, Gibson 2013, Goldstein 2013). Transgendered and intersexed persons are rarely found on the faculty of these schools or, if they are present, these teachers must ensure their identities remain a secret (see Sinnema 2009).

Young men and women who are LGBTQ fear speaking about parts of themselves not even adults are willing to share. Stuck on an island of solitude, afraid to reach for companionship, too many young people choose silence through suicide (Pike 2012). My voice in this chapter is a loud cry against the damning silence marginalizing *any* person found unacceptable by the dominant culture.

The Need for Diversity and Social Justice

The act of oppression negates humanity, and "with the establishment of a relationship of oppression, violence has already begun" (Freire 1970/2005, 55). Combatting this is the inclusion of multicultural education that "is by definition inclusive. Because it is about all people, it is also for all people, regardless of their ethnicity, language, sexual orientation, religion, gender, race, class, or other difference" (Nieto 2002, 38). The need for diversity and social justice within education emphasizes two points: (1) the importance of voice, and (2) the reality of heteronormative oppression.

The Importance of Voice

There is a regular absence of voice throughout education. This silencing begins with the political machinations of educational crises and the projection of misplaced blame upon and non-professionalization of teachers (Pinar 2012). Promoting oppression and silencing teachers, the absence of voice filters down to the silencing of the student voices so important in developing a sense of connection and relationship affecting student success (Bishop and Berryman 2006).

Teachers should be able to manage change (Fullan 1993), and question current practices (Fullan 1993, Lane, Lacefield-Parachini, and Isken 2003), but the use of politics to "solve" the "problems" of education has resulted repeatedly in political agendas framing the social context of education (Pinar 2012, Tye 2000), taking stances and directions that serve to further degrade, denounce, and oppress certain populations. "The suppression of culture and voice, and the promotion of hegemonic practices increase educational problems" (Fisher 2009, 13). The calls for educational reform that focus on curriculum, "accountability" (aka: high stakes testing), and standardization are often politically motivated (Pinar 2012) and structured to support one part of the population while oppressing others (Apple 2006), promoting the dominant voice (Darder, Baltodano, and Torres 2009). Such reforms often fail due to top-down changers who assume they are not part of the problem; instead, promoting the perception that teachers are not "good enough" (thus, deskilling teachers), without taking into account lack of funding and the tendency to drop responsibility upon teachers without the power, training, and tools necessary to implement change effectively (Tye 2000). "Unless solutions to the classroom and school problems under study tap into the complex theories of action that underlie and maintain the status quo, problems will only be solved in a superficial and temporary manner" (Anderson, Herr, and Nihlen 1994, 27).

When teachers are voiceless in education (Nieto 2002), and "with sanctions and economic penalties dangling overhead, job evaluations hanging in the balance, and the results of each school's performance printed in the newspaper" (Gallagher and Allington 2009, 10), the focus of education loses sight of the children, bending to the stupidities in education (Kohl 2003) and promoting hegemonic practices (Macedo, Dendrinos, and Gounari 2003) instead of advocating for children and embracing cultural diversity (Eisner 2002, Guisbond et al. 2006). This silencing is doubly compounded for the LGBTQ teacher in a private or religious institution who is contractually bound to promote doctrinally sound formulations of sexuality and gender. The silencing of these voices is conspicuous and oppressive. Similarly, teaching within a community with a high religious or conservative population may result in school board or administrative pressures toward silencing at all levels (Reichman 2012).

Student voices are typically left out of educational discussions where "the voices of students are rarely heard in the debates about school failure and success, and the perspectives of students from disempowered and dominated communities are even more invisible" (Nieto 2002, 123). This pattern of silencing and disconnection flows throughout the classroom where student success is strongly affected by student and teacher relationships and a sense of connection and safety engendered through these relationships (Bishop and Berryman 2006). "It is the absence of a feeling of safety that often promotes prolonged silence or lack of student engagement" (hooks 1994, 39). This silencing of children who do not see themselves within the mainstream is exacerbated for children who do not see themselves within established gender identities (Gallas 1998) or do not see their families within portrayed family structures (Reichman 2012).

Heteronormative Oppression

There is always a need to address patterns of heteronormative oppression in education (Koschoreck and Slattery 2006). "Schools can either be part of the solution or a part of the problem in addressing heterosexism and bigotry against LGBTIQ students, staff, and parents" (151). Sixty-nine percent of students perceived to be LGBTQ experience harassment (Koschoreck and Slattery 2006). When homophobic harassment through verbal slurs, anti-gay jokes, or homophobic ridicule is not addressed (Meyer 2009), then a "'societal sense of permission' to marginalize, abuse, or assault gay men, lesbians, bisexuals, and transgendered individuals—or the children of LGBTIQ parents" (155) is created, developing a culture of fear and oppression—promoted by the institution—for the average LGBTQ student (see Figure 4.1). "This condemnation of gay students in schools is pervasive and damaging. The isolation and vulnerability experienced by these students is exacerbated by the refusal of teachers and administrators to intervene on their behalf" (Meyer 2009, 5). Thus, not only do students who identify as LGBTQ or come from LGBTQ forms of non-traditional families find themselves in an institution promoting the silencing of student voices, but they are in a climate allowing for intolerance and the possible flourishing of oppression and bullying (Koschoreck and Slattery 2006).

The Purpose of Story

Stories serve a number of purposes involving understanding our present and past while imagining our future. "Story is at the heart of who we each are as human beings and who we might become" (Short, Lynch-Brown, and Tomlinson 2005/2014, 6). Unfortunately, what we usually see is how "literacy programs generally give people access to a predetermined and preestablished discourse while silencing their own voices" (Freire and Macedo 2003, 360).

It is important that children of all forms of diversity see themselves within the stories they read (Short, Lynch-Brown, and Tomlinson 2005/2014):

> Stories that are handed down from one generation to the next connect us to our past, to the roots of our cultural identities and national heritage, and to the general human condition. Readers grow in their own identities by finding themselves and their families and communities within books and

Experiences of Bullying and Harassment for Students Grades 6–12

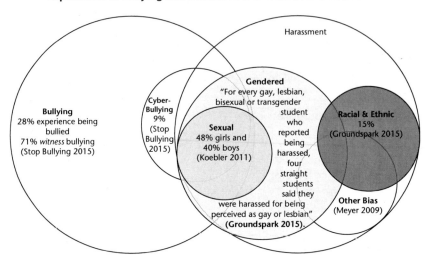

Experiences of Bullying and Harassment for LGBTQ Students

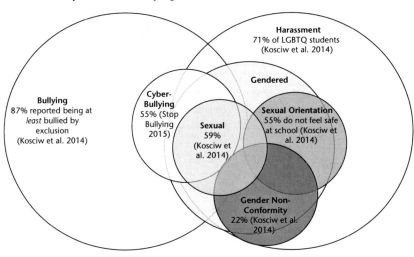

Note: Statistics are pulled from a variety of sources and years. Statistics reports can vary between sources, since a percentage of incidents of bullying and harassment are never reported. However, these numbers still demonstrate the patterns of bullying and harassment as well as the increased risk for LGBTQ students.

FIGURE 4.1 The Relation of Bullying, Harassment, and Gendered Harassment

exploring the multiple connections of their identities, including race, ethnicity, nationality, gender, religion, language, disability, region, family structures, and social class.

(6)

Thus, the stories we read and tell support our understanding of ourselves both within the world of the story and within our lives as readers (Mooney 2004). Additionally, "a good book encourages you to think not only about what you know but also about what you feel, and to remind you that it is acceptable to feel that way and that someone else understands" (28).

The Conspiracy of Silence

The stories we read and tell in education, whether fiction or non-fiction, offer a place for students to find themselves and understand the world around them. What, then, are we offering students who never see themselves and/or their family structures within the educational stories?

Both curriculum and textbooks are predominantly mainstream, and 83 percent of teachers are European American with suburban backgrounds (Short, Lynch-Brown, and Tomlinson 2005/2014). Within this setting, "literacy becomes a weapon that can be used against those groups who are 'culturally illiterate,' whose social class, race, or gender renders their own experiences and stories as too unimportant to be worthy of investigation" (McLaren 2003, 80).

Within many private or religiously based schools, there appears a dichotomy of acceptance, "brotherly love," and social justice paired with intolerance toward the LGBTQ community. In Catholic schools this dual message is a result of theological condemnation of homosexual behaviors and the call to be pastorally responsive to the individual (Martin and Litton 2004). This dichotomy seems to say: love one another and accept those who are different *as long as they agree with me*. Limiting the teaching of social justice to "poverty" or multicultural literature tied to language and culture or ability fails the tenets of social justice when a portion of the population is forced into aligning with dominant culturally normed roles of gender and family.

Multiculturalism recommends including literature, allowing the marginalized to develop understanding of themselves, their cultures, histories, traditions, and people (Nieto 2002), while including and addressing "issues of race, religion, poverty, exceptionalities, and sexual orientation ... to provide a more complete understanding of current issues and of the people who belong to these groups ... challenging prejudice and discrimination" (Short, Lynch-Brown, and Tomlinson 2005/2014, 219), developing historical perspectives, and understanding injustice and bonds of experiences. While the LGBTQ community is and should be included within diversity, material reflecting the LGBTQ community, LGBTQ issues, and gender differences are often considered controversial instead of diverse and subject to censorship as

> an offending object in order to encourage and perpetuate public outcry against transgressive behavior [creating] what Stan Cohen has termed moral panic … most censorship of homosexed art and literature occurs at cultural moments when the fear of corruption by sexually deviant material is framed as a pervasive social problem.
>
> (Meem, Gibson, and Alexander 2010, 309)

Queer-themed books are easily found for young adults (ages 12 and up). However, according to a 2004 poll, teaching about homosexuality at the high school level was acceptable by three out of four parents, and at the middle school level by 50 percent of parents, but LGBTQ subject matter at the elementary level was only acceptable by a few parents (319). Books geared for younger audiences, like *Heather Has Two Mommies* (Newman and Cornell 2009), *In Our Mothers' House* (Polacco 2009), *King and King* (Nijland and DeHaan 2003), and *And Tango Makes Three* (Richardson, Parnell, and Cole 2012) are more likely to appear on banned books lists.

Including LGBTQ literature, historical experiences, and media within the classroom combats the uses of literacy to limit other voices (Koschoreck and Slattery 2006, Short, Lynch-Brown, and Tomlinson 2005/2014). At the same time, it promotes the value of other voices, accepting the LGBTQ culture and existence. Nonetheless, some teachers face restricted literary selection due to administrative and community pressure. This limitation, however, does not mean a moratorium on creating spaces for children to find and express their voices.

Creating Spaces

We want to create spaces for those who are silent and do not see themselves within the dominant discourses, particularly students who are queer and questioning. Our subjectivities as teachers and as students come into play when creating spaces, as do the subjectivities of our students.

As teachers, we need to develop social awareness both in ourselves and within our students (Fullan 1993, Lane, Lacefield-Parachini, and Isken 2003, Lindsey, Campbell-Jones, and Roberts 2005, Marshall and Oliva 2010). This includes promoting understanding and respect for difference. Ideally, this respect should be sourced within the administration, since the morals and values of the leadership affects the entire school: leaders, teachers, staff, parents, and students (Marshall and Oliva 2010). However, we do not all teach within the ideal school. When "injustice and inequality are taken for granted as natural, commonsense realities" (Sehr 1997, 19), the burden then falls upon the teachers, particularly with the teachers who identify as LGBTQ, to create those safe spaces for students.

Creative Spaces

Marni. Until I began teaching at the university level, I had never taught in a school where the creation of safe spaces extended beyond the dominant heteronormative gender and family roles. Having taught kindergarten through first grade for seven years and middle school for six years, mostly in private or religious institutions, roles outside of established heteronormativity were missing from the first seven years of my teaching career, and I accepted this lack as the norm. During my last six years while teaching within a school that punished individuality and difference at any level, I also studied leadership and social justice, and grew increasingly aware of and uncomfortable with the established dominant norms.

What I always could, and did, offer my students was a space where they could safely express their thoughts and ideas, creating a harbor where student personalities emerged without disrupting the learning. The development of a democratic community (Apple and Beane 1995, Dewey 1916, Sehr 1997) promoted intrinsic student ownership of learning (Bishop and Berryman 2006) and established the value of student voice (hooks 1994, Nieto 2005). Listening to students and giving them legitimate choices established teacher–student relationships while collaborative activities and activities promoting student interaction enhanced student–student relationships (Ackerman 2003, Apple and Beane 1995, Dewey 1916, Eisner 2002, Nieto 2002). Employing a pedagogy that was creative (Ackerman 2003, Dewey 1916, Eisner 2002, hooks 1994), engaged, multimodal (Gardner 2011), culturally diverse (Guisbond et al. 2006, Nieto 2002, Shaffer 2001), differentiated (Tomlinson et al. 2003), active (Dewey 1916) and required higher level thinking skills (Bloom 1956) established a class culture where creativity and difference were treasured and accepted:

> [The most caring and compassionate teachers] believe that supporting and affirming students' identities while at the same time encouraging students to become members of the larger community when they are ready and able is in the long run a better way to help students adjust to school and, ultimately, to life beyond school.
>
> (Nieto 2003, 39)

There was a digital class camera for students to use freely to document learning when they used non-traditional tools, but they could also use the camera for posed and humorous photos. Classroom spaces established areas where students were allowed (and expected) to discuss learning, understanding, and application of concepts. Meeting at the front of the room or in small groups with the teacher determined when students were to sit and listen, ask questions, or interact in modeled activities for short 15–20 minute lessons, as did using the SmartBoard or Overhead Projector. These were mixed up with a variety of materials, games, and activities for pairs, groups, and individually.

We established ground rules of what needed to be reported by law (topics reflecting suicide, abuse, or threats) and school consequences. Any other topic could emerge in their writing safely. Immediate reading (ideally the same day) of any writing was required to ensure nothing reportable had emerged, but the alternative of creating spaces where students were safe to write was worth the extra work. Where we could, classes followed the guidelines of applied critical pedagogy and democracy, allowing students' voices in developing course/topic structure and guidelines (Boutelier et al. 2009, Luschei et al. 2013). The reward? Later, one of my students explained they were middle school students who did not feel comfortable with themselves, with how they thought, and with who they were. At a time when they felt different and were struggling to find themselves, I let them know I was different, so it was okay if they were different, too.

Why I'm Hearing Voices

Kevin. In the religious institution where I am a service coordinator and theology teacher, there has been a great conversation about creating safe places for students who remain silent. It is easier for a school to respond with love to defend the outspoken activist student who may proclaim his/her non-heteronormative identity than to ensure that those who remain quiet find acceptance and security to be themselves. Called by the church to ensure "every sign of unjust discrimination in their regard should be avoided" (Sacred Congregation for the Doctrine of the Faith 1994, para. 2358), we sought ways to open spaces in the curriculum and in school life to counteract the social oppression of these students. Yet, outright approval of homosexual acts from the school would be in contradiction to the belief that homosexual conjugal love is "intrinsically disordered" (Sacred Congregation for the Doctrine of the Faith 1994, para. 2357).

Despite nuances and divergent voices in the field (e.g., Althaus-Reid 2003, Boff and Boff 1987, Cheng 2011, Gutierrez 2014), limiting the scope of theological inquiry is often an unquestioned and insufficient pedagogical method. It became clear that one vital safe space must be the theology classes, which could not be taught one-dimensionally or statically, or, like other forms of repression, "their historical character is forgotten, and they become reduced to patterns of habit" (Giroux 2003, 49). Choosing only one theological lens to explain religious belief would silence those deemed "unacceptable." Instead, the theology department introduced other viewpoints through class conversations or readings.

Queer and liberation theologians offer a different perspective on theological inquiry and, perhaps, invite LGBTQ students to identify themselves as valuable members of the religious world. The sounding of the voices of these theologians creates a safe place in which the silent student might feel freer to offer his/her experiences and insights.

The school also realized silencing the student body comes from the pressures of the existent peer group. The pressure to conform to a sense of proper masculinity seemed palpable in this all-male school. Maher's (2004) study of Catholic school graduates showed those coming from single-sex high schools were less positive toward homosexuality than their co-ed counterparts. My school believed safe spaces needed to be created outside of the classroom as well as in the curriculum. Following the request of a few students, the school established a faith-sharing organization that met weekly so students could discuss their experiences of many kinds of diversity. In keeping with the mission of the Catholic school, the group would not seek to contradict ecclesial teaching but to provide an open space for young men to discuss how their experience of the world affects their faith. This proved to be a wonderful space for some of our most silenced students, particularly gay and queer ones, to find voice and acceptance among their peers.

Conclusion

The creation of safe spaces within all schools and classrooms ideally falls within the purview of the entire school. Leaders and teachers should be concerned with providing a safe environment where students can find themselves and identify outside dominant norms. When the values, character, and morals of the leadership that permeate the entire structure of the school (Marshall and Oliva 2010) enforce patterns of silence, the burden falls upon the teacher to create these spaces of safety and points of change within the arena where teachers *have* the power to create change: their own classrooms (Ayers 2012).

When the straight (or passing) teacher fails to support places of safety, they fail to support all students, especially those outside the dominant patterns of heteronormativity. When that teacher fails to speak up, then heteronormative oppression is enforced.

When leaders and teachers who are openly LGBTQ remain silent or fail to act, then silence is further enforced. The burden often falls upon these teachers to create change, but this does not exempt other educators from the responsibility of creating safe spaces for students. Whether these spaces are concerned with embracing difference, diversity, or creativity, our success or failure is measured in the opportunity for or oppression of voice in our students.

Note

1   "Prism theory is grounded in a contemporary surrealist foundation that blends the philosophical and psychological factors of Breton (1924, 1929/1969, 1934/1936) and Deleuze and Guattari (1987), then explores other frameworks, such as grounded theory, critical theory, feminist theory, and arts-based research … Prism theory … includes: (1) [a] call to action, (2) mapping of the inside/outside, (3) freedom and expression, (4) *praxis*, and (5) convergence and divergence … Prismatic inquiry methodology utilizes the convergence, divergence and juxtaposition of data in the

exploration of hidden or unexpected relationships, opening the paths to other ways of knowing while maintaining a criterion of quality and definitions of success" (Fisher 2013b, vii).

References

Ackerman, D. B. 2003. "Taproots for a New Century: Tapping the Best of Traditional and Progressive Education." *Phi Delta Kappan* no. 84 (5): 344–349.

ALAOIF. 2010. *Banned Books Week: Celebrating 30 Years of Liberating Literature* [Timeline]. American Library Association [cited June 25 2013]. Available from http://www.tiki-toki.com/timeline/entry/51787/Banned-Books-Week-Celebrating-30-Years-of-Liberating-Literature/ - vars!date=1982-10-29_03:04:18!

Althaus-Reid, M. 2003. *The Queer God*. New York: Routledge.

Anderson, Gary L., Kathryn Herr, and Ann Sigrid Nihlen. 1994. *Studying Your Own School: An Educator's Guide to Qualitative Practitioner Research*. Thousand Oaks, CA: Corwin Press.

Apple, Michael W. 2006. *Educating the "Right" Way: Markets, Standards, God, and Inequality*. 2nd ed. New York: Routledge.

Apple, Michael W., and James A. Beane. 1995. *Democratic Schools*. Alexandria, VA: Association for Supervision and Curriculum Development.

Ayers, William. 2012. "Occupy your Imagination/Occupy the Future: Building an Activist Movement for Radical School Reform." Paper read at JCT Conference, at Dayton, OH.

Best, Rickey. 2010. "Censorship or Selection? Academic Library Holdings of the Top Ten Most Challenged Books of 2007." *Education Libraries* no. 33 (2): 18–35.

Bishop, Russell, and Mere Berryman. 2006. *Culture Speaks: Cultural Relationships and Classroom Learning*. Wellington, NZ: Huia Publishers.

Bloom, Benjamin S. 1956. *Taxonomy of Educational Objectives: The Classification of Educational Goals*. 1st ed. New York: Longmans, Green.

Boff, Leonardo, and Clodoris Boff. 1987. *Introducing Liberation Theology*. Maryknoll, NY: Orbis Books.

Boutelier, Stefani, Dina Eletreby, Marni E. Fisher, Ndindi Kitonga, Suzanne SooHoo, and Amy Tanner. 2009. Freaky Freire: Applications of Critical Pedagogy in the Classroom. Paper read at American Association for the Advancement of Curricular Studies Conference, April 10–13, 2009, at San Diego, CA.

Breton, Andre. 1924, 1929/1969. *Manifestoes of Surrealism*. Translated by R. Seaver and H. R. Lane. Ann Arbor: University of Michigan Press.

Breton, Andre. 1934/1936. *What is Surrealism?* Translated by D. Gascoyne. London: Faber & Faber.

Brown, Jean E., and Elaine C. Stephens. 1998. *United in Diversity: Using Multicultural Young Adult Literature in the Classroom*. Ubana, IL: National Council of Teachers of English.

Cheng, P. S. 2011. *Radical Love: Introduction to Queer Theology*. New York: Seabury Books.

Corliss, Julia Candance. 1998. *Crossing Borders with Literature of Diversity*. Norwood, MA: Christopher-Gordon Publishers.

Darder, Antonia, Marta Baltodano, and Rudolpho D. Torres. 2009. *The Critical Pedagogy Reader*. 2nd ed. New York: Routledge.

Dei, Seffa J. George. 2005. "Introduction." In *Indigenous Philosophies and Critical Education: A Reader*, edited by George J. Seffa Dei, 1–13. New York: Peter Lang.

Deleuze, Gilles, and Feliz Guattari. 1987. *A Thousand Plateaus: Capitalism and Schizophrenia*. Minneapolis: University of Minnesota Press.

Dewey, John. 1916. *Democracy and Education: An Introduction to the Philosophy of Education, Text-Book Series in Education*. New York: The Macmillan Company.

Eisner, Elliot W. 2002. "The Kind of Schools We Need." *Phi Delta Kappan* no. 83 (8): 576–584.

Fisher, Marni E. 2009. "Traits of Social Justice and Democracy." In the *American Association for the Advancement of Curricular Studies Conference*. San Diego, CA: AAACS

Fisher, Marni E. 2013a. "A Gift for Enlightenment: Exploration of Student Experience of 'Othering' through Poetic Surrealism." In the *American Association for the Advancement of Curricular Studies Conference*. San Francisco, CA: AAACS.

Fisher, Marni E. 2013b. "Here There be Dragons: The Initial Defining of Prism Theory and Prismatic Inquiry." Dissertation, College of Educational Studies, Chapman University, Orange, CA.

Freire, Paulo. 1970/2005. *Pedagogy of the Oppressed*. Translated by M. B. Ramos. 30th Anniversary ed. New York: Continuum. Original edition, 1970. Reprint, 30th Aniversary.

Freire, Paulo, and Donald P. Macedo. 2003. "Rethinking Literacy: A Dialogue." In *The Critical Pedagogy Reader*, edited by A. Darder, M. Baltodano and R. D. Torres, 354–364. New York: RoutledgeFalmer.

Fullan, Michael. 1993. "Why Teachers Must Become Change Agents." *Educational Leadership* no. 50 (6): 12–18.

Gallagher, Kelly, and R. L. Allington. 2009. "The Elephant in the Room." In *Readicide: How Schools are Killing Reading and What You Can Do About It*, 7–26. Portland, ME: Stenhouse Publishers.

Gallas, Karen. 1998. *"Sometimes I Can Be Anything": Power, Gender, and Identity in a Primary Classroom*. New York: Teacher's College Press.

Gardner, Howard. 2011. *Frames of Mind: The Theory of Multiple Intelligences*. New York: Basic Books.

Gibson, David. 2013. *Gay Catholic School Teacher Loses Job*. District Chronicles, December 25 [cited November 11 2015]. Available from http://www.districtchronicles.com/news/view.php/421283/Gay-Catholic-school-teacher-loses-job.

Giroux, Henry A. 2003. "Critical Theory and Educational Practice." In *The Critical Pedagogy Reader*, edited by Antonia Darder, Marta Baltodano and Rodolfo D. Torres, 27–56. New York: RoutledgeFalmer.

Goldstein, Sasha. 2013. "Ohio Catholic School Teacher Fired after 'Appalled' Parent Learned She was Gay." *NY Daily News*, April 18.

Groundspark. 2015. *Bullying and School Climate Statistics*. Groundspark [cited July 26 2015]. Available from http://groundspark.org/our-films-and-campaigns/lets-get-real/lgr_stats.

Guisbond, L., P. Dunphy, J. Johnson, K. Kaplan, M. Neill, M. Segal, N. Shapiro, and L. Valentine. 2006. "The Campaign for the Education of the Whole Child." In *A Report from the Alliance for the Education of the Whole Child*. Boston, MA: Alliance for the Education of the Whole Child.

Gutierrez, Gustavo. 2014. *A Rheology of Liberation*. 15th ed. Maryknoll, NY: Orbis Books.

hooks, bell. 1994. *Teaching to Transgress: Education as the Practice of Freedom*. New York: Routledge.

Janke, D. 2004. "'Tell Me Who You Are': Problemizing the Construction and Positionalities of 'Insider'/'Outsider' of a 'Native' Ethnographer in a Postcolonial Context." In *Decolonizing Research in Cross-Cultural Contexts*, edited by K. Mutua and B. B. Swadener, 87–103. Albany, NY: State University Press.

Jipson, Janice, and Nicholas Paley. 1997. *Daredevil Research: Re-creating Analytic Practice, Counterpoints*. New York: P. Lang.

Koebler, Jason. 2011. Survey: Nearly Half of Students Sexually Harassed in School. *U.S. News and World Report*, http://www.usnews.com/education/blogs/high-school-notes/2011/11/09/survey-nearly-half-of-students-sexually-harassed-in-school.

Kohl, Herbert R. 2003. *Stupidity and Tears: Teaching and Learning in Troubled Times*. New York: New Press, distributed by W.W. Norton.

Koschoreck, James W., and Patrick Slattery. 2006. "Meeting *All* Students' Needs: Transforming the Unjust Normativity of Heterosexism." In *Leadership for Social Justice: Making Revolutions in Education*, edited by C. Marshall and M. Oliva, 145–166. Boston, MA: Pearson/Allyn and Bacon.

Kosciw, Joseph G., Emily A. Greytak, Neal A. Palmer, and Madelyn J. Boesen. 2014. The 2013 *National School Climate Survey: The Experiences of Lesbian, Gay, Bisexual and Transgender Youth in Our Nation's Schools*. New York: Gay, Lesbian and Straight Education Network (GLSEN).

Lane, S., N. Lacefield-Parachini, and J. Isken. 2003. "Developing Novice Teachers as Change Agents: Student Teacher Placements 'Against the Grain'." *Teacher Education Quarterly* no. 30 (2): 55–68.

Lindsey, Randall B., Franklin Campbell-Jones, and Laraine M. Roberts. 2005. *The Culturally Proficient School: An Implementation Guide for School Leaders*. Thousand Oaks, CA: Corwin Press.

Luschei, Savannah, Ashleigh Luschei, Katherine Nowicki, and Marni E. Fisher. 2013. Even When Castles Fall: Collaborative Practitioner Action Research between Students and Teachers. In *American Educational Research Association Conference*. San Francisco, CA: AERA.

Macedo, Donald P., Bessie Dendrinos, and Panayota Gounari. 2003. *The Hegemony of English*. Boulder, CO: Paradigm.

Maher, Michael J. 2004. "Catholic High School Students' Attitudes toward Homosexuality: A Snapshot of Incoming College Freshmen." *Catholic Education: A Journal of Inquiry and Practice* no. 7 (4): 462–478.

Marshall, C., and M. Oliva. 2010. *Leadership for Social Justice: Making Revolutions in Education*. 2nd ed. Boston, MA: Pearson/Allyn and Bacon.

Martin, Shane, and E. F. Litton. 2004. *Equity, Advocacy and Diversity: New Directions for Catholic Schools*. Washington, DC: National Catholic Education Association.

McLaren, Peter. 2003. "Critical Pedagogy." In *The Critical Pedagogy Reader*, edited by Antonia Darder, Marta Baltodano and Rodolfo D. Torres, 69–96. New York: Routledge.

McLaren, Peter. 2009. "Critical Pedagogy." In *The Critical Pedagogy Reader*, edited by Antonia Darder, Marta Baltodano and Rodolfo D. Torres, 62–83. New York: Routledge.

Meem, Deborah T., Michelle A. Gibson, and Jonathan F. Alexander. 2010. "Censorship and Moral Panic." In *Finding Out: An Introduction to LGBT Studies*. Thousand Oaks, CA: Sage.

Meyer, Elizabeth J. 2009. *Gender, Bullying and Harassment: Strategies to End Sexism and Homophobia in Schools*. New York: Teachers College Press.

Mooney, M. 2004. "A book is a present..." In *A Book is a Present: Selecting Text for Intentional Teaching*, 27–30. New York: Richard C. Owen Publishers.

Newman, Leslea, and Laura Cornell. 2009. *Heather Has Two Mommies*. Boston: Alyson Publications.

Nieto, Sonia. 2002. *Language, Culture, and Teaching: Critical Perspectives for a New Century, Language, Culture, and Teaching*. Mahwah, NJ: L. Erlbaum.

Nieto, Sonia. 2003. *What Keeps Teachers Going?* New York: Teachers College Press.

Nieto, Sonia. 2005. *Why We Teach*. New York: Teachers College Press.

Nijland, Stern, and Linda DeHaan. 2003. *King and King*: Random House Children's Books.

Pike, Deirdre. 2012. "The Gift of Positive Space Groups: A Transformation for LGBTQ Students." *Education Canada* no. 52 (3): 28–31.

Pinar, William. 2012. *What is Curriculum Theory?* 2nd ed. New York and London: Routledge.

Polacco, Patricia. 2009. *In Our Mothers' House*. New York: Philomel Productions.

Reichman, Henry. 2012. "Censorship dateline." *Newsletter on Intellectual Freedom* no. 61 (5): 201–227.

Richardson, Justin, Peter Parnell, and Henry Cole. 2012. *And Tango Makes Three*. New York: Simon & Schuster.

Sacred Congregation for the Doctrine of the Faith. 1994. *Catechism of the Catholic Church*. Rome: Sacred Congregation for the Doctrine of the Faith.

Sehr, David T. 1997. *Education for Public Democracy*. New York: State University of New York.

Shaffer, G. 2001. "Cookie Cutter Education." *The Humanist* no. 6 (3): 14–19.

Short, Kathy G., Carol G. Lynch-Brown, and Carl M. Tomlinson. 2005/2014. *Essentials of Children's Literature*. New York: Pearson Education.

Sinnema, J. 2009. "Transgendered Teacher Files Complaint Over Work Loss: Woman Now a Man; Catholic Board Says Move Goes against Church." *National Post*, 5.

SooHoo, Suzanne. 2006. *Talking Leaves: Narratives of Otherness*. AnnArbor, MI: Hampton Press.

Stop Bullying. 2015. Facts About Bullying. Edited by U.S. Department of Health & Human Services. Washington, DC: Stopbullying.gov Editorial Board.

Tomlinson, Carol Ann, Catherine Brighton, Holly Hertberg, Carolyn M. Callahan, Tonya R. Moon, Kay Brimijoin, Lynda A. Conover, and Timothy Reynolds. 2003. "Differentiating Instruction in Response to Student Readiness, Interest, and Learning Profile in Academically Diverse Classrooms: A Review of Literature." *Journal for the Education of the Gifted* no. 27 (2/3): 119–145.

Tye, Barbara B. 2000. *Hard Truths: Uncovering the Deep Structure of Schooling*. New York: Teachers College Press.

Interlude I

TRAVELING POET AND BRIDGE OVER TROUBLED WATERS

Stacy E. Schupmann

Traveling Poet

The sign on your door says no solicitors.
You see, I am just a friendly little visitor
I'm just peddling my goods
I'm not from the backwoods
Although you might think again when you hear what I'm bringin' in.
I am going door-to-door selling equal rights.
Just trying to do my part for the fight.
Oh no…don't be scared…let me get you prepared
All I have to tell you is my story—in all its glory…
I call it—THE TRAVELING LESBIAN POET

They say that the cute girl made me move here
Well, isn't that queer?
You see, they should 'a got in my face, told me to stay out of this place
They don't want my kind
They want to leave me behind
They want me to hide like I got a secret inside.
Are you just homophobic? Is that it?
Well, that's just pathetic
See, you think that secret is dirty
If I let it out you will hurt me because
Homophobia is your weapon
Your sword, your gun, your word
But, I just need to be HEARD!

I need to speak
I need to believe
You see, my secret is no disease
I am okay
I just happen to love "that way"
I'm just looking for a town that will let me be
You see I just want to be me
You don't have to put up a sign that says
NO DYKES ALLOWED
I'm pretty well known for getting lost in a crowd
I am a mellow activist
You won't see my fists
I don't have a reason to hate
I will always listen to the straight
I've heard it's okay to call you that
Don't worry; you won't be the one that I wink at.
I don't really play for your team
Nothing against you, I just like my extreme
You see, I'm going to start new trends
I'm trying to get everyone to make amends
The problem is living in hate is a bad mistake
Hate Crimes are no fun, they are soooo overdone
Can't you come up with a different idea?
Blood and Death can be found at the galleria
Just consult the shoppers of the S & M shop
At least they have fun before they drop
Oh no, I'm not trying to offend
God forbid you feel hurt—THAT, I do not intend
I'm just going door-to-door selling equal rights
Just doing my part for the fight
I'm just a butch poet
Wouldn't you know it?
I'm not asking for a donation
Just trying to give the world an education
We dykes don't bite—well some of us might
But that's for another trip
You don't need to hear that bit
We aren't asking you to agree
But could you at least let us be free
Let us have kids
Let us get married
Let us walk down the street without getting beat
You see, I'm tired of feeling trapped

I'm trying to get out of that
With every slanderous word you make a deposit
The extreme right will pay to keep me in the closet
I just want to stop hearing the word gay
When you mean it in a bad way
Because I don't think food or movies really want to live with the
    "Homo-Scandal"
I don't think it is something they can handle
Okay, okay, I will get to the point
Give me a sec and I will be out of this joint
Here is my hope
Don't treat us like we are a joke
The butch, dyke, lipstick lesbian, baby dyke, muff divers and carpet
    munchers are here to stay
Just let us BE—because we didn't have a choice to be gay
We were just born this way
Now that you have heard my rhyme
I will thank you for your time
I'm on to the next town because
No matter what, I'm never going to back down
I'm just a traveling lesbian poet going door-to-door selling equal rights
At least I am trying to do something for the fight.

Bridge Over Troubled Waters: Letters from the Lesbian Underground

I Never Imagined My Life Would Be a Political Statement

Don't worry; you won't be the one that I wink at.
I don't really play for your team
Nothing against you, I just like my extreme

On December 25, 2007 I became engaged to my wife. Six months later, I had a conversation with my mother that brought up feelings most people don't or will never have to think about in their lifetime:

ME: It's interesting … I never, in my wildest dreams, would have imagined my life to be a political statement.
MOM: Well, me either.
ME: Hmm … just very crazy.

I wonder about this all the time. I wake up in the morning knowing living my life the only way I know how is a political statement. Giving my partner a hug and kiss and telling her I love her offends people. I make people mad by being alive. How many people wake up thinking this?

Am I a political statement? Yes. I am walking politics. Are you a political statement? Are you protected by the law? Are you worried about what someone might do to you based on who you love?

I want my life to be real and meaningful. I just want it to be equal. I would like to not fear having children and worrying about them getting hurt because the laws don't side in their parents' favor. I want them to be protected. I want to be protected.

> They say that the cute girl made me move here
> Well, isn't that queer?

On July 8, 2008 my wife and I were legally married at a California courthouse. We had already filled out the paperwork online, so when we arrived at the Norwalk Superior Court, all we had to do was sign the paper and tell the guy we wanted to get married, get an additional copy of the license, and pay for the same-day ceremony service in the tents. My wife didn't like the idea of getting married in a tent, but I thought there was so much sanctity in the process, it had to be done. We then had to swear we were telling the truth (on the marriage license) by raising our right hand in front of the Plexiglas window. I almost swooned right then.

When we were done paying our bill, we were told to exit out the back door and go over to the tent where they would call our number at 12pm. My mom asked if we wanted to request a woman to do the ceremony, but I didn't care, so we just took whoever came up to us. A very Abe Lincoln looking man, named Jim, sworn to perform ceremonies especially for the big gay rush, greeted us. He informed us this was his first official gay ceremony, and he was tired of doing heterosexual marriages all day. He said the most beautiful things in our cubicle with paper wedding bells and hearts attached to the walls under the tent.

In the past, California voted to make marriage between a man and a woman. This vote was overturned due to a ruling in the court. We did not really know what would happen to the status of marriages taking place before November, but we wanted the possible security of "real" marriage for just a little while. If, by doing this, we could change the mind of one voter, we were all set to go. This was a very political move for me. One that I am not used to. I am really not that political. I try to be as open as possible about my life and help students achieve success. If that's political, then I'd chalk this up to one more notch on my belt.

If our marriage would be overturned, I would deal with it. We would deal with it. We were ready for whatever might come. We would be sad, but we have been sad before. We would overcome. What we knew was that we both wanted kids. We wanted those kids and ourselves to be protected. We also wanted people to know how much this meant to us, as we moved our wedding up much sooner than we had planned because we hoped we might be a part of the movement, to be one of the couples who would be able to stay married. Since we believed marriage officially happened in the court, and the ceremony was a completely different celebration, we made the commitment early.

Amidst this, I must acknowledge there are still people who believe gay people need exorcisms (because we are being taken by the devil), shock therapy, counseling, and other forms of torture to get over "this thing." It's crazy for me to think that some people still believe I am choosing this "lifestyle."

Proposition 8: Denying Me the Same Rights

> They don't want my kind
> They want to leave me behind
> They want me to hide like I got a secret inside.

On November 4, 2008 I didn't even know how to describe my feelings. On the one hand, I had never been happier to elect a president than I was that day. I felt somewhat represented in him and his ideological beliefs.

Yet during this same election, California's Proposition 8 passed, denying me the same rights as others.

So, I sat there watching an African American man be elected president, knowing my civil rights had been taken away. It was a bittersweet, heartbreaking moment. I cried all morning and night. I cried because there should not be a fight in the first place.

When do we learn our lesson?

Was it not enough that we fought a battle on American soil for civil rights for African Americans?

When we took the ban off interracial marriage?

When women finally achieved the vote?

How many laws can be overturned and injustices be righted before you get the picture?

EVERYONE DESERVES THE SAME RIGHTS UNDER THE LAW!!! Women are protected, interracial marriages are protected, African Americans are protected ... We are still fighting for equality, but we are not protected. Wouldn't it be nice if everyone were protected and equal?

I am a lesbian woman fighting for equality in an uncertain time. In California, my marriage to my wife was tested. We took the plunge early to establish a bond between each other and our families. We promised to love one another through all things, to support one another in the struggles and the happiness. On election night, we were met with bitter feelings of a nation who refused to support that marriage. Proposition 8 led in the polls. The California television commercials that featured lush lands and beautiful oceans were tarnished in hate and fear. We were a state saying, "Come visit! We support 3/4 of you!"

What I know is I have an obligation to keep fighting. I have the power to make a difference, and I will. I have friends who have been supportive and have made me cry by just saying, "I support you!" They don't do this for my approval; they do this because they don't see me as anything less than myself. A friend. A wife. A partner. A daughter. A teacher. A student. A spiritual being.

I have an obligation to not back down. I have that obligation to them and to myself. The minute I let myself believe that I am not equal, I have lost. We cannot forget our role in making history, but we cannot be complacent and stop fighting.

Years from now, I will take my children and wife on a trip to the past. I will walk them over to the apartment where I used to live and show them the place where I heard that their mom and I would possibly not be married anymore. I will tell them, "I was standing right here when they elected an African American man as President of the United States. I also was right here when they tried to take my rights as a Californian away. I will never forget that day." And then my children will take me and my wife aside and say, "Wow! How could people have done that? We will never do that to anyone." And I will say, "It was a different time. A time of much fear and of much more hope. We have come a long way, but must never forget the past and where we once were. What you can never forget are those people who are a part of your lives and once supported, and still support, your mom and I. They are the real heroes."

During the days following the election I was bombarded by comments of sadness and joy. I heard people attack the Mormon Church and African American and Latino communities with letters and words of hate. I heard people attack their own friends, relatives, associates, and congregations with hate. This gets us nowhere. There is nothing to fear by supporting a human being and loving them just as any other. This was not a time for blame, but for reason and understanding. This was a time for the ultimate act of love … treating others as you would have them treat you.

Open the lines of communication and tell your story. Do it with compassion for the other person. Tell them there is nothing to fear. This is about love for fellow human beings and the American dream. We can do this by being honest and open. The fight is not over and does not have to be filled with anger. This movement is truly about hope. There is a hope for a better tomorrow where everyone is treated equally and loved equally.

I do not think this is a battle over religious values in America, but a battle over the manipulation and lies that religious organizations use in politics and elections. To attack faith is to attack the person. To attack the doctrine or the laws which have been made by political and religious ideologies is the winning ticket. To attack the people who incur those gets us nowhere. Set the record straight. When opponents of gay marriage say, "We don't hate gay people. We are just trying to protect marriage." We can firmly say, "We don't hate the church. We are just trying to protect our rights as American citizens."

In Return, I Was Ashamed I Was a Christian

> I am okay
> I just happen to love "that way"
> I'm just looking for a town that will let me be
> You see I just want to be me

For years, I was ashamed I was gay.

For years, in return, I was ashamed I was a Christian.

It has taken multiple years to make sense of these emotions. This dichotomous subjection of alternate ideological and personal identities is confusing to me on multiple levels. It has been for years.

I was "saved" on six different occasions. Even after being saved and opening up my heart to God and Christ, I was, each and every time, still gay. I was still myself. I was Christian and gay. I was told this wasn't possible.

Even though I had been saved, I felt dark. I was tired. I was empty. I was gay. I felt ashamed. I felt ashamed through years in Christian School, in Christian Club in High School, and Christian Club in College … I felt ashamed in church. I was living two separate lives: the sinner and the saint.

When I was growing up, we didn't have "It Gets Better" campaigns. We didn't have Ellen being the most loved television personality. We had Ellen getting canceled for being gay. Our representation was the person who got beat up and ridiculed in school. Our stories were morose and not joyful. We were kicked out of houses, killed, and hated. We were the characters to laugh at on the fringe. We didn't have lives filled with love. We didn't get the girl. We didn't get the guy. We didn't get it.

In college I didn't feel anything toward men. I didn't understand. I just felt darkness when I was alone.

Then it happened. I fell for my best friend. I fell hard for a woman. I would sit next to her and my stomach would burn and hurt. I felt the desire to kiss her … to be close to this wonderful woman. I longed for something … I ached in ways I didn't understand. When I wasn't with her, I wanted to be with her. I wanted to know everything about her. I wanted to share everything with her. We never dated but remained friends. I knew what I felt. It wasn't about the other person, in the end. It never would be about them. This was about me. This was the first time I felt something. I really felt something. I felt what others talked about feeling. Except, I was told, what they were feeling was love and what I was feeling was a choice. I was ashamed.

How dare you? These tears, the butterflies, the passion, the love, and the complete compassion I am feeling doesn't feel shameful. These feelings feel right.

I tried to distance myself from Christianity when I left college. I felt unwelcome in Christian Club. I felt unwelcome in Bible study because I was cast aside. You weren't able to be Christian and Gay. You had to pick. "One is a sin, the other is salvation."

How could I have been part of a religion that would get rid of me so quickly if I were unwilling to let go of the love I felt in my heart? How could this group of people talk about the love of Jesus and then shun me?

I was ashamed of all the years I put into a religion that didn't care about me. They cared about me for numbers, but they didn't care that I had a full and whole life. They didn't care if I ever felt the love of another. They were willing to take me in if I was willing to give up such a large part of what makes me a human being.

We are too evolved to be lost in a world that restricts us from the very deepest part of our soul that longs to feel a connection.

It's tough enough to be a human in a politically and religiously unjust world. It's hard enough to make it day-to-day, keeping your head up in the midst of pain, loss, and pressure to be successful.

The answer lies within us and within our ability to be good to others. Instead of building up walls, we should tear them down. We should surrender our lives to the love of one another.

It's been a long and hard road. The tears are my way of no longer hiding. Each tear heals the wounds of the heart and rids my body of the shame the people of the "church" have placed on my body.

Because We Love Each Other and Believe in Each Other

We aren't asking you to agree
But could you at least let us be free
Let us have kids
Let us get married
Let us walk down the street without getting beat

Marriage is about love, commitment, support, and a bond between two people. Thank you to all that continue to support our cause. I encourage others to show the many faces of marriage!

My wife and I work hard to grow together, and not leave the other one out in the cold. We talk about life, love, fears, hate, adversity, and the struggle to be authentic. We process my desire to be a vocal advocate for the LGBT community, sharing so much about ourselves. We talk about our vulnerabilities and our past. We argue over who picks the movie and who should be taking down the water glasses in the morning. We argue over small things and big things. We laugh over small little things. We laugh with our friends. We have cuddle time with our dogs.

We are not married because of monetary benefits, or because we were accidentally pregnant and want to make it legitimate. We are not married because we are trying to be the downfall of Western society or because we want to end marriage. We are married because we love each other and believe in each other. We believe that we can make a go of this and have decided on waking up next to each other. We want to support each other, and enjoy each other. We want our kids to have two people to love and be a part of their lives. We got married because we believe in who we are when we are together.

When I Walked into a Room, People Would Stop Talking

> We dykes don't bite—well some of us might
> But that's for another trip
> You don't need to hear that bit

On October 25, 2011 I attended a wedding on my wife's side of the family in Minnesota. The whole family is supportive of us as a married couple under the law. I have not actually asked any questions to anyone in the family or allowed their opinion to be stated, because I feel if I give room to do so, I might get an answer I don't like. As a gay person, I keep a running track record in my head for safety purposes. It's what you do as a defense mechanism and I haven't quite learned how to turn it off and I am not sure the world we live in is one where I could actually turn it off.

At the wedding, I wore my extremely awesome button-downs, my Jason Priestly-esque haircut, and my men's shirts. I looked incredibly normal for me, dyke-style-awesomeness. For the people in Minnesota, I was Bigfoot/Voldemort/Pink Elephant. When I walked into a room, people would stop talking. All the bridesmaids looked at me like I was crazy when I entered the women's restroom. One guy on the groom's side spoke to me; all the rest ignored me. I kept track. It was that noticeable.

When I married my wife, her fight became my fight. My life became her life. I made a vow, for better or for worse, to defend her and love her in a world that doesn't really love us, and I thought I could handle it. I still think I can, but I understand how difficult that will be. Encouraging someone to just be normal in a sea of people whose stares say, "You are not normal" is very difficult. It hurts you. It challenges you. It defines you.

I often feel the same way about the words my community uses to describe themselves. Gay, Straight, LGBT, Queer, and acronym-upon-acronym that somehow adds to our already complex world. These are not just words. These are deep meaningful lives. They are a deep and meaningful self-expression of a culture, hope, faith, religion, love, and soul that is indescribably permanent and indelibly marked on us.

I sometimes wonder why so many people want to think about my life, to make judgments. They declare wrongful ideals and spend more time telling me about my shoes than getting in and walking around in them.

I am deeply blessed to have so many people care for me and love me, to have the support system I have, because it keeps me going. It lifts me up when I am struggling in a world that uses my life for political gain or hateful rhetoric. I have lived all over the country and, in the midst of individuals who perpetuate hate, there are always the few who stand up and fight back. They use their power and influence to take a stand for those who are dismissed because they are only seen as the label that oppresses them.

I know the world will evolve and make this a safe place because I have seen it take place. I have seen people challenge their misconceptions and extend their hearts in order to make a difference.

For all those who took a stand in their states, I thank you. For all those who are still fighting the injustices in other states, I thank you for continuing to support my wife and I by standing up and telling our truth. We were married by a pastor four years ago, under God, and in the presence of all our friends and family. I thank all who continue to do the work and speak the truth for us and who stand with us and not against us. You have made a difference with your actions. It will not be forgotten.

There are still more milestones to achieve, equality to create, and people to reach. There are those who still wish to place our status below their own. There are those who rely on their feelings and beliefs to establish a different reality for our brothers and sisters. There are those who still feel we are unable to have faith, be faithful, and make decisions for our own lives.

I celebrate and I hope. I hope for more love, more acceptances, and more conversation. I celebrate for the people who continue to fight. I celebrate for the people who challenge. I celebrate for the people who love beyond what their heart can imagine. And most importantly, I continue to hope for equality.

My Marriage Utility Belt is Locked and Loaded!

> Just let us be—because we didn't have a choice to be gay
> We were just born this way

On May 26, 2009. That's right California … you still have to call us Mrs. and Mrs.! My marriage utility belt is locked and loaded! It's ON! After that wonderful day, we heard Mormon leaders, Focus on the Family, and other religious leaders talk about us as if we were animals who didn't deserve the same rights as others. They called us, in every way, separate but equal. Abomination, sinner, future pedophile, not of God … you name it, we heard it. The same church I grew up in told me I was not allowed to share the same fundamental rights because of who I loved, not who I was. We stood up to take a stand against that. My wife and I love each other and will fight for our marriage and our faith every chance we get.

What I don't think people understand is what this does to those around me and those families I deeply care about. I am lucky to have friends and family that care about me, but they also have to see me struggle. They have to see me cry. They have to see us go through discrimination. They also have to see all of this under the shroud of religious law.

Here's what I know is certain. If you kick us down, we will stand back up again. You can make me cry, hate me, yell at me, say terrible things to me, you can disown me, but you CAN NOT break my spirit. I will be who I am forever. My spirit will not break. My God loves me, and your "pick-and-choose" religion will not break me.

I'm on to the next town because
No matter what, I'm never going to back down
I'm just a traveling lesbian poet going door-to-door selling equal rights
At least I am trying to do something for the fight.

SECTION II

Climate and Culture
Fostering Positive Identities

Veronica E. Bloomfield and Marni E. Fisher

Beginning the conversation in teacher education programs to raise awareness about the history, needs, and experiences of LGBTQ youth in schools is necessary, and some of the most important educational experiences can take place *on campus*, in *real time*. Having learned to trouble the waters, we shift our focus to the treasures of climate and culture as the dance challenges the dragons of previously held beliefs. Section II addresses how integrating LGBTQ into education can positively impact the climate and culture of schools.

Melissa Smith and Elizabethe Payne explain the discourse of bullying in schools, directly addressing its roots in heteronormativity. They found that the dominant discourse on bullying shapes educators' conceptualization of "the problem," and does not sufficiently address day-to-day marginalization and stigmatization of LGBTQ students. Their concerns include the power of language, the silence (or inconsistent interventions) of educators, and what environmental factors can alleviate the negative experience of LGBTQ students in schools.

Elise Paradis explores the use of the Internet by LGBTQ youth. Due to their marginalization and invisibility at school, LGBTQ youth are more likely to seek comfort and community online. Paradis' work de-pathologizes and de-sexualizes the role of the Internet with these youth, instead addressing how, for LGBTQ youth, use of the Internet creates a sense of belonging, and how educators and allies can support this use.

Gay–Straight Alliances (GSA) have been in existence for years, yet rarely is there a GSA founded without some type of difficulty. Markus Bidell describes the history and legality of these organizations and their potential to impact the culture of school as an extra-curricular, interest-based organization. GSAs can provide a safe and supportive space; a community within the larger community of school.

These organizations can counteract the widespread hostility often faced by LGBTQ youth and provide a system of support and security.

In the final chapter of this section, Danné Davis examines children's literature, offering insight into the search, and types of books available, and resources for lesson plans. Her chapter offers a starting place for teachers integrating diverse texts into the curriculum and classroom library. One of the greatest concerns and challenges in addressing sexual diversity is age and developmental appropriateness. How does one broach this subject appropriately with kindergarteners? What material does one use as curriculum for elementary age students? Davis offers ways to challenge heteronormativity in both age appropriate and culturally relevant ways. The use of children's literature allows students and teachers to see "queer people" in normative situations. Not only does Davis describe how to do this, she also indicates by name, publisher, and plot summary a wide variety of children's titles. In addition, she provides a helpful script for questions or challenges teachers may face as they queer literature for children.

Each of these chapters indicates how educators can play an active and effective role in cultivating a climate of safety and respect on their school campuses. Addressing and challenging topics such as bullying and sexual diversity, and advocating for the creation of communities, both virtual and face to face, can help foster positive identities for LGBTQ youth and transform the space of school from one of hostility to that of camaraderie.

5

EDUCATOR EVALUATIONS OF SCHOOL CLIMATE FOR LGBTQ STUDENTS

A Reiteration of the Bullying Discourse

Melissa J. Smith and Elizabethe Payne

During the 2010–2011 academic year, the Department of Education (DOE) distributed two "Dear Colleague"[1] letters to U.S. schools reminding educators of their responsibilities to address harassment and support LGBTQ students. The October 2010 letter educated school personnel about their "legal obligations to address harassment under [civil rights law]" (Ali 2010, 1) and reminded schools that LGBTQ harassment may be addressed by Title IX's prohibition of gender-based harassment—as victims are often targeted for "failing to conform to stereotypical notions of masculinity and femininity" (8). The June 2011 letter defined the Obama Administration's position on Gay–Straight Alliances (GSAs)[2]—they play an important role in creating safe and affirming learning environments—and reminded schools that the Equal Access Act "protects student-initiated groups of all types" (Duncan 2011, para. 4).

These letters are indicative of taken-for-granted methods for addressing LGBTQ bias in schools: violence intervention and increased awareness of discrimination. In other words, the position taken by Obama's DOE—while admirable for its explicit recognition of LGBTQ youth—reflects dominant themes in educational research on LGBTQ youth's school experiences, which focus on (1) the correlation between victimization and negative psychosocial outcomes (Poteat and Espelage 2007; others); and (2) environmental factors that can be manipulated to "improve" school climate and temper the effects of homophobic harassment (Goodenow, Szalacha, and Westheimer 2006; others). This definition of "the problem" of in-school harassment and marginalization of LGBTQ youth reproduces bullying discourses, which are so powerful that it has become practically impossible to understand victimization outside "the binary logic of protection (i.e. 'victims' of bullying) and vilification (i.e. pathologising 'the bully')" (Ringrose and Renold 2010, 574). LGBTQ youth are defined as victims, bullies as anti-social "bad kids," and schools as negligent due to their ineffective support systems and methods for intervention (Payne and Smith 2012a, 2014). Further, this narrative makes the costly assumption that schools are neutral sites where all students have equal opportunities, and that barriers to success appear when injurious behavior or attitudes infiltrate schools and create "negative" climates. Overt acts of violence against LGBTQ youth (or those who are perceived to be) are surface-level, explicit effects of heteronormative school cultures that are not neutral but, in fact, privilege idealized (hetero) gender performances and create social benefits for peer-to-peer policing of non-normative sexualities and genders (Payne 2007, Payne and Smith 2012a, 2014).

This chapter explores how dominant discourses of bullying, school climate, and LGBTQ students' victimization shape how educators understand negative school climates for LGBTQ youth and envision possibilities for change. We argue that school climate and bullying discourses reproduce an oversimplified narrative of how LGBTQ students are stigmatized and marginalized in the day-to-day operations of schools. Further, this worldview limits the possibilities for effective interventions, lending itself to anti-bullying programs designed to address visible and "measurable" indicators of homophobia or hostile climate. Such programs fail to address how and why LGBTQ students are systematically excluded through "mundane and everyday practices inside school" (Youdell 2006, 5) and why sexual minority and gender non-conforming students are persistently targeted. In other words, anti-bullying programs, GSAs, and other such interventions fail to be disruptive. LGBTQ and gender non-conforming students' positions in social hierarchies remain largely unchanged, and systems of power that put them there remain intact.

"Bullying" and "School Climate" Discourses

Research on bullying is shaped by a bully–victim binary in which "power is conceptualized mostly as the capacity of an individual student for abusing another who is perceived by the bully as being weaker or deficient in some way" (Walton 2005, 105). Olweus (2010) defines bullying as aggressive behavior characterized by intent, repetition, and imbalance of power between bully and victim. Other researchers have added to this baseline definition: bullies are also understood as individuals who exhibit anti-social behavior, report low levels of empathy (Hymel et al. 2010), exhibit aggression to gain social status (Faris and Femelee 2011, Pellegrini et al. 2010), and/or live in an environment that supports the development of aggressive behavior (Espelage and Swearer 2010, Green et al. 2011). These conceptualizations of bullying assume individual-to-individual relationships between bullies and victims—one child imposes power over another, and the victim suffers psychosocial consequences. This binary construction carries powerful implications for possible interventions: bullies need rehabilitation and victims need protection.

Research on bullying reflects cultural myths about who bullies are, what they look like, and whom they target. A large body of work aims to identify factors that increase students' risk for engaging in bullying behaviors, and research-informed interventions typically aim to manage the behavior and change the attitudes of students who are identified as bullies (Espelage and Swearer 2010, Orphinas and Horne 2010, Swearer et al. 2010). However, researchers have also attempted to complicate projects that focus solely on overt aggression, are overly dependent on the bully–victim binary, or presume peer-to-peer aggression is always anti-social. Areas of inquiry include relational bullying (Goldstein, Young, and Boyd 2008), bullying roles (i.e. bystanders) (Frey et al. 2009, Twemlow, Fonagy, and Sacco 2010), bullying norms in individual school contexts (Gendron, Williams, and Guerra 2011, Waasdrop et al. 2011), gender differences in experiences with bullying (Faris and Femelee 2011, Felix and Green 2010, Garandeau, Wilson, and Rodkin 2010) and the social purposes of bullying (Faris and Femelee 2011, Garandeau, Wilson, and Rodkin 2010, Pellegrini et al. 2010). Significantly, Faris and Femelee (2011) speak against "psychological literature on aggression, which views [bullying] as a reaction to psychological problems, social insecurities, or troubled home lives" (51), and advocate for further examination of in-school aggression as a social phenomenon that finds its purpose in students' battles for social power.

"Positive" School Climate for LGBTQ Youth

Gendron, Williams, and Guerra (2011) claim, "school climate [is] the most frequently studied school characteristic linked to bullying" (151), because "a comprehensive understanding of bullying requires the identification of how student and school characteristics interact" (152). But what is *school climate*, and how is it characterized as *positive*? *Culture* and *climate* are often conflated in educational discourse, collapsed under the umbrella of *school climate* (Van Houtte 2005, Welsh 2000). Climate research intends to identify "mediating variables between the structural features of the school and the outcomes for pupils and teachers" (Van Houtte 2005, 71). Climate assessment tools measure student and faculty perceptions of factors such as school attachment, school involvement, clarity and fairness of rules, parental involvement, safety, respect between students and staff, strength of leadership, student and staff morale, and clarity of educational mission (Gottfredson et al. 2005, Stewart 2003, Welsh 2000). The implication is if there are deficiencies in any of these factors, designated elements of the school will need to be altered to "fix" the climate. Anti-bullying and school climate interventions often go hand in hand, as many school safety studies argue causal relationships between decreases in violent behavior and improved school climate.

The questions unifying research on LGBTQ bullying are: in what ways are LGBTQ students "at risk," and what environmental changes could alleviate that risk? Goodenow, Szalacha, and Westheimer (2006) examined LGB students' reports of suicidality and victimization as it related to their perceptions of school safety and the presence of GSAs, staff training around supporting LGB youth, or inclusive school policies. Murdoch and Bolch (2005) investigated correlations between various environmental elements (experiences with victimization, social exclusion, teacher support) and "school belonging, school disruptive behavior, and academic achievement" (160). Birkett, Espelage, and Koenig (2009) explored how school contextual factors are related to negative outcomes for LGBTQ youth such as victimization, drug use, suicidality, and truancy. These studies draw connections between negative social and psychological effects that LGBTQ students may experience when they are victimized in their school and the possibility of positive change through policy, educator training, and school-based support networks.

The literature reviewed here illustrates the discourse that is shaping conversations in the United States about schools' responsibilities to LGBTQ students. "The problem" is understood in terms of aggressive or intolerant students' anti-social behaviors. The presence of a problem is determined by visual or audible evidence of bias in the school environment—homophobic language or overt aggression—and visibility (or not) of LGBTQ students. This chapter will argue that these dominant bodies of research are defining the creation of safe and supportive schools in a way that is too narrow and simplistic, and that the U.S. anti-bullying discourse has placed costly limitations on discursive and practical tools available for educators to conceptualize the social marginalization of LGBTQ students. Participants' understanding of "the problem" in terms of biased language and bullying "reflects a shallow understanding of the social processes underpinning these phenomena and the subtle ways in which schools are complicit in sustaining them" (DePalma and Jennett 2010, 16). By examining the narratives of three educators who (1) claim to understand "the problem" and (2) are engaged in the work of intervening when they witness the problem in their schools, we aim to explicate how their understandings of what is happening and their visions for change are shaped by educational discourses that are narrowly focused on addressing behavioral *symptoms* of cultural, systemic problems.

Methods

The data are part of a larger evaluation study of the first three years of the Reduction of Stigma in Schools© (RSIS)—a Queering Education Research Institute[3] program that provides professional development about creating LGBTQ-affirming K–12 school environments. All research participants had previously attended RSIS training. The larger data set consisted of workshop evaluations, semi-structured interviews, and questionnaires completed by past participants of the RSIS workshops. Data were initially analyzed using the program evaluation criteria and subsequently analyzed using emergent processes reflective of Carspecken's (1996) critical ethnography. Full descriptions of the research methods are available in the program design and evaluation papers (Payne and Smith 2010, 2011).

Findings

The participants were interviewed to gain insight to their experiences of participating in the RSIS program. However, all participants also devoted significant interview time to connecting RSIS program content to the "state of things" in their respective school contexts. All spent time discussing "the problem" of LGBTQ students' school experiences in terms of the normalized presence of homophobic language in the school environment and the need to take consistent, organized, and focused action to disrupt this pattern of student behavior. The three "problem/solution" narratives presented here are indicative of the larger participant pools' overall framing of the problems to be solved in their schools, strategies for doing so, and visions of success.

Normalization of Homophobic Language

Donna evaluates her high school's climate in terms of student and staff behavior and defines "the problem" in her school as the constant use of homophobic language among students. She perceives that students are not concerned about consequences for using such language because it is a "normal" part of their daily interactions:

> And I think that mostly kids see [homophobic language] as normal ... Even if they're calling 'em a fag, or whatever, that and another big term now is "no homo." So kids say that all the time. It's in some movie.

She also sees this issue of language "normalization" in teachers' responses to student usage of homophobic pejoratives:

> I think, pretty much, people do kind of see it as a normalized, you know, behavior. That, I don't know if anybody's ears go (*surprised sound*). You know what I mean? Like profanity, they would. You know? Umm, and not [to] say that they like it or accept it or say that that's okay, but I just don't know if people would go out of their way to go over to somebody that they don't know [and correct them].

The claim that anti-LGBTQ language is normal implies neutral effects—its usage does not *do* anything to the environment or the people within it. Donna's concern is that normalization has made it unlikely that students will recognize the *wrongness* of using words that communicate bias. Additionally, she sees students receiving cultural support for using these terms. Her perception is students who say "that's so gay" or "no homo" and teachers who do not intervene do not understand the severity of the offense because they are not aware of the pernicious effects of biased speech.

Donna's analysis of why homophobic language is present in her school focuses on two issues. First is students' widespread unawareness that their language *is* biased or that language's effects could extend beyond their intentions. Students' references to movies or their (out) gay friends' use of the same biased language are offered as permission and rationale for using the language.

> And kids will tell me, "I have a friend who's gay and they say it all the time too." I go, "Well, I think that a lot of people may be offended," I go, "I guess maybe it depends on how they're saying it, or maybe because they are gay they feel it's okay to say it," you know, I go, "so I think that when you go out into public, you have to watch what you're saying, you know, 'cause other people may be offended … So … and you could be talking about my relative or my friend or, you know, my child. You know, and I could be offended."

Students who cite their gay peers' use of homophobic epithets as "proof" that the language is "normal" and harmless try to divorce themselves from possible wrong doing. While she does not challenge the logic of their rationale or question gay students' use of the language, she does deflect the argument and reiterate her position that using the language is unacceptable in any context. Second, Donna attributes students' failure to consider others' perspectives to intellectual and emotional immaturity—which is apparent in their lack of empathy:

> I mean, I can sit and try to tell kids how it is, you know, and like say, you know, "suicide rates are higher" and all that kind of stuff, but I think the general kid is like, "Oh well. Too bad." You know what I mean? Like, they don't understand and they don't, they don't have that empathy and I think that probably, that empathy would be important to our kids.

Her strategy for disrupting this pattern with her students is to raise their awareness of their own language use and how others might perceive it:

> So, I mean, we talk about it in [my classes] and I talk to the kids about how, you know, if somebody came in from the outside … Do they really think that the person who comes in from the outside would think that we are an accepting environment and that we're kind to each other and, you know, are not saying derogatory things in the hall? And they're like, "No, I think they would not think that at all." (laughs) "They'd pick up on some things and hear them." And I'm like, "Okay, well then we probably shouldn't be saying those things," you know.

When Donna has this discussion with her students, she asks them to do as she does: evaluate the quality of the school environment based on behavior. When the students acknowledge the problem of homophobic language and behavior in their school, she teaches them that the solution to this problem is students correcting their own behavior and asking their peers to do the same. She proposes taken-for-granted behavior modification solutions as defined by anti-bullying scholars, but this strategy fails to extend students' analysis of the language patterns to address the ways it reinforces the stigmatization and marginalization of LGBTQ identities.

Donna's definition of "the problem" and vision for solving it are reflective of messages within the bullying discourse which claim that students who engage in aggressive behavior do so because of negative attitudes or poor social skills learned from family and other cultural sources (Espelage and Swearer 2010; others). Further, concern about absence of empathy reflects a belief that the problem of bias and violence in schools is one that only has effects on the feelings and self-worth of individuals who may be personally injured—either by being directly targeted or by hearing the language circulating in their environment. Her interpretation does *not* account for the power of language in systematic marginalization of LGBTQ youth or valorization of heterosexuality. Homophobic speech used in reference to something students deem abnormal or unpleasant implicitly cites heteronormative discourse—which defines heterosexuality and stereotypical gender roles as normal (Ngo 2003, using Butler).

Inconsistent Intervention

Amy's descriptions of her school's level of support for LGBTQ students also focus on the normalized presence of homophobic language in classrooms and hallways. Like Donna, she finds it difficult to explain to students why they should not use anti-LGBTQ speech:

> It's like, I was just down the hallway today and some girl used ["That's so gay"], and I said, "I find that offensive, please don't use it. Do you understand why I find it offensive?" And she's like, "I gotta get to class" and she kept walking. I was like fine, I'm done with this discussion but I don't think she had [understood] … [A]nother teacher was walking up behind her and heard her say, "I don't understand what's offensive about the word." She thinks I was thinking she swore and the kids know not to swear. But when I say I find ["that's so gay"] offensive, and I go to explain why, sometimes they'll listen but sometimes they don't understand.

Both Donna and Amy express concern about issues of student "understanding," indicating a belief that *someone* needs to teach youth that language has consequences. While Donna is concerned with developing empathy in her students, Amy is concerned with students understanding political correctness. Both of these positions are invested in "efforts to minimize intergroup conflict by improving interpersonal relationships" (Mayo 2001, 78)—the goal being to eliminate the possibility of offending or hurting someone who may hear the language. This approach aims to "cur[e] social ills through mannered response [rather] than political challenge" (78). Such an approach may eliminate homophobic language but it also reinforces LGBTQ students as cultural "Other" because ceasing to use the language means dominant-group students "tolerate" or "empathize" with an unfamiliar, marginalized group.

Both teachers' visions for improving school climate are reflective of the bullying discourse's claim that peer-to-peer aggression "is something that can be observed, discovered, found, analyzed, reported and ultimately stopped" (Walton 2005, 92). A key component to this approach is raising awareness and diligence of *all* educators. Amy's interview was riddled with frustration about her colleagues' inconsistency:

> And I know other teachers tend not to hear it and I think, because I do the [GSA], I'm more aware of it, and after [the RSIS workshop] in November I know, um, teachers were aware of it for a while, but then they kind of forget and, like the woman that was in the hallway after that student that I corrected, she goes, "I didn't even hear it. I had no idea that she even said that."

By separating herself from those who do not take action, Amy establishes a professional and ethical standard for fulfilling responsibilities to LGBTQ students and maintaining the overall school climate. These standards are similar to those established by educational and political discourses on bullying—both of which look to educators to set an example.

Based on Amy's explanation of "the problem" in her school, it is possible to draw some conclusions about her vision of a positive school climate for LGBTQ youth. First, faculty and students need a collective understanding that homophobic language is not tolerated. Second, all school staff should address biased language every time it occurs. Third, the consistent effort will teach students a lesson about language that is permissible in schools and other social spaces. Her goal is a "measurable outcome," and her vision of an effective strategy is to *contain, regulate,* and *manage* behavior (Walton 2005, 112). The vision reflects research on LGBTQ youth's school experiences, which uses statistics such as *frequency of homophobic language* or *victimization* measurements to indicate the quality of the school climate (Birkett, Espelage, and Koenig 2009, Goodenow, Szalacha, and Westheimer 2006). The implication is that ending the behavior ends the problem, but this perspective fails to address *why* students use this language to target one another or express general displeasure, how this language cites gender stereotypes and heteronormative discourse, and how it reinforces social stigma around LGBTQ identities and gender transgressions.

Visibility as Solution

In Cheryl's story of her school's improving climate, the parameters of the bullying discourse are clear—bullies are students who bring negative attitudes and behaviors with them from outside the school environment and the school tries to mitigate their effects. Through those efforts, the frequency of negative events decreases. This reliance on decreasing frequency of negative incidents to signal climate improvement cites and inscribes the school climate discourse and reliance on number of reportable offenses as a viable measure of climate quality.

Cheryl notes the presence of normalized anti-LGBTQ language as a significant problem in her school, and she links it to larger cultural and student developmental factors—outside the school:

> We get so frustrated with, um, you know, the fag word, the gay word on a regular basis and so many kids would say, "Oh I don't mean anything by it" … Um, so I think we are like any other high school where that still is … it's still prevalent. Kids still use that term, "You're so gay." I mean, it's a formative time in their lives when some kids are so, especially boys, are so homophobic.

Cheryl's description of problems in her school focuses on behaviors of students whose homophobia leads them to target peers and/or prevents them from considering the significance of their derogatory speech. Her re-telling of students' claims that "injurious speech" (McInnes and Couch 2004) "doesn't mean anything" and her reference to homophobia in adolescent boys' peer groups defines the problem to be solved in terms of the students' normalized behavior and biased attitudes—problems located within the students themselves:

> Um … I think that no matter what programs you have instilled you are going to have kids in a school environment that come from homes that are … prejudiced against types of differences … And [LGBT students] are going to meet some resistance along the way, you are going to meet some … people that are just bigots or whatever.

Cheryl follows the anti-bullying discourse's assertion that students bring intolerance with them from outside the school. In turn, the strategies she proposes to address it are designed to generate empathy and dispel homophobia by raising awareness and educating youth about tragic consequences of bias:

> I think that continuing to do the Day of Silence[4] … this year, we did a Transgender Day of Remembrance.[5] We did that too! So, we had posters around talking about the different, the people who were killed for various reasons.

These one-day events draw attention to the violence experienced by LGBTQ people, and they are commonly used in schools to increase awareness about homophobia/transphobia and develop empathy in students. They rely on the belief that environmental factors (such as increased visibility) can be added or altered to shift school climate. However, these approaches fail to address the systemic privileging of gender and sexual conformity (Ngo 2010) and their transformative potential is limited because they "reinforce the position of the LGBTQ student as a 'cultural other' rather than shifting the cultural norms or creating alternative paths to power and prestige in the school environment" (Payne and Smith 2012b, 266). Consequently, the figure of the LGBTQ youth is being positioned as "a subject who needs to be saved" (Marshall 2010, 65) rather than integrating these students into the school environment by "honor[ing] the smartness of queer youth as instructors in an everyday pedagogy of sexual and gender diversity" (82).

To illustrate her point about the value of these visibility events, Cheryl described changes she has observed in the years her school has participated in Day of Silence events.

> Um, but the first year we had a lot of issues of kids being called "faggots" if they were, if they ... [participating in the Day of Silence] ... The first year was definitely our toughest. Signs were pulled down from the, from the walls and they were marked on a lot, you know, "you faggots" or whatever, that kind of thing. So there was a lot of resistance the first year. And each year as we've gone along, we've been, I think, pleasantly surprised that it's a little bit better ... number one, the signs are not being pulled down. I mean, you might have maybe one, now. It, it would be much, much less than that first year.

Despite the continued presence of anti-LGBTQ language in her school, Cheryl believes that the long-term effect of visibility events has been to increase awareness, reduce the prevalence of negative language, and increase tolerance and empathy. She gives no indication of any awareness that publicly and repeatedly linking LGBTQ identities with victimization and murder continues to reinforce the marginalization of these students and to mark LGBTQ identities as dangerous and at-risk (Payne and Smith 2012b).

In Cheryl's narrative, there is only so much the school can do. Educating bullies and trying to increase diversity awareness are the limits of the school capabilities to improve the situation. Stopping the verbal violence is imperative, but simply educating students on the harm it causes fails to make visible the value system that stigmatizes "gay" or that provides popularity and prestige to the harasser (Mahan et al. 2006, Payne and Smith 2012b).

Conclusion

Consistently, participants' evaluations of school climate and their actions to improve it reflected awareness of anti-LGBTQ language in their schools, inconsistent educator intervention, and a belief that increasing empathy in individual students would improve school climate. However, portions of their interviews revealed that they recognized problems that will require more complex solutions. These issues included patterns of exclusion in students' social groups, the stigmatization of attending GSA meetings, and silencing of LGBTQ voices in curriculum. These issues were often posed as unsolvable or overwhelming problems, and strategies for intervening were just beyond their reach.

The anti-bullying paradigm does not offer the requisite insight for designing interventions that can interrupt marginalization and create sustainable change (Payne and Smith 2014). These teachers intuitively understand that pervasive homophobic language has negative effects on schools, but they do not have the tools for "examining the underlying power dynamics that such behaviors build and reinforce" (Meyer 2008, 44). Sustainable change requires interventions that account for both the lived experiences of students and the processes through which cultural systems reward hegemonic gender and heterosexuality (Youdell 2006). Educators who can make meaning of their schools using these lenses will experience new possibilities for making meaning of the peer-to-peer aggression they are observing and gain new insight to innovative, transformative intervention.

Notes

1   The October 2010 "Dear Colleague" letter was written to address all forms of bullying and harassment. However, it was released just weeks after a rash of highly publicized LGBTQ youth suicides—all of which were attributed (by the media) to the grave effects of in-school victimization.
2   A Gay–Straight Alliance is a student organization that aims to provide support and affirmation to LGBTQ students and their allies.
3   The Queering Education Research Institute© (QuERI) is an independent think-tank, qualitative research, training, and policy center. The prime purpose of QuERI is to bridge the gap between research and practice in the teaching of LGBTQ students and the creation of LGBTQ youth-affirming schools. www.queeringeducation.org.
4   Day of Silence is an annual, nation-wide in-schools event when U.S. students take a vow of silence to raise awareness about anti-LGBTQ harassment in schools.
5   Transgender Day of Remembrance is an annual U.S. event to memorialize transgender people who have been killed or otherwise victimized.

References

Ali, Russlynn. 2010. Dear Colleague Letter; Harassment and Bullying, October 26.

Birkett, Michelle, Dorothy L. Espelage, and Brian Koenig. 2009. "LGB and Questioning Students in Schools: The Moderating Effects of Homophobic Bullying and School Climate on Negative Outcomes." *Journal of Youth and Adolescence* no. 38 (7): 989–1000. doi: 10.1007/s10964–008–9389–1.

Carspecken, P. F. 1996. *Critical Ethnography in Educational Research*. New York: Routledge.

DePalma, Renee, and Mark Jennett. 2010. "Homophobia, Transphobia and Culture: Deconstructing Heteronormativity in English Primary Schools." *Intercultural Education* no. 21: 15–26.

Duncan, Arne. 2011. Letter to Colleagues Announcing Release of Legal Guidelines Regarding the Equal Access Act and Recognition of Student-Led Noncurricular Groups.

Espelage, Dorothy L., and Susan M. Swearer. 2010. "A Socio-ecological Model for Bullying Prevention and Intervention: Understanding the Impact of Adults in the Social Ecology of Youngsters." In *Handbook of Bullying in Schools: An International Perspective*, edited by Shane R. Jimerson, Susan M. Swearer and Dorothy L. Espelage, 61–72. New York: Routledge.

Faris, Robert, and Diane Femelee. 2011. "Status Struggles: Network Centrality and Gender Segregation in Same- and Cross-gender Aggression." *American Sociological Review* no. 76: 48–73.

Felix, Erika D., and Jennifer Greif Green. 2010. "Popular Girls and Brawny Boys: The Role of Gender in Bullying and Victimization Experiences." In *Handbook of Bullying in Schools: An International Perspective*, edited by Shane R. Jimerson, Susan M. Swearer and Dorothy L. Espelage, 173–185. New York: Routledge.

Frey, Karin S., Miriam K. Hirschstein, Leihua V. Edstrom, and Jennie L. Snell. 2009. "Observed Redctions in School Bullying, Nonbullying Aggression, and Destructive Bystander Behavior." *Journal of Educational Psychology* no. 101: 466–481.

Garandeau, Claire F., Travis Wilson, and Phillip C. Rodkin. 2010. "The Popularity of Elementary School Bullies in Gender and Racial Context." In *Handbook of Bullying in Schools: An International Perspective*, edited by Shane R. Jimerson, Susan M. Swearer and Dorothy L. Espelage, 119–136. New York: Routledge.

Gendron, Brian P., Kirk R. Williams, and Nancy G. Guerra. 2011. "An Analysis of Bullying Among Students within Schools: Estimating the Effects of Individual Normative Beliefs, Self-Esteem, and School Climate." *Journal of School Violence* no. 10: 150–164.

Goldstein, Sara E., Amy Young, and Carol Boyd. 2008. "Relational Aggression at School: Associations with School Safety and Social Climate." *Journal of Youth and Adolescence* no. 37: 641–654.

Goodenow, Carol, Laura Szalacha, and Kim Westheimer. 2006. "School Support Groups, Other School Factors, and the Safety of Sexual Minority Adolescents." *Psychology in the Schools* no. 43: 573–589.

Gottfredson, Gary D., Diane C. Gottfredson, Allison Ann Payne, and Nisha C. Gottfredson. 2005. "School Climate Predictors fo School Disorder: Deliquency Prevention in Schools." *Journal of Research in Crime and Delinquency* no. 42: 421–444.

Green, Jennifer Greif, Erin C. Dunn, R. M. Johnson, and Beth E. Molnar. 2011. "A Multilevel Investigation of the Association between School Context and Adolescent Nonphysical Bullying." *Journal of School Violence* no. 10: 135–149.

Hymel, Shelley, Kimberly A. Schonert-Reicl, Rina A. Bonanno, Tracy Vaillancourt, and Natalie Rocke Henderson. 2010. "Bullying and Morality: Understanding How Good Kids Can Behave Badly." In *Handbook of Bullying in Schools: An International Perspective*, edited by Shane R. Jimerson, Susan M. Swearer and Dorothy L. Espelage, 101–118. New York: Routledge.

Mahan, Wil C., Kris Varjas, Brian J. Drew, Joel Meyers, Anneliese Singh, Megan L. Marshall, and Emily C. Graybill. 2006. "Adult Providers' Perspectives on Bullying Toward GLBTQI Youth." *Journal of GLBT Issues in Counseling* no. 1: 45–66.

Marshall, Daniel. 2010. "Popular Culture, the 'Victim' Trope and Queer Youth Analytics." *International Journal of Qualitative Studies in Education* no. 23: 65–85.

Mayo, Cris. 2001. "Civility and its Discontents: Sexuality, Race, and the Lure of Beautiful Manners." *Philosophy of Education 2001*, edited by Suzanne Rice, 78–87. Urbana, IL: Philosophy of Education Society.

McInnes, David, and Murray Couch. 2004. "Quiet Please! There's a Lady on the Stage—Boys, Gender and Sexuality Non-conformity and Class." *Discouse: Studies in the Cultural Politics of Education* no. 25: 431–443.

Meyer, Elizabeth J. 2008. "A Feminist Reframing of Bullying and Harrassment: Transforming Schools Through Critical Pedagogy." *McGill Journal of Education* no. 47: 33–48.

Murdoch, Tamera B., and Megan B. Bolch. 2005. "Risk and Protective Factors for Poor School Adjustment in Lesbian, Gay, and Bisexual (LGB) High School Youth: Variable and Person-centered Analysis." *Psychology in the Schools* no. 42: 159–172.

Ngo, Bic. 2003. "Citing Discourses: Making Sense of Homophobia and Heteronormativity at Dynamic High School." *Equity and Excellence in Education* no. 36: 115–124.

Ngo, Bic. 2010. "Doing 'Diversity' at Dynamic High: Problems and Possibilities of Multicultural Education in practice." *Education and Urban Society* no. 42: 473–495.

Olweus, Dan. 2010. "Understanding and Researching Bullying: Some Critical Issues." In *Handbook of Bullying in Schools: An International Perspective*, edited by Shane R. Jimerson, Susan M. Swearer and Dorothy L. Espelage, 9–33. New York: Routledge.

Orphinas, P., and A. M. Horne. 2010. "Creating a Positive School Climate and Developing Social Competence." In *Handbook of Bullying in Schools: An International Perspective*, edited by S. R. Jimerson, S. M. Swearer and D. L. Espelage, 49–60. New York: Routledge.

Payne, Elizabethe C. 2007. "Heterosexism, Prefection and Popularity: You Lesbian's Experiences of the High School Social Scene." *Educational Studies* no. 41: 60–79.

Payne, Elizabethe C., and Melissa Smith. 2010. "Reduction of Stigma in Schools: An Evaluation of the First Three Years." *Issues in Teacher Education* no. 19: 11–36.

Payne, Elizabethe C., and Melissa Smith. 2011. "The Reduction of Stigma in Schools: A New Profesional Development Model for Empowering Educators to Support LGBTQ Students." *Journal of LGBTQ Youth* no. 8: 174–200.

Payne, Elizabethe C., and Melissa Smith. 2012a. "Rethinking Safe Schools Approaches for LGBTQ Students: Changing the Questions We Ask." *Multicultural Perspectives* no. 14 (4): 187–193.

Payne, Elizabethe C., and Melissa Smith. 2012b. "Safety, Celebration and Risk: Educator Responses LGBTQ Professional Development." *Teaching Education* no. 23 (3): 265–285.

Payne, Elizabethe C., and Melissa Smith. 2014. "LGBTQ Kids, School Safety, and Missing the Big Picture: How the Dominant Bullying Discourse Prevents School Professionals from Thinking about Systemic Marginalization or … Why We Need to Rethink LGBTQ Bullying." *QED: A Journal of GLBTQ Worldmaking* no. 1: 1–36.

Pellegrini, Anthony D., Jeffrey D. Long, David Solderg, Carry Roseth, Danielle Dupuis, Catherine Bohn, and Mehgan Hickey. 2010. "Bullying and Social Status During School Transitions." In *Handbook of Bullying in Schools: An International Perspective*, edited by Shane R. Jimerson, Susan M. Swearer and Dorothy L. Espelage, 199–209. New York: Routledge.

Poteat, V. Paul, and Dorothy L. Espelage. 2007. "Predicting Psychosocial Consequences of Homophobic Victimization in Middle School Students." *The Journal of Early Adolescence* no. 27: 175–191.

Ringrose, Jessica, and Emma Renold. 2010. "Normative Cruelties and Gender Deviants: The Performative Effects of Bully Discourses for Girls and Boys in School." *British Educational Research Journal* no. 36: 573–596.

Stewart, Eric A. 2003. "School Social Bonds, School Climate, and School Misbehavior: A Multilevel Analysis." *Justice Quarterly* no. 20: 575–604.

Swearer, Susan M., Dorothy L. Espelage, Tracy Vaillancourt, and Shelley Hymel. 2010. "What Can be Done about School Bullying?" *Educational Researcher* no. 30: 38–47.

Twemlow, Stuart W., Peter Fonagy, and Frank C. Sacco. 2010. "The Etiological Cast to the Role of the Bystander in the School Architecture of Bullying and Violence in Schools and Communities." In *Handbook of Bullying in Schools: An International Perspective*, edited by Shane R. Jimerson, Susan M. Swearer and Dorothy L. Espelage, 73–86. New York: Routledge.

Van Houtte, Mieke. 2005. "Climate or Culture? A Plea for Conceptual Clarity in School Effectiveness Research." *School Effectiveness and School Improvement* no. 16: 71–89.

Waasdrop, Tracy Evian, Elise T. Pas, Lindsey M. O'Brennan, and C. P. Catherine P. Bradshaw. 2011. "A Multilevel Perspective on the Climate of Bullying: Discrepancies Among Students, School Staff, and Parents." *Journal of School Violence* no. 10: 115–132.

Walton, Gerald. 2005. "'Bullying Widespread': A Critical Analysis of Research and Public Discourse on Bullying." *Journal of School Violence* no. 4: 91–118.

Welsh, Wayne N. 2000. "The Effects of School Climate on School Disorder." *Annals of the American Academy of Political and Social Science* no. 567: 88–107.

Youdell, Deborah. 2006. *Impossible Bodies, Impossible Selves: Exclusions and Student Subjectivities*. The Netherlands: Springer.

6

SEARCHING FOR SELF AND SOCIETY

Sexual and Gender Minority Youth Online

Elise Paradis

While American research on gay, lesbian, bisexual, transgender, intersex, queer, and questioning (LGBTQ) adults has taken up the challenge of studying the new "Cyberqueer" phenomenon since the mid-1990s, there is a dearth of research on LGBTQ youth online, especially as it pertains to their usage of community networking services and other online environments. The current generation of American LGBTQ youth aged 13–21 grew up with the Internet. According to results from the 2006 Pew Internet and American Life Project survey, more than half (55%) of all American youths aged 12–17 who use the Internet also use online social networking sites (Lenhart and Madden 2007, 5), including Facebook, MySpace, and others. A large-scale study of a social networking site by Piskorski (2007) has shown that people reporting same-sex attraction were close to two times more likely to have logged into a networking site over a two-day period than those who did not report same-sex attraction. As Mike Glatze, founder of the activist website Young Gay America, noted: "Gay youth use the web like no other subset of the population … What exists today was completely unheard-of even 10 years ago" (cited in Alexander 2004, 5).

Indeed, while LGBTQ youth occupy shrunken public spaces in school (Irvine 1997, Macgillivray 2004, Muñoz-Plaza, Quinn, and Rounds 2002) and in their families, there are countless LGBTQ-friendly websites where they can claim their identity, learn from, and relate to LGBTQ peers. As Cohler and Hammack (2007) have argued, "social change such as that inspired by the internet, which has made available accounts by sexual minority youth overcoming obstacles and coping with minority stress … has led to changes in the manner in which sexual minority youth narrate their life stories" (49).

I investigate this phenomenon using a large-scale online survey of American LGBTQ youth. While a growing number of small-scale qualitative studies discuss the online experiences of LGBTQ youth (Alexander 2004, Curry 2005, Driver 2005, 2007, Egan 2000, Gray 1999, Laukkanen 2007, Rothbauer 2004, Silberman 1997) and investigate whether or how they come out online (Cohler and Hammack 2007, Driver 2005, Munt, Bassett, and O'Riordan 2002), there is a paucity of survey research addressing these issues. In a world where policy is most often dictated by a combination of both qualitative data and quantitative data, it is surprising that no study has yet been published that combines both approaches in investigating the online behaviors and communities of LGBTQ youth. My study tries specifically to answer the following questions:

1. How important are certain key features (see below) of LGBTQ online environments to LGBTQ youth?
2. What factors do LGBTQ youth identify as reasons for why they participate in LGBTQ online environments?

This chapter is a preliminary attempt to document quantitatively and qualitatively how American LGBTQ youth make use of the Internet. Further research will be required to address the same or similar research questions internationally.

Literature Review

Many accounts of the lives of LGBTQ youth in relation to the Internet are qualitative, written in a provocative journalistic style (e.g. Egan 2000, Silberman 1997), or are concerned mostly with access to information questions. Curry (2005), for example, worried whether librarians would help LGBTQ youth find answers to their questions in (queer) cyberspace, and Rothbauer (2004) showed the extent to which library- and Internet-savvy young lesbians struggle to find lesbian literature online. Laermer's (1997) *Get On With It: The Gay and Lesbian Guide to Getting Online* and other such reference books are mostly resource guides for LGBTQ Internet users that list queer-friendly sites. Of those, very few are specific to LGBTQ *youth* (an exception is Ellis et al. 2002).

In most studies, treatment of the importance of the Internet in LGBTQ youth's lives is almost accidental. For example, out of the 15 LGBTQ youth cited in the very influential book by Mary Gray (1999), only five discuss their Internet experiences. Indeed, her chapter on LGBTQ youth and the Internet is one of the shortest in the book. One of the most telling quotes is from "Ernie Hsiung." A first-generation Chinese American who grew up in a suburb of Berkeley, California, Ernie sees the Internet as a necessary space for social encounters: "As far as meeting other gay folks are concerned, I meet other people through the Internet" (Gray 1999, 100). Similarly, of the 54 youth featured in the LGBTQ youth anthology *Revolutionary Voices* (Sonnie 2000), only two mentioned the Internet, and wrote about their online experiences only in passing.

More recent studies (post-2000) are typically part of the new field of "cyberstudies," and so is this chapter. Kick-started in the early 1990s, this emerging field treats online behavior as a topic of interest in its own right. Two main themes emerged from the early cyberstudies work: identity and community. While Bruckman (1992) and Turkle (1995) focused on the development and management of identities online (a common theme in cyberstudies), Rheingold (1993) discussed the potential of the Internet for community-building and community-development. He defined virtual communities as:

> the social aggregations that emerge from the Net when enough people carry on those public discussions long enough, with sufficient human feeling, to form webs of personal relationships in cyberspace.
>
> (1993, 5)

In general, such cyberstudies legitimize identity and community experiences on the Internet as more than merely cold and artificial. Walther (1996), for example, refused to accept that Internet interactions are by definition "impersonal," and argued that, in some cases, computer-mediated communication could lead to "hyperpersonal" interactions and associated deep feelings of intimacy, without the need for a bodily presence.

The subfield of cyberqueer studies, constructed upon the foundations laid by pioneer Nina Wakeford (1997), examines the tensions of LGBTQ identities and communities online. Among cyberqueer studies of LGBTQ youth, the work of Driver (2005, 2007), Hillier and Harrison (2007), Laukkanen (2007), and Munt, Bassett, and O'Riordan (2002) deserve further mention.

British researchers Munt, Bassett, and O'Riordan (2002) discussed the way young women attracted to women "came out" and used identity labels on an American website which they dubbed "gaygirls.com." Their study of forum postings by 66 women allowed them to claim that women's queer identities are built online in a "discursive community" (136). Coming out, being out, and understanding what it means to be a woman attracted to women is thus seen as a critical component of LGBTQ online forums.

In "Out, Creative and Questioning," Driver (2005) provides the reader with glimpses of the homepages of queer and trans girls. For Driver, homepages serve as flexible spaces where youth create and display identities and desire, halfway between perfect anonymity and self-disclosure, away from the pressures of adults. Her later account of two LiveJournal.com communities of queer girls—"I kiss girls" and "birls"—is part of a larger study of queer girls and popular culture which argues that queer girls, who live in relative geographical and cultural isolation, and sometimes in fear, need these safe spaces as they explore their gender and sexual orientation identities. As such, "while the turn to online communities may seem like a poor substitute for face-to-face interactions, it becomes crucial to rethink simple divisions between real and virtual sociality" (Driver 2007, 174).

Laukkanen (2007) questions the apparent unlimited possibilities for queer self-representation on the Internet. Her analysis of the online experiences of a group of 14 Finnish youth underscored the heterosexual and gendered normativity of youth online services, most of which are or have become in Finland, as in the United States, commercial sites with limited and limiting features.

Open-coding the qualitative data in their survey, Hillier and Harrison (2007) identified six aspects of non-heterosexual life that LGBTQ youth "practice" online and offline: sexual identity, same-sex friendship, disclosure (coming out), same-sex intimacy, "homosex," and finding out about and practicing living as part of the gay community. The Internet, in Hillier and Harrison's view, exists as a "practice" field for youth, in prevision for their "real" offline lives. Similarly, Munt, Bassett, and O'Riordan (2002) and Driver (2005) see the Internet as practice ground or backstage arena but nevertheless see online experiences as real.

These studies emphasize the distinction between online and offline behavior, in contradistinction with other studies that see online and offline lives as inseparably interconnected, both part of "real" life. Berry and Martin (2000), for example, argue that "the net is neither a substitute for nor an escape from real life. Nor is it simply an extension of existing offline communities and identities. Instead, it is part of lived culture, informed by and informing other parts of users' lives" (cited in Alexander 2002, 80).

Finally, in their manifesto for the empirical study of online networking sites by queer researchers, MacIntosh and Bryson (2007) forcefully argue that educators need to pay greater attention to social networking sites and their significance for LGBTQ youth, and understand these sites as "constitutive of everyday locations of engagement and signification" (141) rather than as threats or trends.

Methods

This chapter presents quantitative and qualitative results based on a large-scale online survey, whose target population consists of American self-identified LGBTQ youth aged 13–21 who use the Internet. The survey questionnaire went through five different iterations, including focus group and pre-testing, following the methodological steps generally agreed on for survey design (Fink 1995, Fowler Jr. 1998, Iarossi 2006, Preece and Maloney-Krichmar 2005, Riggle, Rostosky, and Reedy 2005).[1]

The final version of the survey questionnaire consisted of 120 questions, divided into seven sections. A *Personal Information* section asked youth about their age, grade level, current state, ethnic origin, religiosity, family tensions, whether they were "out" to their parents, etc. A *Gender and Sexuality* section asked about gender identities, sexual orientations, and attraction to same and other genders. An *Online Habits* section asked questions about access to computers, privacy while using the Internet, number of hours spent online per day, etc. If youth said they accessed LGBTQ sites, they filled in an *LGBT Online Environment* section, where they were asked a plurality of questions about their online behavior. If youth said they felt they were part of an LGBTQ online community, they filled an *Online Communities* section, where they were asked how often they participate, completed a Sense of Community Index test (Chavis and Pretty 1999), and were asked to rate the importance, absolute and relative, of their online communities in their lives currently. The *Friends and Acquaintances* section asked youth where they meet their LGBTQ friends, if they meet offline people they first meet online and, if so, to describe one such experience. It also asked them whether they see a difference between online and offline friendships and, if yes, how so. Another section, *Offline Communities and Overall Support*, asked questions about LGBTQ offline support networks, including trustworthy adults, Gay–Straight Alliances (GSAs) and offline communities. The final section, *Discrimination against LGBT Youth*, asked about perceived levels of safety, openness, and discrimination online and offline.

I was careful in my approach to the "boxing" of identity in the *Personal Information* section. Queer researchers have documented the symbolic violence of forcing queer identities into binaries (Gosine 2007, Laukkanen 2007, O'Riordan and Phillips 2007). In order to better accommodate queer identities, I suggested pre-defined identity categorizations, but respondents were allowed to provide multiple answers for identity questions involving sexual orientation, gender identity and race, and could elect to fill an "other" text box.

Evidence that youth demand greater choice in the way they identify—or to not identify—with any of the LGBTQ labels (Cohler and Hammack 2007, Savin-Williams 2005) can be seen in the distribution of answers that I obtained for gender identity and sexual orientation. While the great majority of youth checked only one box for gender identity (80.5%), close to 20 percent of all respondents checked more than one box, with an average number of 1.34 responses for gender per youth (S.D. = 0.85). The picture is even more striking for sexual orientation. Only 57.1 percent of respondents checked a single box, such that more than two out of five youth in the sample chose more than one label for themselves.[2] On average, youth checked 1.63 boxes for sexual orientation (S.D. = 0.90).

These numbers are important warning signs for researchers who study LGBTQ youth, and further evidence of what scholars in the field previously found with regards to the changing relationship of youth to identity labels (Cohler and Hammack 2007, Laukkanen 2007, Savin-Williams 2005). In my survey, youth identified as "pansexual," "heteroflexible," "bicurious," "omnisexual," "sexually disoriented," "fluid," or simply wrote: "I don't identify with labels."

I used a snowball sampling technique (Fink 1995) to find my research subjects. Starting with LGBTQ online resources listed on popular LGBTQ websites and in Ellis et al. (2002), I sent 225 individual emails, 35 of which bounced, for a total of 190 LGBTQ resources across the country. LGBTQ youth, activists, researchers, and allies were asked to forward the online survey link to the LGBTQ youth they know, and to any contacts they might have in schools, GSAs, and LGBTQ organizations across the United States. The American national organization of Gay, Lesbian and Straight Educators Network (GLSEN) agreed to distribute my survey to its youth members. Between November 19, 2007 and October 17, 2008, 696 valid questionnaires were completed.

One of my main hypotheses was that the online experience of LGBTQ youth would be different depending on whether youth are in college, or in middle through high school. I therefore present separately the results obtained for college and non-college youth. In order to test this hypothesis, mean differences between both samples and t-test results are also reported. These statistics allow me to highlight the direction and magnitude of the difference, as well as the extent to which the difference in means between the two samples is statistically significant, reflecting non-random differences in online behavior.

The non-probabilistic nature of the sample prevents me from generalizing results to all LGBTQ youth, and the fact that all youth included in the analysis were currently living in the United States of America limits the validity of my findings to this demographic. While a study that would compare the online behaviors of LGBTQ youth to the online behaviors of non-LGBTQ youth could have yielded interesting insights comparing the two populations, the object of the present study lay elsewhere. It aimed at giving voice to LGBTQ youth and, as the analyses below will show, many of the questions would have had no immediate translation for non-LGBTQ youth. What would it mean, for example, to ask non-LGBTQ youth how often they go online "to feel like they belong," or "to explore their identity"? How does the need for belonging of a youth marginalized based on race, weight, or ability compare to that of LGBTQ youth? Comparing different types of marginalization was beyond the scope of the present research project.

Results

How Important are Certain Key Features of Online Environments to LGBTQ Youth?

LGBTQ youth were asked to rank 12 features of LGBTQ online environments to evaluate how important these features are to them (see Table 6.1). College-attending LGBTQ youth listed in descending importance inclusive spaces for all queer people (3.73 out of 5), socializing spaces (3.67), LGBTQ-specific health information (3.40), communities of interest (3.09) and support groups (3.06). Youth who are not in college listed as the most important features inclusive spaces (4.03 out of five), socializing spaces (4.02), support groups (3.68), communities of interest (3.66) and spaces shared with straight allies (3.44).

TABLE 6.1 How Important are the Following Features of Online Environments to LGBT Youth?

Features	College Mean	SD	Not in College Mean	SD	Difference	T-Test Significance
An inclusive space for all queer people	3.73	1.26	4.03	1.23	0.30	★★★
Socializing	3.67	1.20	4.02	1.10	0.34	★★★
LGBT-specific health information	3.40	1.22	3.28	1.30	−0.12	
Communities of interest (e.g. music, pop culture, travel)	3.09	1.34	3.66	1.28	0.58	★★★
Support groups	3.06	1.35	3.68	1.30	0.62	★★★
Legal advice	3.03	1.28	3.07	1.42	0.04	
An online community that organizes offline group events	2.96	1.37	3.26	1.41	0.30	★★
Spaces shared with straight allies	2.90	1.37	3.44	1.32	0.54	★★★
Networking/business/ housing opportunities	2.74	1.35	2.54	1.36	−0.21	★
A crisis center	2.68	1.37	3.08	1.45	0.40	★★★
Formal peer counseling spaces	2.46	1.27	3.08	1.42	0.62	★★★
Dating sites	2.09	1.22	1.94	1.20	−0.15	

Note. SD: Standard Deviation. Results reported on scale: 1 = not at all important, 2 = slightly important, 3 = moderately important, 4 = very important, and 5 = extremely important.

Significance levels of t-test: ★ $p < 0.1$; ★★ $p < 0.05$; ★★★ $p < 0.01$

If not for the importance accorded to LGBTQ-specific health information, the difference in rating between college- and non-college-attending youth for the top five most important features is statistically significant, and non-college attending youth almost always rate these features higher (i.e., more important) than their college-attending counterparts. The only features for which college-attending youth gave significantly higher ratings were networking/business and housing opportunities. In general, then, younger respondents seem to have more pressing needs for, and demand more from, online environments. They also tend to value socializing online with LGBTQ people and allies more than college-attending youth.

Overall, what is striking in those results is the predominance for LGBTQ youth of socializing needs over other types of needs—including dating and counseling needs, as well as crisis centers—regardless of educational level.

What Factors Do LGBTQ Youth Identify as Reasons Why They Participate in LGBTQ Online Environments?

I used two different approaches to evaluate why LGBTQ youth participate in LGBTQ online environments. I first looked at how often they indicated going online for a set of reasons chosen from the literature and during a focus group with LGBTQ youth. These results are quantitative. I then coded 155 responses to the question "What is the number one reason you use LGBT online environments?"

I asked youth how often they go online for 16 different reasons including "to ask questions" and "to find a date or a hook-up" (see Table 6.2).

The youth in my sample tell a clear story: their online lives mostly fulfill their need to be themselves, to belong, to socialize and be out. Non-college-attending youth report going online most often to be themselves (6.31 out of 7),

TABLE 6.2 How Often Do LGBT Youth Go Online for the Following Reasons?

Reasons	College Mean	SD	Not in College Mean	SD	Difference	T-Test Significance
To be yourself	4.73	2.83	6.31	2.36	1.59	★★★
To feel like you belong	3.92	2.77	5.07	2.84	1.15	★★★
Get information	3.92	1.80	4.12	1.80	0.20	
To explore my identity	3.81	2.53	4.28	2.63	0.47	★★
To come out and/or be out	3.73	2.73	4.88	2.75	1.15	★★★
To understand what it means to be LGBT	3.37	2.38	3.98	2.61	0.61	★★★
Meet LGBT people and socialize	3.35	1.99	3.84	2.30	0.49	★★★
To feel normal	3.32	2.68	4.48	2.92	1.16	★★★
To be anonymous	3.14	2.45	3.56	2.54	0.43	★
Get advice, support	2.88	1.80	3.57	2.00	0.69	★★★
Ask questions	2.41	1.62	2.98	1.86	0.57	★★★
To practice socializing for when I meet LGBT people offline	2.12	2.08	2.92	2.59	0.80	★★★
Meet people you can then meet offline	1.82	1.42	1.62	1.38	−0.20	★
Find a date or a hook-up	1.76	1.49	1.65	1.41	−0.13	
Play out fantasies	1.45	1.24	1.70	1.53	0.26	★★
Have online sex	1.32	0.91	1.47	1.27	0.15	

Note. SD: Standard Deviation. Results reported on scale: 1 = never, 2 = less than once a month, 3 = once a month, 4 = 2 or 3 times per month, 5 = once or twice a week, 6 = 3–6 times per week, 7 = once per day, and 8 = more than once a day.

Significance levels of t-test: ★ p < 0.1; ★★ p < 0.05; ★★★ p < 0.01

feel like they belong (5.07), come out/be out (4.88), feel normal (4.48), and explore their identity (4.28). College students report going online most often to be themselves (4.73 out of 7), feel like they belong (3.92), get information (3.92), explore their identity (3.81) and come out/be out (3.73). Here again, younger youth seem to have more pressing needs to go online, as they report on average much higher frequencies of usage. The differences between both sub-samples are almost always positive and significant: youth in middle and high school go online more often to meet most of their identity and community needs.

A notable exception lies with the frequency at which they go online to meet people face-to-face (mean difference = -0.20, significant at the 0.10 level), indicating that younger LGBTQ youth are more likely to want to meet offline the strangers they meet online. This could testify either to the greater social isolation of the younger youth as they discover their non-mainstream sexuality or gender identity, or to younger youth's less cautious online usage, greater gullibility or greater need for adventure.

Another striking observation is the very low frequencies that sex-related items obtained in this survey. College-attending youth reported going online to find a date or a hook-up, to play out fantasies, or to have online sex less than once per month (college youth: 1.76, 1.45, and 1.32 out of 7, respectively; non-college attending youth: 1.65, 1.70, and 1.47 out of 7, respectively; 1 = never, 2 = less than once a month). These results are in line with the qualitative results of Driver (2007) and others, but in stark contrast with cultural stereotypes about the sexual lives of LGBTQ people. Social desirability and self-disclosure biases cannot be excluded as an explanation of these observations, although the self-administration and total anonymity of the online survey limited its likelihood, and many youth shared details about their experiences with face-to-face meetings after online interactions.

To give the LGBTQ youth in my sample a chance to express themselves freely on the reasons why they go online, I offered them a text box for written responses to the open-ended question: "What is the number one reason why you use LGBT online environments?" From the 198 possible respondents who had viewed this question when I started coding the data, I obtained 155 answers (response rate of 78.3%) and a total of 202 reasons. Frequencies for each code can be found in Table 6.3.

Unsurprisingly, a majority of youth (54.2%) who answered this question mentioned socializing in one form or another as the number one reason why they go online. Some youth answered with a short "Socialize" to the question, while others provided more details: they organize LGBTQ events, learn about such events, meet LGBTQ people, or keep in touch with friends.

Some 31 percent of youth go online mostly to gain information about LGBTQ lives, people, culture, or history. For example, a 19-year-old bisexual Asian American woman attending college in California responded: "To stay up-to-date on queer-related pop culture or entertainment news in the lesbian community."

TABLE 6.3 Qualitative Coding of "Number One Reason" to Go Online Cited by LGBT Youth

Purpose	N	%
Socialize	84	54.2
Gain information	48	31.0
Feel a sense of belonging	37	23.9
Cope with a difficult life	16	10.3
Get advice	13	8.4
Pornography	4	2.6
Total	202	130.4

Note. Sample size is 155. Some youth listed more than one reason, resulting in a total of 202 reasons, and a total percentage greater than 100%.

Similarly, a 19-year-old gay Latino male wrote: "It's where I can get information about cultural and sexual practices without feeling any cultural pressure." Others reported going online to find LGBTQ contents for school-related purposes.

A total of 24 percent of youth reported going online to find a sense of belonging or to be themselves. They wrote, for example, that they wanted to "feel a part of something," want to "[m]eet people who identify with me" or "I want to feel like I belong." That one in four youth hinted at issues of belonging and/or identity is quite telling of the role that relationships to peers play in their lives as sexual or gender minorities. Many youth are indeed explicit about this need to relate to "like-minded people" or "[t]o be in a place where I feel like I belong and where I can find/chat with fellow LGBT people" (19-year-old white lesbian college student in Vermont).

A significant 10 percent of youth alluded to the difficulties of their lives offline. Some youth mentioned distance and isolation. A 17-year-old Washington State high school student of mixed race who identifies as male/gender neutral and gay wrote that he goes on the Internet "[b]ecause many people are not out in real life and we are spread apart by distance." Others mentioned the lack of LGBTQ people nearby, including one youth, a 19-year-old Colorado college white lesbian/bisexual who wrote that online environments "supplement the lack of the homosexual lifestyle in my life. I don't have any lesbian friends or love interests, [so] the internet offers a way for me to still be active in the community." Some responses were altogether heartbreaking, such as the isolation and pain felt by this 18-year-old white college-attending gay male: "To meet people. I want friends, dates, anything. I want to feel like I'm not some ugly fag that no one wants to be around or date. In Utah, that's all I feel like. There's no 'love' for 'our kind' and there aren't people I like that like me back." Finally, some youth mentioned the need to escape discrimination, sanctions, and the judgments of others. They go online, they write, "To make friends that won't judge me" (white 20-year-old lesbian from Florida).

Less than 10 percent of youth who answered the question mentioned going online to get advice. This category was coded in contrast with the "gain information" category in that it had to imply active seeking of advice from peers, and not mere reading of information online. As such, this code means interacting with peers to obtain guidance, and when contrasted with the information and socializing categories, it becomes clear that youth mostly go online to "hang out" and "chat" with peers. A 14-year-old white Massachusetts bisexual male provided an elaborate answer:

> Again, I use LGBTQIQQ (or, LGBTQQIA, as I have heard it) environments to meet other people and discuss with them their own experiences, especially in comparison and contrast to my own experiences. I often find myself conversing with other people about coming out, being out, having a significant other, their first time with sexual intercourse, etc. In the end, I most usually find that I simply converse and confer with other persons.

Others wrote that they go online to "listen to and learn from others' experiences" or to "give support to the people I left behind in my high school or in the old groups where I used to need support. Now I get my support in real life instead of [online], though, so I don't really need any." Once again, we get hints of changing needs and changing lives.

Finally, only 2.6 percent of respondents mentioned pornography or erotica as one of the main reasons they use the Internet, and when they did, it was often with a single word: "porn."

Conclusion

Much of the literature on LGBTQ youth indicates that they occupy shrunken public spaces in the offline world, when compared to non-LGBTQ youth. School, for many LGBTQ youth, is one such shrunken space. Whereas schools should be safe spaces for all adolescents, school authorities are currently not universally able to provide an adequate level of resources to LGBTQ youth, be it physical safe space or sense of community (Irvine 1997, Macgillivray 2004, Muñoz-Plaza, Quinn, and Rounds 2002). Indeed,

> Many researchers have particularly focused on the lack of social support systems for lesbian and gay youth within my schools, identifying the classroom as the most homophobic of all social institutions.
>
> (Muñoz-Plaza, Quinn, and Rounds 2002, 53)

In such a context, it is reasonable to think that a significant portion of these youth will find their community through other avenues, such as offline community centers, or online-based LGBTQ communities. My survey results go against pathologizing interpretations of the over-sexualized cyberqueer such as those found in the study by Wolak, Mitchell, and Finkelhor (2003): "normal" kids should be able to make "real-life" friends; the others—the "abnormal"— should compensate this lack of social skills with "non-real-life" behavior. Given that homosexuality and gender non-conformity are often pathologized, this discourse is potentially harmful to LGBTQ youth, and at any rate quite troubling. Rather than positing youth as lacking in social skills (a deficit model), my data shows that LGBTQ youth use the Internet to socialize and to feel a sense of belonging over any other purpose, echoing the work of Driver (2005, 2007) and Laukkanen (2007). They are not primarily going online to find dates, to have sex, or to look at pornography. They are searching for self and society.

What is clear, then, is that even when life is rough for some LGBTQ youth in their offline lives, they do find comfort, support, and community online. Those youth who do not speak of lacking communities use the Internet to keep in touch with friends. Overall, my data shows LGBTQ youth find the Internet an inclusive social space for expression, acceptance, and exploration of their queer identities; it shows that the Internet's queer-friendly features are more important to youth in middle through high school than they are for their college-attending counterparts; and that younger youth seem to use LGBTQ websites more often and more intensely than college-aged youth.

While one could argue that the nature of the topic or of the survey biases youth against honestly reporting sexual behavior, the prominence of belonging and identity in youth's answers is constant, however you probe for youth's online behavior on LGBTQ websites. "Sex" is thus disconfirmed as the central element of LGBTQ youth's online behavior. When asked openly about the reasons they go online, youth deny it is for sex, and confirm time and again that they are doing this to look for LGBTQ peers, to socialize, to belong, or to escape the stresses and distresses of their lives. Further analyses are still required to assert a connection between the presence or absence of offline LGBTQ communities and friends in these youth's use of the Internet, and subsequent research should identify the factors that influence online behavior and sense of community for LGBTQ youth. This chapter, however, is a first step in setting a new research agenda about LGBTQ youth and their communities: one that is less pathologizing, that focuses more on issues of relatedness, identity and belonging.

Teachers and other adults interested in helping LGBTQ youth explore their identities and find community should feel comfortable to direct these youth to the Internet. This work will be particularly critical for younger youth, youth outside urban centers, and youth who choose to attend college at more conservative institutions. Allies should work with school authorities to make sure that LGBTQ-friendly sites are not blocked by content filters, and to publicize the names of allies with whom youth can speak for guidance in exploring the wealth of information available to them online. The numbers presented here should add to educators' argumentation tools by depathologizing and desexualizing youth's online explorations, while simultaneously emphasizing the productive uses youth make of new technologies.

Notes

1   Readers interested to read detailed information about the survey design and its different versions, or are curious about the demographics related to the sample, are invited to inquire with the author.
2   In cases where both the "Lesbian" and the "Gay/Homosexual" boxes were simultaneously checked, the number of boxes reported here is the total number of boxes minus one. The numbers for each category, however, have not been transformed.

References

Alexander, Jonathan. 2002. "Queer Webs: Representations of LGBTQ People and Communities on the World Wide Web." *International Journal of Sexuality and Gender Studies* no. 7 (2 and 3): 77–84.

Alexander, Jonathan. 2004. *In Their Own Words: LGBTQ Youth Writing the World Wide Web*. New York: GLAAD Center for the Study of Media and Society.

Berry, C., and F. Martin. 2000. "Queer 'N' Asian On—and Off—the Net: The Role of Cyberspace in Queer Taiwan and Korea." In *Web Studies: Rewiring Media Studies for the Digital Age*, edited by D. Gauntlett, 74–81. London: Arnold.

Bruckman, Amy. 1992. *Identity Workshop: Emergent Social and Psychological Phenomena in Text-Based Virtual Reality* [cited July 27 2007]. Available from http://www.nicoladoering.net/Hogrefe/bruckman92.rtf/.

Chavis, David M., and Grace M. H. Pretty. 1999. "Sense of Community: Advances in Measurement and Application." *Journal of Community Psychology* no. 27 (6): 635–642.

Cohler, Bertram J., and Phillip L. Hammack. 2007. "The Psychological World of the Gay Teenager: Social Change, Narrative, and 'Normality'." *Journal of Youth Adolescence* no. 36: 47–59.

Curry, Ann. 2005. "If I Ask, Will They Answer? Evaluating Public Library Reference Service to Gay and Lesbian Students." *Reference and User Services Quarterly* no. 45 (1): 65–74.

Driver, Susan. 2005. "Out, Creative and Questioning: Reflexive Self-Representations in Queer Youth Homepages." *Canadian Women Studies* no. 24 (2/3): 111–116.

Driver, Susan. 2007. *Queer Girls and Popular Culture: Reading, Resisting, and Creating Media*. New York: Peter Lang.

Egan, Jennifer. 2000. "Lonely Gay Teen Seeking Same." *New York Times Magazine*, 10 December, 110.

Ellis, Alan, Liz Highleyman, Kevin Schaub, and Melissa White. 2002. *The Harvey Milk Institute Guide to Lesbian, Gay, Bisexual, Transgender and Queer Internet Research*: New York: Harrington Park Press.

Fink, Arlene (ed.). 1995. *How to Sample in Surveys*, Vol. 6. Thousand Oaks, CA: Sage.

Fowler Jr., Floyd J. 1998. *Handbook of Applied Social Research Methods.* Thousand Oaks, CA: Sage.

Gosine, Andil. 2007. "Brown to Blonde at Gay.com: Passing White in Queer Cyberspace." In *Queer Online: Media, Technology & Sexuality,* edited by Kate O'Riordan and David J. Phillips, 139–154. New York: Peter Lang.

Gray, M. L. 1999. *In Your Face: Stories from the Lives of Queer Youth.* New York: Haworth Press.

Hillier, Lynne, and Lyn Harrison. 2007. "Building Realities Less Limited than Their Own: Young People Practising Same-Sex Attraction on the Internet." *Sexualities* no. 10 (1): 82–100.

Iarossi, Giuseppe. 2006. *The Power of Survey Design: A User's Guide for Managing Surveys, Interpreting Results, and Influencing Respondents.* Washington, DC: World Bank.

Irvine, J. M. 1997. "One Generation post-Stonewall: Political Contests over Lesbian and Gay School Reform." In *A Queer World: The Center for Lesbian and Gay Studies Reader,* edited by M. Duberman, 572–588. New York: New York University Press.

Laermer, Richard. 1997. *Get On With It: The Gay and Lesbian Guide to Getting Online.* New York: Broadway Books.

Laukkanen, Marjo. 2007. "Young Queers Online: The Limits and Possibilities of Non-Heterosexual Self-Representation in Online Conversations." In *Queer Online: Media, Technology & Sexuality,* edited by Kate O'Riordan and David J. Phillips, 81–100. New York: Peter Lang.

Lenhart, Amanda, and Mary Madden. 2007. *Social Networking Websites and Teens: An Overview.* Washington, DC: Pew Internet & American Life Project.

Macgillivray, I. K. 2004. "Gay Rights and School Policy: A Case Study in Community Factors that Facilitate or Impede Educational Change." *International Journal of Qualitative Studies in Education* no. 17 (3): 347–370.

MacIntosh, Lori, and Mary Bryson. 2007. "Youth, MySpace, and the Interstitial Spaces of Becoming and Belonging." *Journal of LGBTQ Youth* no. 5 (1): 133–142.

Muñoz-Plaza, Corrine, Sandra Crouse Quinn, and Kathleen A. Rounds. 2002. "Lesbian, Gay, Bisexual and Transgender Students: Perceived Social Support in the High School Environment." *High School Journal* no. 85 (4): 52–63.

Munt, Sally R., Elizabeth H. Bassett, and Kate O'Riordan. 2002. "Virtually Belonging: Risk, Connectivity, and Coming Out On-line." *International Journal of Sexuality and Gender Studies* no. 7 (2/3): 125–137.

O'Riordan, Kate, and David J. Phillips. 2007. *Queer Online: Media, Technology & Sexuality.* Edited by Steve Jones. Vol. 40, *Digital Formations.* New York: Peter Lang.

Piskorski, Mikolaj Jan. 2007. "I Am Not on the Market, I Am Here with Friends: Finding a Job or a Spouse on an On-line Social Network." In *Conference of the American Sociological Association,* August 11–14, New York.

Preece, Jenny, and Diane Maloney-Krichmar. 2005. "Online Communities: Design, Theory, and Practice." *Journal of Computer-Mediated Communication* no. 10 (4): Article 1 [cited November 19 2015]. Available from http://jcmc.indiana.edu/vol10/issue4/.

Rheingold, Howard. 1993. *The Virtual Community: Homesteading on the Electronic Frontier.* Reading, MA: Addison-Wesley.

Riggle, Ellen D. B., Sharon S. Rostosky, and C. Stuart Reedy. 2005. "Online Surveys for BGLT Research: Issues and Techniques." *Journal of Homosexuality* no. 49 (2): 1–21.

Rothbauer, Paulette. 2004. "The Internet in the Reading Accounts of Lesbian and Queer Young Women: Failed Searches and Unsanctioned Reading." *The Canadian Journal of Information and Library Science* no. 28 (4): 89–110.

Savin-Williams, Ritch C. 2005. *The New Gay Teenager*. Cambridge, MA: Harvard University Press.

Silberman, Steve. 1997. "We're Teen, We're Queer, and We've got E-mail." *Wired*, December, 1–3.

Sonnie, Amy. 2000. *Revolutionary Voices: A Multicultural Queer Youth Anthology*. Los Angeles, CA: Alyson Publications.

Turkle, Shelley. 1995. *Life on the Screen: Identity in the Age of the Internet*. New York: Simon and Schuster.

Wakeford, Nina. 1997. "Cyberqueer." In *The Lesbian and Gay Studies Reader: A Critical Introduction*, edited by Sally R. Munt and A. Medhurst, 20–38. Washington, DC: Cassell.

Walther, J. B. 1996. "Computer-Mediated Communication: Impersonal, Interpersonal, and Hyperpersonal Interaction." *Communication Research* no. 23 (1): 3–43.

Wolak, Janis, Kimberly J. Mitchell, and David Finkelhor. 2003. "Escaping or Connecting? Characteristics of Youth Who Form Close Online Relationships." *Journal of Adolescence* no. 26 (1): 105–119.

7

CHANGING SCHOOL CULTURE THROUGH GAY–STRAIGHT ALLIANCES

Markus Bidell

Gay–straight alliances (GSAs) are one of the fastest growing school-based organizations in the United States and are also being formed internationally. They embody a paradigm shift away from the problems facing lesbian, gay, bisexual, transgender, and queer/questioning (LGBTQ) youth toward one of resiliency and empowerment (Griffin et al. 2004, Russell et al. 2009). GSAs are non-curricular social and advocacy groups for LGBTQ students and allies (Bidell 2011a). They offer students a safe and supportive space in schools and often provide LGBTQ education, activism, and advocacy for students and school personnel. When students and school staff support GSAs, they participate in a growing social justice movement to counteract many of the problems and prejudice facing LGBTQ young people in our schools (Bidell 2011b).

The Need for GSAs: A Crisis in Our Schools

Middle and high schools can be treacherous environments for LGBTQ youth. Numerous studies document LGBTQ students overwhelmingly report exceptionally high levels of verbal and physical harassment and abuse as well as cyberbullying while at school (e.g., Berlan et al. 2010, Institute of Medicine 2011, Kosciw et al. 2014). Unfortunately, school personnel can be direct or passive contributors by making prejudicial remarks themselves or failing to intervene when others do so. In the GLSEN 2013 National School Climate Survey (Kosciw et al. 2014), over half of LGBTQ students reported hearing school staff using prejudicial remarks, and approximately 40 percent said school personnel failed to intervene when in the presence of others making such comments (Kosciw et al. 2014). It is not surprising the majority of LGBTQ students didn't report these incidents and believed telling school staff would result in either little to no action or make the situation worse (Kosciw et al. 2014).

Verbal and physical harassment directed toward LGBTQ students takes a profound psychosocial toll. LGBTQ students who are bullied are far more likely to experience educational problems including absenteeism, poor academic performance and achievement, and even diminished educational aspirations to post-secondary studies (e.g., Berlan et al. 2010, Institute of Medicine 2011, Kosciw et al. 2014). And as levels of verbal and physical abuse increase, so do the negative academic and emotional outcomes. LGBTQ students describing more frequent levels of harassment due to their sexual orientation or gender identity missed considerably more school, had lower grade point averages, and described a diminished desire to enter college than LGBTQ students experiencing lower levels of harassment at school (e.g., Berlan et al. 2010, Institute of Medicine 2011, Kosciw et al. 2014). LGBTQ students experiencing high amounts of school bullying and abuse also had significantly higher rates of depression, anxiety, substance abuse, low self-esteem, self-harm, suicidality, and isolation (Almeida et al. 2009, Bontempo and D'Augelli 2002, Kosciw et al. 2014).

For LGBTQ students, school-based harassment and bullying creates a hostile educational environment to navigate, and exacerbates the multiple risks and psychosocial problems they already face. There is a consensus among health and human service researchers that LGBTQ youth, regardless of school experiences, are at heightened risk for a host of serious psychosocial and health problems, including: (a) mental health problems, such as depression and anxiety, (b) eating disorders, (c) violence and abuse, (d) substance use and abuse, (e) risky sexual behaviors and HIV infection, (f) suicidal ideation and attempts, as well as (g) homelessness and the resultant problems LGBTQ youth face on the streets (Institute of Medicine 2011).

The Emergence of Gay–Straight Alliances

While there is debate over the first emergence of GSAs, no one disputes these organizations are one of the fastest growing student-led groups and are "one of the most visible manifestations of the contemporary movement for social justice … across the United States" (Russell et al. 2009, 892). There are well over 4,000 registered GSAs throughout the United States (GLSEN 2003–2012a) and similar organizations are spreading internationally. The overwhelming majority of GSAs are found on high school campuses, and there is increasing recognition for GSAs at the middle school level (Kilman 2007). Even though middle school LGBTQ youth report some of the highest levels of bullying and abuse based on their sexual orientation and gender identity, they have far fewer resources and sources of support (e.g., GSAs, LGBTQ curriculum, supportive school staff) versus those found in high schools (Kosciw et al. 2014)

Johnson (2007) states the first GSA was started in 1972 at the George Washington High School in New York City shortly after the 1969 Stonewall riots, considered the pivotal event marking the start of the LGBTQ civil rights movement in the United States. The group was a student-led extracurricular organization to support and address the needs of LGBTQ youth and consisted of "20 student activist group members who were predominantly self-identified as Third World, with 15 gay members, nine women and six men, and six straight allies" (382). The organization also published a school pamphlet called *George Washington Goes Gay*. The origins of GSAs are also traced to Fairfax High School in California and three Boston area high schools.

In 1985, Dr. Virginia Uribe started Project 10 at Fairfax High School in California after faculty and school staff became enraged about the experiences of an African American gay male transfer student (Uribe and Harbeck 1991). The student

> was physically abused by peers, and verbally abused by teachers and peers alike … dropped out … becoming one more casualty of a system that neither understood, nor cared about him. His rejection was a systematic repeat of his experiences at four previous schools.
>
> (10)

In response, a comprehensive counseling and education program was developed in 1985 for LGBTQ students called Project 10. The program's name represents the percentage of the population thought to be lesbian, gay, or bisexual (Kinsey, Pomeroy, and Martin 1948). Project 10 is still active within the Los Angeles Unified School District.

Three groups were formed in the Boston area during the late 1980s and coined the term *gay–straight alliance*. Kevin Jennings is often credited with founding the first GSA in 1988 at Concord Academy in Massachusetts. Jennings was a history teacher and a female student approached him about dealing with LGBTQ bullying at the school. She proposed a club saying, "you're gay and I'm straight, so let's call it a Gay–Straight Alliance" (GLSEN 2003–2012b). In 1990, Jennings went on to co-found the Gay and Lesbian Independent School Teachers Network with other gay and lesbian educators in Massachusetts to support LGBTQ youth and worked with the state department of education to adopt the GSA-model in their Safe School Program. By 1995, the network became a national origination and changed its name to the Gay, Lesbian and Straight Education Network or GLSEN in 1997. GLSEN is the largest organization in the United States supporting LGBTQ students and GSAs. Similar to GLSEN, the Gay–Straight Alliance Network helps students establish and maintain GSAs and provides leadership, networking, and advocacy regarding safe school environments for LGBTQ students. The organization was started in 1998 to support GSAs in the San Francisco Bay Area and is now a national organization (GSA Network 2009).

Communities across the United States vary widely in their views and treatment of sexual orientation and gender identity, which can have real, significant, and even dramatic consequences for LGBTQ youth. Where a young LGBTQ person lives can be a significant factor regarding access to LGBTQ community support services and the presence of a GSA in their local school. Fetner and Kush (2008) found larger schools in wealthier urban and suburban communities with more liberal or progressive politics are more likely to start a GSA. The researchers concluded that students "in small schools, poor neighborhoods, rural areas, or the South or the Midwest were significantly less likely to have a GSA [and] because young people have little say in where their families live, these inequalities of place and of resources can be insurmountable" (128).

In addition, location is a major factor regarding community hostility and litigious actions to block the formation of GSAs. Exploring the legal cases brought by school districts to prevent GSAs in their schools, Mercier (2009) notes:

> the geographical locations where these disputes have arisen suggests that this increase in litigation is partially the result of increased student assertiveness to form GSAs in locales where their message is most controversial … and an absence of such litigation in more liberal parts of the country.
>
> (178)

Legal Issues and GSAs

It was not until the mid-1990s that legal challenges to ban GSA organizations on school campuses arose in the courts, garnering an unprecedented level of legal attention and activity for a non-curricular student organization. Parents, school administrators, and politicians opposed to GSAs utilized a variety of legal methods and arguments. Primarily motivated by conservative religious and political beliefs, opponents claimed GSAs promoted homosexuality and promiscuity as well as acted as recruiting beacons for students confused about their sexuality or gender identity. After the U.S. Supreme Court invalidated the 13 remaining state sodomy laws in the 2003 Lawrence v. Texas ruling, GSA adversaries could no longer argue that allowing these student organizations was tantamount to the sanctioning of illegal and criminal behavior on school campuses. Without the ability to use state sodomy laws and a criminality argument to ban GSAs, school boards and politicians developed other means to prohibit or curtail GSAs.

Efforts to ban GSAs have been struck down by federal court rulings based primarily on the protections afforded in the 1984 Equal Access Act as well as the First Amendment of the United States Constitution (Mercier 2009). Passed by the 98th Congress in 1984, the intent of the Equal Access Act was to oblige federally funded schools in providing equal access to all extra or non-curricular student clubs. Ironically, conservative religious groups supported the Equal

Access Act and extensively lobbied the United States Congress for its passage, as these groups wanted to guarantee the rights of students to form extra-curricular Bible study and other religious groups on school campuses. Specifically, the law applies to any school that accepts federal funding and has a limited open forum. The limited open forum criteria means at least one student-led non-curricular organization or club is granted permission by the school to meet outside of instructional periods (e.g., drama club, debate club, cheerleading, or school yearbook committee). So, if a school receives federal support and permits at least one non-curricular group to meet, they cannot deny, restrict, or discriminate against any students wishing to meet on the basis of "religious, political, philosophical, or other content of speech at such meetings" (EAA 1984). In 1990, the U.S. Supreme Court ruled the Equal Access Act was constitutional in the case Westside Community Schools v. Mergens (496 U.S. 226, 1990). The Supreme Court ruling confirmed that any schools receiving federal aid and having at least one student-led non-curriculum club can not discriminate against student organizations and must give each group equal access to school resources such as meeting spaces, public address systems, and school publications.

Two important U.S. Federal Court cases originating in California and Utah were largely argued using the 1984 Equal Access Act. The Orange Unified School District in California unanimously voted to prohibit a GSA at El Modena High School in 1999. The students went to court arguing violations of the Equal Access Act and First Amendment. In 2000, U.S. District Court Judge David Carter issued a preliminary injunction ordering the Orange Unified School District to permit the GSA at El Modena High School. After the injunction, the Orange County School Board settled the case by agreeing to recognize the GSA organization. Judge Carter's ruling, based on the 1984 Equal Access Act, was the first of its kind in favor of GSAs. As a way to maintain compliance with the Equal Access Act and also prohibit the GSA formed in 1995 at East High School, the Salt Lake City School District took the unprecedented step of banning all extracurricular student groups in February 1996. In 1998, the American Civil Liberties Union of Utah and Northern California, the Lambda Legal Defense and Education Fund, and the National Center for Lesbian Rights along with cooperating attorneys filed a lawsuit on behalf of East High School-GSA members Keysha Barnes, Leah Farrell, and Ivy Fox. The suit argued that the Salt Lake City School District was in violation of the Equal Access Act since some non-curricular groups were still meeting at the school. In addition, the lawsuit charged that banning all school clubs was in actuality a policy aimed at prohibiting GSAs, and hence a violation of the students' First Amendment rights to freedom of speech regarding LGBTQ positive viewpoints.

In November 1999, U.S. District Judge Bruce Jenkins rendered a judgment that the rights of Keysha Barnes and Ivy Fox were violated, but only for the 1997–1998 school year. It was discovered that during this school year, some non-curricular student groups were continuing to meet, which meant the Salt Lake

City School District was in violation of the Equal Access Act. While the judge ordered the school district to pay the plaintiffs' legal fees, he also found the school district had corrected the Equal Access Act violations by assuring the court all non-curricular student groups were no longer meeting. This prohibited GSAs from forming or meeting in the Salt Lake City School District.

A notice was filed in the United States 10th Circuit Court of Appeals in December 1999 challenging the judge's finding that all non-curricular student groups had in actuality stopped meeting after the 1997–1998 school year. The National Association of Social Workers, the School Social Work Association of America, the American Counseling Association, and the National Association of School Psychologists submitted a friend of the court brief stating the need for and importance of GSAs in public schools. Several other organizations (Asian American Legal Defense and Education Fund, Hispanic Bar Association of the District of Colombia, National Asian Pacific American Legal Consortium, and National Organization for Women Legal Defense and Education Fund) also submitted a friend of the court brief outlining the benefits of non-curricular clubs and argued the district ban was especially detrimental for minority students.

The challenge was fully briefed on appeal and in November 2000, the Salt Lake City School District decided to allow non-curricular student groups, including GSAs, to meet and the case was voluntarily dismissed. While such legal challenges might have dampened the development of supportive LGBTQ school policies and GSAs in Utah, the opposite seems to have occurred throughout the state. About a decade later, the same organization that fought to prohibit GSAs (i.e., the Salt Lake City School District) by banning all non-curricular student clubs and organizations in Salt Lake City passed a policy protecting LGBTQ students against discrimination and harassment at school. In December 2010, the Salt Lake City School Board approved the first such policy in the state of Utah (Drake 2010) and the number of new Utah GSAs have risen dramatically in the wake of these legal issues (Eckholm 2011).

Despite nearly unanimous support of GSAs by the courts, local and state politicians as well as school boards continue efforts to circumvent the legal protections afforded GSAs, such as developing district policies and state laws requiring students to obtain parental consent to join or participate in non-curricular clubs and organizations. Georgia passed legislation requiring school districts to distribute a list describing the purpose and mission of each non-curricular student organization to parents. The law also stipulates parents must be given the opportunity to decline permission for their child's participation in any non-curricular clubs and organizations. Lawmakers in several other states have considered similar legislation. Whittaker (2009) argues that parental consent legislation to thwart GSAs are a direct violation of the freedom to associate provision in the First Amendment and that "requiring students to gain a parent's consent to join a GSA will have a chilling effect on GSA membership" (51). Legal rulings concerning these parental notification and consent policies for GSAs have yet to come about. Irrespective of legal actions, some students have elected to create unique and creative names for their GSA organizations that place less emphasis, and hence potential backlash, on the use of the word "gay" as one strategy to avoid confrontation with conservative school personnel and parents.

The Impact of GSAs

Even with aggressive legal attempts to limit or ban them, school GSAs are flourishing across the country. And evidence is mounting that GSAs and other LGBTQ forms of support can have dramatically positive benefits on school climate and on the health, education, and psychosocial well-being of LGBTQ youth (Griffin et al. 2004, Kosciw et al. 2014, Russell et al. 2009, Walls, Kane, and Wisneski 2010). Schools with GSAs and other forms of LGBTQ supports (i.e., supportive curricula, staff, and policies) have a significantly improved LGBTQ school climate where students report they feel safer and have a stronger sense of belonging to their school community (e.g. Berlan et al. 2010, Williams et al. 2003). Moreover, students attending a school with a GSA reported school staff were more likely to intervene when hearing anti-LGBTQ comments and, in turn, these youth were less likely to experience verbal harassment and physical assault (e.g., Berlan et al. 2010, Williams et al. 2003).

LGBTQ students in schools with GSAs also have better academic performance and attendance even if they have limited (or no) participation in the organization at their school (Walls, Kane, and Wisneski 2010). Griffin and colleagues (2004) found that GSAs provided support and safe spaces, raised LGBTQ visibility and awareness, and played a role in wider school education and advocacy efforts about LGBTQ issues on campus. GSAs also have a positive impact on personal, academic, relational, and social aspects of LGBTQ students' lives. Participation in a school's GSA can lead to improvements in academic performance, self-acceptance, self-worth, and sense of belonging as well as with LGBTQ students' social relationships at school and home (Griffin et al. 2004, Kosciw et al. 2014, Lee 2002, Walls, Kane, and Wisneski 2010). Conversely, lack of GSAs and supportive school staff may have harmful consequences, especial for LGBT youth at risk for homelessness, a considerable problem amongst LGBT young people (Institute of Medicine 2011). In one study, the overwhelming majority of LGBT homeless youth reported they attended a high school without a GSA and few sought out school personnel for support (Bidell 2014). The researcher concluded that the "limited level of school support reported by the LGBT homeless youth may have played a deleterious role in their ability to successfully complete high school" (373).

Russell and colleagues (2009) have documented how GSAs can also foster youth empowerment. Youth leaders described a personal, relational, and strategic empowerment trifecta in having "connected the knowledge received from GSA leadership to larger movements for social change ... and ... a possible means to changing the school climate" (896). Intrapersonal empowerment helped youth feel good about themselves and gain a sense they had a voice as well as personal agency. Relational empowerment increased through feeling part of a community and experiencing the social support GSA membership can bring. The descriptions of empowerment by the GSA youth leaders were seen as unique by the researchers as they did not include the aspect of shared power with adults, often seen as a key element in youth empowerment models. Through GSA involvement, the youth leaders

> did not share power with adults at their school; rather, most were engaged in challenging the adult-defined school systems … and highlights the GSA as a unique historical moment in which, in many cases, young people are leading adults rather than partnering with them.
>
> (902)

School Personnel and GSAs

We know supportive, accepting, and inclusive school professionals and environments that promote the overall development of LGBTQ students can have powerful academic, career, personal, psychosocial, health and social benefits (Crowley, Harré, and Lunt 2007, Detrie and Lease 2007, Grossman and Kerner 1998, Institute of Medicine 2011, Kosciw et al. 2014, Muñoz-Plaza, Quinn, and Rounds 2002, Nesmith, Burton, and Cosgrove 1999, Vincke and Van Heeringen 2002). Central to the creation of such educative environments are teachers, counselors, administrators, and other school staff. Supportive teachers and other school staff are integral to LGBTQ students' well-being (Kosciw et al. 2014) and LGBTQ students might be more likely to seek support from school staff compared to their non-LGBTQ counterparts, likely due to their unique concerns and issues about being LGBTQ (Rivers and Noret 2008). Researchers have shown LGBTQ youth have significantly lower levels of mental health problems, feelings of social isolation, and school absenteeism as well as stronger overall academic performance and aspirations for post-secondary education if they can identify the presence of supportive school educators and staff (Kosciw et al. 2014, Russell, Seif, and Truong 2001).

Regrettably, school staff can also be direct or passive contributors to engendering or maintaining a hostile environment for LGBTQ students. In the GLSEN 2013 National School Climate Survey, over half of LGBTQ students reported hearing prejudicial remarks about sexual orientation and gender identity from school staff (Kosciw et al. 2014). Equally troubling, the majority of students didn't report LGBTQ bullying and harassment to school staff because of "doubts that staff would effectively address the situation and fears that reporting would make the situation worse" (27). Considering the importance of supportive school professionals, it's troubling to find that among a group of LGBTQ homeless youth "80.9% reported they never talked to a teacher, 70.8% never talked to a school/

mental health counselor, and 86.5% never talked to a school administrator about issues related to their sexual orientation or gender identity" (Bidell 2014, 371).

School teachers, administrators, and counselors, along with those educating such professionals, might be grappling or catching up with LGBTQ affirmative social, policy, and attitudinal changes. Numerous research studies support this supposition and outline problems regarding school personnel's professional training and competency when working with LGBTQ youth (Bidell 2012, Farmer, Welfare, and Burge 2013, Jennings and Sherwin 2008, McCabe and Rubinson 2008, Mudrey and Medina-Adams 2006, Zavalkoff 2002). For example, school counselor trainees reported significantly lower sexual orientation competence compared with other counseling specializations (Bidell 2012, Farmer, Welfare, and Burge 2013). These results are worrisome, especially considering that "professional school counselors are uniquely situated to play a vital role in supporting LGBTQ youth" (Bidell 2012, 206). Moreover, school professionals and trainees can and do hold biased and prejudicial views regarding LGBTQ issues that are often based on conservative sociopolitical and religious beliefs (Bidell and Whitman 2013, Farmer, Welfare, and Burge 2013, Henke, Carlson, and McGeorge 2009, McCabe and Rubinson 2008, Mudrey and Medina-Adams 2006, White 2009, Wyatt et al. 2008, Zavalkoff 2002). Faculty that train future teachers, administrators, and school counselors have a crucial role to play by helping future school professionals explore their attitudes regarding LGBTQ issues as well as develop the requisite knowledge and skill to support their LGBTQ students (Bidell 2012).

One of the most direct ways school personnel can support LGBTQ students is to become a GSA advisor at their school. Yet for some school staff, this can be a difficult decision that often presents both real and perceived professional risks. School professionals can fear for important aspects of their job such as tenure, dismissal, or retribution if they became a GSA advisor (Valenti and Campbell 2009). They might also worry their credibility could be undermined in the school, and that some colleagues may automatically assume that either they are LGBTQ or want to convert students if they become a GSA advisor or mentor (Valenti and Campbell 2009). Obtaining support and guidance from professionals and organizations that already have experience in developing LGBTQ school-based programs can be especially helpful. For school counselors, "networking was vital when supporting, developing, and maintaining a GSA in their school … [and] networking efforts provided [them] with needed information and resources as well as personal and political support for their GSA endeavors" (Bidell and Garfield 2012, 27).

School personnel considering ways to support their LGBTQ students through becoming a GSA advisor or implementing other LGBTQ programs and policies can tap into a considerable array of resources from national organizations (e.g., GLSEN, Gay–Straight Alliance Network, and Project 10). If new to or unsure about starting a GSA, school professionals can consider beginning with a host of existing LGBTQ school-based programming. For example, GLSEN has developed downloadable resources such as the GLSEN Safe Space Kit, The Day of Silence, No-name Calling Week, GLSEN Lunchbox, or GLSEN K-12 Lesson Plans. Utilizing such aides might be less risky than starting a GSA and provide an initial and visible way to become a LGBTQ ally. It can also begin the process of change and help teachers, counselors, or administrators gain a sense of the political climate at their school and within their community before undertaking the larger task of creating and advising a GSA. However, the most important point is for school staff to embark on tangible and visible efforts to support their LGBTQ student. Martha Langmuir from GLSEN notes:

> One of the most important ways a teacher or one educating teachers can support LGBTQ students and GSAs is to be a visible ally in all the ways it seems appropriate and safe to be. If LGBTQ students don't know you are an ally, your support is invisible. There are many, many ways teachers can begin the process of being an LGBTQ student ally and pave the road for the creation of a GSA in their school. GLSEN has multiple resources for teachers that can facilitate this process but teachers can also cover topics during LGBT history month, use LGBTQ examples in their teaching, and even more important, confront LGBTQ harassment and bullying by other students and staff.
>
> (Langmuir 2011)

Implementing any of these school-based interventions to support LGBTQ students can be important steps toward the development of a GSA, and will likely foster a more positive LGBTQ school climate. LGBTQ affirmative curricula, policies, and advocacy programs in schools can significantly improve a school's climate, helping LGBTQ students to feel safer and more comfortable to talk with teachers about LGBTQ (Horowitz and Hansen 2008, Kosciw et al. 2014). Students enrolled in schools with an LGBTQ-inclusive curriculum and supportive administrations describe better school attendance; more accepting peers; greater feelings of school safety and belonging; higher levels of LGBTQ school resources; and more responsive school staff to incidents of sexual orientation and gender identity harassment.

Conclusion

Over the last two decades, academic research has primarily centered on the serious psychosocial, educational, and developmental risk factors impacting many LGBTQ youth. While immensely valuable, there is a growing reevaluation of such scientific inquiry as now being redundant as well as inadvertently supporting problem-based views of LGBTQ youth. Scholars are beginning to shift their focus away from the now well-documented risks associated with being a LGBTQ adolescent to a more holistic assessment of "the ways in which [LGBTQ] youth negotiate their development within various social contexts" (Horn, Kosciw, and Russell 2009, 863). GSAs represent such an approach and are a positive way that LGBTQ students and their allies can create a safe and supportive school environment.

LGBTQ youth face extraordinary educational, social, and emotional stressors often with few or no resources, allies, or mentors available to help them. This lack of support can fuel intense isolation. Unlike ethnic and cultural minority young people, LGBTQ youth typically do not have parents, siblings, and extended family members that share their minority status. Hence, LGBTQ youth cannot draw on the support, experience, and wisdom of their family regarding how to navigate a minority identity within a hetero and gender normative culture. When school professionals and educators support GSAs and other types of LGBTQ affirmative school programs and policies, they are directly contributing to the psychological, physical, emotional, social, and academic well-being of their LGBTQ students. By taking incremental, tangible, and concrete steps to support LGBTQ students and establish a GSA, those working in schools can become a pivotal and powerful resource and source of support for LGBTQ students. One teacher that became a GSA advisor stated it well:

> Somebody needs to do it. I was very nervous and anxious about [becoming a GSA advisor] because I just never did it before and I am all alone doing it, but somebody has to do it and boy I just love these kids ... I [didn't] know exactly what I [was] doing ... but we [were] going to figure it out together.
>
> (Valenti and Campbell 2009, 238).

GSAs draw on the best in teachers, administrators, counselors, and students. Through the courageous commitment of youth and adults, GSAs build bridges that offer tangible ways to improve schools for LGBTQ students. A strong well-supported GSA can not only transmute a school's climate and culture, but also be individually transformative, helping to ameliorate many of the problems facing LGBTQ youth in our nation's schools.

Resources for School Teachers and Staff

Amplify-LGBTQ Youth Resource: www.youthresource.com
Gay and Lesbian Alliance Against Defamation (GLAAD): www.glaad.org
Gay, Lesbian and Straight Education Network: www.glsen.org
Gay–Straight Alliance Network: www.gsanetwork.org
The Hetrick-Martin Institute (Home of The Harvey Milk High School): www.hmi.org
Lambda Legal Defense and Education Fund: www.lambdalegal.org
Lavender Youth Recreation and Information Center (LYRIC): www.lyric.org

The National Youth Advocacy Coalition (NYAC): www.nyacyouth.org
Parent, Families and Friends of Lesbians and Gays: www.pflag.org
Project 10: www.project10.org

Legal Rulings

Colin ex rel. *Colin v. Orange Unified School District*, 83 F. Supp. 2d 1135 (C.D. Cal. 2000)
East High v. Board of Education, 2:98-CV-193J (S. D. C. Ut, 1999)
Equal Access Act of 1984, 20 U.S.C. § 4071 *et seq.* (20 U.S.C. §§ 4071–74)
Lawrence v. Texas, 539 U.S. 558 (2003)
Westside Community Schools v. Mergens (496 U.S. 226, 1990)

References

Almeida, Joanna, Renee M. Johnson, Heather L. Corliss, Beth E. Molnar, and Deborah Azrael. 2009. "Emotional Distress Among LGBT Youth: The Influence of Perceived Discrimination Based on Sexual Orientation." *Journal of Youth and Adolescence* no. 38 (7): 1001–1014. doi: 10.1007/s10964–009–9397–9.

Berlan, E. D., H. L. Corliss, A. E. Field, E. Goodman, and S. B. Austin. 2010. "Sexual Orientation and Bullying among Adolescents in the Growing Up Today Study." *The Journal of Adolescent Health* no. 46 (4): 366–371. doi: 10.1016/j.jadohealth.2009.10.015.

Bidell, Markus P. 2011a. "Gay-Straight Alliances and School Counselors: Social Justice Advocacy for Lesbian, Gay, Bisexual, Transgender and Questioning Students." *New York State School Counseling Journal* no. 8 (1): 9–15.

Bidell, Markus P. 2011b. "School Counselors and Social Justice Advocacy for Lesbian, Gay, Bisexual, Transgender, and Questioning Students." *Journal of School Counseling* no. 9 (10): 1–22.

Bidell, Markus P. 2012. "Examining School Counseling Students' Multicultural and Sexual Orientation Competencies through a Cross-Specialization Comparison." *Journal of Counseling and Development* no. 90: 200–207. doi: 10.1111/j.1556–6676. 2012.00025.x.

Bidell, Markus P. 2014. "Is There an Emotional Cost to Completing High School? Ecological Factors and Psychological Distress among LGBT Homeless Youth." *Journal of Homosexuality* no. 61 (3): 366–381. doi: 10.1080/00918369.2013.842425.

Bidell, Markus P., and A. R. Garfield. 2012. "Networking in New York State Schools: Supporting Gay-Straight Alliances." *New York State School Counseling Journal* no. 9 (1): 27–34.

Bidell, Markus P., and J. S. Whitman. 2013. "A review of Lesbian, Gay, and Bisexual Affirmative Counseling Assessments." *Counseling Outcome Research and Evaluation* no. 4: 112–126. doi: 10.1177/2150137 813496423.

Bontempo, D. E., and A. R. D'Augelli. 2002. "Effects of At-school Victimization and Sexual Orientation on Lesbian, Gay, or Bisexual Youths' Health Risk Behavior." *The Journal of Adolescent Health* no. 30 (5): 364–374. doi: 10.1016/S1054–139X(01) 00415–3.

Crowley, Colm, Rom Harré, and Ingrid Lunt. 2007. "Safe Spaces and Sense of Identity: Views and Experiences of Lesbian, Gay and Bisexual Young People." *Journal of Gay & Lesbian Psychotherapy* no. 11 (1/2): 127–143.

Detrie, Pamela M., and Suzanne H. Lease. 2007. "The Relation of Social Support, Connectedness, and Collective Self-Esteem to the Psychological Well-Being of Lesbian, Gay, and Bisexual Youth." *Journal of Homosexuality* no. 53 (4): 173–199.

Drake, Katie. 2010. "Salt Lake City School Board Passes Antidiscrimination Policy." *The Salt Lake Tribune*, December 7.

EAA. 1984. Equal Access Act of 1984.

Eckholm, Erik. 2011. "In Isolated Utah City, New Clubs for Gay Students." *The New York Times*, January 1.

Farmer, L. B., L. E. Welfare, and P. L. Burge. 2013. "Counselor Competence with Lesbian, Gay, and Bisexual Clients: Differences among Practice Settings." *Journal of Multicultural Counseling and Development* no. 41: 194–209. doi: 10.1002/j.2161–1912. 2013.00036.x.

Fetner, Tina, and Kristin Kush. 2008. "Gay-Straight Alliances in High Schools: Social Predictors of Early Adoption." *Youth & Society* no. 40 (1): 114–130.

GLSEN. 2003–2012a. *Get the Facts about GSAs*. Gay, Lesbian, and Straight Education Network (GLSEN) [cited July 17 2014]. Available from http://glsen.customer.def6. com/participate/gsa/about-gsas.

GLSEN. 2003–2012b. *Who We Are*. Gay, Lesbian, and Straight Education Network (GLSEN) [cited July 17 2014]. Available from http://glsen.customer.def6.com/learn/ about-glsen.

Griffin, Pat, Camille Lee, Jeffrey Waugh, and Chad Beyer. 2004. "Describing Roles that Gay-Straight Alliances Play in Schools: From Individual Support to School Change." *Journal of Gay & Lesbian Issues In Education* no. 1 (3): 7–22.

Grossman, Arnold H., and Matthew S. Kerner. 1998. "Self-esteem and Supportiveness as Predictors of Emotional Distress in Gay Male and Lesbian Youth." *Journal of Homosexuality* no. 35 (2): 25–39.

GSA Network. 2009. *History*. Gay–Straight Alliance Network [cited June 29 2015]. Available from http://gsanetwork.org/about-us/history.

Henke, Tegan, Thomas Stone Carlson, and Christi R. McGeorge. 2009. "Homophobia and Clinical Competency: An Exploration of Couple and Family Therapists' Beliefs." *Journal of Couple & Relationship Therapy* no. 8 (4): 325–342. doi: 10.1080/ 15332690903246101.

Horn, Stacey S., Joseph G. Kosciw, and Stephen T. Russell. 2009. "Special Issue Introduction: New Research on Lesbian, Gay, Bisexual, and Transgender Youth: Studying Lives in Context." *Journal of Youth and Adolescence* no. 38 (7): 863–866. doi: 10.1007/s10964–009–9420–1.

Horowitz, Alan, and Anastasia Hansen. 2008. "Out for Equity: School-based Support for LGBTQA Youth." *Journal of LGBT Youth* no. 5 (2): 73–85.

Institute of Medicine. 2011. *The Health of Lesbian, Gay, Bisexual, and Transgender People: Building a Foundation for Better Understanding*. Washington, DC: National Academies Press.

Jennings, Todd, and Gary Sherwin. 2008. "Sexual Orientation Topics in Elementary Teacher Preparation Programs in the USA." *Teaching Education* no. 19 (4): 261–278.

Johnson, Dominique. 2007. "'This Is Political!' Negotiating the Legacies of the First School-Based Gay Youth Group." *Children, Youth & Environments* no. 17 (2): 380–387.

Kilman, Carrie. 2007. "This Is Why We Need a GSA." *Teaching Tolerance* (31): 30–36.

Kinsey, Alfred C., M. Pomeroy, and C. E. Martin. 1948. *Sexual Behavior in the Human Male*. Philadelphia, PA: Saunders.

Kosciw, Joseph G., Emily A. Greytak, Neal A. Palmer, and Madelyn J. Boesen. 2014. *The 2013 National School Climate Survey: The Experiences of Lesbian, Gay, Bisexual and Transgender Youth in Our Nation's Schools*. New York: Gay, Lesbian and Straight Education Network (GLSEN).

Langmuir, Martha. 2011. Personal Communication, May 19.

Lee, Camille. 2002. "The Impact of Belonging to a High School Gay/Straight Alliance." *High School Journal* no. 85 (3): 13–26.

McCabe, Paul C., and Florence Rubinson. 2008. "Committing to Social Justice: The Behavioral Intention of School Psychology and Education Trainees to Advocate for Lesbian, Gay, Bisexual, and Transgendered Youth." *School Psychology Review* no. 37 (4): 469–486.

Mercier, Matthew T. 2009. "Fighting to Fit In: Gay-Straight Alliances in Schools under United States Jurisprudence." *International Journal of Human Rights* no. 13 (2/3): 177–191. doi: 10.1080/13642980902758101.

Mudrey, Renée, and Aida Medina-Adams. 2006. "Attitudes, Perceptions, and Knowledge of Pre-Service Teachers Regarding the Educational Isolation of Sexual Minority Youth." *Journal of Homosexuality* no. 51 (4): 63–90.

Muñoz-Plaza, Corrine, Sandra Crouse Quinn, and Kathleen A. Rounds. 2002. "Lesbian, Gay, Bisexual and Transgender Students: Perceived Social Support in the High School Environment." *High School Journal* no. 85 (4): 52–63.

Nesmith, A. A., D. L. Burton, and T. J. Cosgrove. 1999. "Gay, Lesbian, and Bisexual Youth and Young Adults: Social Aupport in Their Own Words." *Journal of Homosexuality* no. 37 (1): 95–108.

Rivers, Ian, and Nathalie Noret. 2008. "Well-Being Among Same-Sex- and Opposite-Sex-Attracted Youth at School." *School Psychology Review* no. 37 (2): 174–187.

Russell, Stephen T., Anna Muraco, Aarti Subramanian, and Carolyn Laub. 2009. "Youth Empowerment and High School Gay-Straight Alliances." *Journal of Youth and Adolescence* no. 38: 891–903. doi: 10.1007/s10964–008–9382–8.

Russell, Stephen T., Hinda Seif, and Nhan Truong. 2001. "School Outcomes of Sexual Minority Youth in the United States: Evidence from a National Survey." *Journal of Adolescence* no. 24: 111–127. doi: 10.1006/jado.2000.0365.

Uribe, Virginia, and Karen M. Harbeck. 1991. "Addressing the Needs of Lesbian, Gay, and Bisexual Youth: The Origins of PROJECT 10 and School-Based Intervention." *Journal of Homosexuality* no. 22 (3/4): 9–28.

Valenti, Maria, and Rebecca Campbell. 2009. "Working with Youth on LGBT Issues: Why Gay–Straight Alliance Advisors Become Involved." *Journal of Community Psychology* no. 37 (2): 228–248. doi: 10.1002/jcop.20290.

Vincke, John, and Kees Van Heeringen. 2002. "Confidant Support and the Mental Wellbeing of Lesbian and Gay Young Adults: A Longitudinal Analysis." *Journal of Community & Applied Social Psychology* no. 12 (3): 181–193. doi: 10.1002/casp.671.

Walls, N. Eugene, Sarah B. Kane, and Hope Wisneski. 2010. "Gay-Straight Alliances and School Experiences of Sexual Minority Youth." *Youth & Society* no. 41 (3): 307–332.

White, Kimberly R. 2009. "Connecting Religion and Teacher Identity: The Unexplored Relationship between Teachers and Religion in Public Schools." *Teaching and Teacher Education* no. 25 (6): 857–866. doi: 10.1016/j.tate.2009.01.004.

Whittaker, Keola R. 2009. "Gay-Straight Alliances and Free Speech: Are Parental Consent Laws Constitutional?" *Berkeley Journal of Gender, Law & Justice* no. 24: 48–67.

Williams, T., J. Connolly, D. Pepler, and W. Craig. 2003. "Questioning and Sexual Minority Adolescents: High School Experiences of Bullying, Sexual Harassment and Physical Abuse." *Canadian Journal of Community Mental Health* no. 22 (2): 47–58.

Wyatt, Tammy Jordan, Sara B. Oswalt, Christopher White, and Fred L. Peterson. 2008. "Are Tomorrow's Teachers Ready to Deal with Diverse Students? Teacher Candidates' Attitudes toward Gay Men and Lesbians." *Teacher Education Quarterly* no. 35 (2): 171–185.

Zavalkoff, Anne. 2002. "Teaching the Teachers: Confronting Homophobia and Heterosexism in Teacher Education Programs." *Journal of Lesbian Studies* no. 6 (3/4): 243–253.

8

QUEERING CHILDREN'S LITERATURE

Rationale and Resources

Danné E. Davis

Introduction

Queering[1] children's literature means to gain awareness of picture books that problematize the pervasive heteronormativity or, challenge oversimplified, homogeneous homosexual relationships in children's literature. Given the growing sexual diversity among schoolchildren, they and their teachers must realize that queer narratives are a subgenre of children's literature. Learning about the existence of such narratives begins to dissolve the prevailing heterosexist hegemony in the genre by expanding people's idea and characterization of children's literature. Moreover, exposure to queer children's narratives is empowering, providing schoolchildren with culturally relevant and profoundly meaningful literature that informs their academic comprehension and worldview.

The term "queer" can mean anyone who is lesbian, gay, bisexual, or transgender (LGBT). At times, and with varying responses, LGBT is used interchangeably with the term queer. For some people—often more conventional in their beliefs—the referent queer is offensive, pejorative, and otherwise unsettling, associating the word with ontological deviance and askewness (Kumashiro 2001, Pinar 2007). Conversely, often among progressive thinkers and radical individuals, queer is an affirming referent. Its cooptation by individuals who identify "as sexual outsiders" (Pinar 2007, 4) and variants, is a welcome and preferable moniker because lesbian, gay, bisexual, or transgender are too restrictive or simply inaccurate (Pinar 2007). In academic contexts, "queer" is used to trouble taken-for-granted epistemologies and customaries (Kumashiro 2002, Mayo 2010) pushing for new understandings and intersections of being and identity critical to education (Meyer 2007). Despite its cooptation by sexual outsiders and gender non-conformity (Huegel 2003, Owens 1998), the term queer often overlooks people of color (Asher 2007), reducing African-Americans, Asians, Latinos/Hispanics, and Indigenous people to an "endnote, footnote" (Han 2009, 111) statistical anomaly, or from the comprehensive discourse of sexual diversity (e.g., Goldstein, Russell, and Daley 2007, Mayo 2010).

Schoolchildren's interaction with queer literature creates opportunities to foster their comprehension and critical literacy. This occurs when young readers make personal, textual, and societal connections to the literature's themes, plots, and characters, in ways similar to culturally relevant, age-appropriate narratives. Furthermore, queer children's narratives provide schoolchildren *and* teachers the opportunity to favorably see people and characters who are queer and in normative situations. Too often this narrative is a footnote, often erased as theme, and rarely accessible en masse, through school, community, and commercial book repositories. This obscurity impedes queer and straight schoolchildren's opportunity to identify and empathize with the narratives in ways beneficial to schoolchildren's development (Escamilla and Nathenson-Mejia 2003). This is troubling, given the increasing sexual diversity in the lives of school-age children.

Straight Youngsters, Queer Parents

For many youngsters, queer identities are a reality of their home life. Since the "gayby boom"—the nickname dubbing the 1990s movement when many people came out as gay, lesbian, or bisexual, and, through in vitro fertilization, single and second parent adoption, and surrogacy, became parents (Jennings 2008, Ryan and Martin 2000, Sears 1999, Snow 2004)—increasing numbers of children under the age of 18 have or live with same-sex (Fox 2008, Kissen 2002, Snow 2004, Tye 2003), single-lesbian/gay, bisexual or transgender parents (Tye 2003). LGBTQ people are continually becoming parents (Fox 2007). Nearly one-quarter of youngsters in the United States are estimated as having same-sex parents (Pawelski et al. 2006) with 40 percent LGBTQ families headed by racially diverse parents (Jennings 2008). The upward trend makes organizations such as Children of Lesbians and Gays Everywhere (COLAGE) an important resource. As a national movement that comprises children with one or more queer caregivers, COLAGE advances social justice ideals through empowerment and education of and advocacy for children (COLAGE 2015).

LGBTQ parents are likely to enroll their children in public elementary schools (Fox 2007, Sears 1999) where youngsters may experience teasing and tormenting by their peers for having LGBTQ caregivers (Mayo 2010, Rowell 2007, Snow 2004). Sometimes unassured or unsavvy youngsters remain silent about having queer parents to avoid harassment and marginalization in school. In fact, being silent about having LGBTQ parents is a common coping strategy for 7, 8 and 10 year olds (Snow 2004). For example, Keila, a 7-year-old, second grade girl with a Mexican American lesbian mother revealed, "The only bad thing about my mom being gay is that I can't tell anyone. I have four best friends, but haven't told anyone" (6). Similarly, this silence prevails in children's queer literature featuring LGBTQ families of color. Despite the minimal presence of queer family structures in actuality and literature, the composition counters the heteronormative image of family that is primary in United States' schools.

Heteronormativity

Heteronormative perspectives are prevalent throughout social and educational contexts in the United States. "There is a belief in the superiority of heterosexuality or heterosexuals" (Sears 1999, 7) as mainstream and privileged. Heternormativity considers affectionate relationships between women and men as normative. Femininity and masculinity are static gendered identities representing conventional expectancies as ways of being (Meyer 2007). Heterosexism, the bias and prejudice that favors heteronormativity, may be due in part to homophobia and ignorance about queer lives (Pinar 2007).

Since classrooms are microcosms of society, heteronormativity exists within the learning environment. Heteronormative perspectives dominate elementary classrooms (Endo, Reece-Miller, and Santavicca 2010, Kissen 2002, Meyer 2007, Sears 1999) and public education (Kissen 2002, Kumashiro 2002, Loutzenheiser and MacIntosh 2004, Morris 2005). While teachers are slowly replacing the referents "mother and father" with "parents and caregiver," the shift in gender and relationship roles of schoolchildren lags. Routinely, teachers presume schoolchildren are or want to be heterosexual (Mayo 2010, Sears 1999). School policies and practices are often heteronormative (Fox 2007, Kissen 2002, Letts and Sears 1999) with "early childhood education … very much a part of this normalisation [sic] process" (Robinson 2002, 422).

Most future teachers in the United States have minimal appreciation for queer perspectives. Many teacher candidates in the United States have been raised homophobic (Clark and Blackburn 2009) or with heteronormative mindsets (Asher 2007, Clark and Blackburn 2009, Kissen 2002, Loutzenheiser and MacIntosh 2004). Future teachers sometimes resist including queer perspectives in the elementary curriculum (Lipkin 2002, Meyer 2007, Robinson and Ferfolja 2001, Sears 1999), asserting that queer perspectives are beyond the scope and comprehension of schoolchildren (Clark and Blackburn 2009). These assertions usually stem from personal religious and ideological differences (Griffin and Ouellett 2003, Mayo 2010) or discomfort with and lack of knowledge about queer perspectives, including appropriate incorporation of queer diversity in the classroom (Clark and Blackburn 2009, Fox 2007, Morris 2005, Robinson 2002).

Customarily, future teachers receive little, if any, significant education and professional development in LGBTQ matters (Kissen 2002, Letts and Sears 1999) including its nexus with race (Griffin and Ouellett 2003, Holmes and Cahill 2004, Ryan 2002, Swartz 2003). "More attention to … teacher education that acknowledge[s] sexual identity … as key aspects of youth identity"

(Hermann-Wilmarth 2010, 188) and as elemental to school literacy (Moje and MuQaribu 2003) is essential. In reality, young children understand sexuality (Morris 2005) and know a lot more about sexual diversity than educators may predict (Bickmore 1999, Meyer 2007, Swartz 2003). Thus, school-age children would be responsive to queer children's literature because it allows them to examine taken-for-granted gender identities and relationship roles (Meyer 2007), which includes the "investigation of ... the ways that sexuality is characterized in those narrow cultural definitions" in the literature (Swartz 2003, 13). For some youngsters, it also offers characters and storylines with which they might personally identify.

Queer Youngsters

Many youngsters, predominantly born male, face contention in their quest to simply attend and experience school like their peers. The youngsters grapple with their non-heterosexual identity, vie for peer acceptance of who they are or are transitioning to become, and yearn for a supportive environment with understanding teachers. The increasing visibility of queer youth in the United States moved the Gay, Lesbian and Straight Educators Network (GLSEN) in 2009 to collect data from 4,356 middle and high gay and lesbian school youth (Kosciw et al. 2010). Today, schoolchildren at younger ages are coming out as lesbian, gay, bisexual (Owens 1998) and transgender (Greytak, Kosciw, and Diaz 2009).

Recently, mass media has been peppered with the voices of youth, prepubescent boys in particular, coming out as transgender or diagnosed with gender dysphoria, also called gender identity disorder, which is a sense of feeling trapped in the wrong gendered body to the point of great dissatisfaction with their birth sex (Blanchard 1988). Some boys, almost from birth, insist they are girls. For example Jazz, who, almost from the moment he could speak, stressed that he wanted to wear dresses and would routinely unsnap his onesies to make it look like a dress. Whenever his parents praised him for being a good boy, Jazz would correct them saying he was a girl (Goldberg and Adriano 2007). As a toddler, Riley exhibited gender non-conforming behaviors. By age six, he verbalized displeasure with his life, prompting his parents to allow Riley to enter school as a female. Eight-year-old male-born Ky, now Kyla, displayed feminine behavior, dress, and desired to join the all-girl cheerleading squad (Keogh 2009). Brandon was born male, but from an early age considered himself female. At home he enjoyed playing with dolls, wearing his mother's heels, lingerie, and dresses, viewing himself a girl.

> When teachers divided the class into boys' and girls' teams, Brandon would stand with the girls. In all of his kindergarten and first-grade self-portraits ... "he" was a girl, often with big red lips, high heels, and a princess dress. Just as often, he drew himself as a mermaid with a sparkly purple tail, or a tail cut out from black velvet.
>
> (Rosin 2008, 57)

Given the opportunity, some youngsters find camaraderie with other transgender females. For example, Lilly and Thomasina, since meeting when aged eight at a conference for families with transgender children, have valued having someone with whom they can identify and self-disclose without humiliation and repercussions (Heroy 2010). However, this opportunity is the exception, underlying the rising need for watchdog and advocacy groups.

Queer perspectives among schoolchildren are often met with contention or crisis, necessitating support. Bullypolice.org advocates for bullied children, reporting on anti-bullying laws across the states (Bully Police USA 2015). To date, all 50 states have anti-bullying legislation. Advocacy groups, such as GLSEN and the Gay–Straight Alliance (GSA), call upon teachers and school administrators to ensure the safety of all schoolchildren, with GLSEN expanding its mission to include LGBTQ children and their parents on the elementary level (Kosciw and Diaz 2008). Yet, many school personnel remain unsupportive of youth who are queer (Mayo 2010) with educators ineffective in keeping youth safe. In the 2009 National School Climate Survey, 84.6 percent of youth reported being verbally harassed at school because of their sexual orientation, with 40 percent verbally harassed and nearly 19 percent physically assaulted. Nearly 64 percent reported being verbally harassed over gender expression, with 27 percent physically harassed and 12 percent physically assaulted. Slightly above 61 percent felt unsafe in school because of their sexual orientation, while close to 40 percent felt unsafe because of their gender expression. Slightly over 62 percent had not reported incidents to teachers or other school personnel because they doubted school adults' ability to effectively address the situation or feared reporting would worsen the situation (Kosciw et al. 2010). "Because name calling and ridicule begin in elementary school … it is vital to begin interrogation of attitudes toward sexuality in elementary education" (Swartz 2003, 11), which may reduce the incidents of harassment and taunting in the upper grades.

While issues of acceptance and safety are usually minimal in schools with GLSEN chapters and GSAs (Mayo 2010, Szalacha 2004), serious harm has resulted from taunting and bullying. Over the years, there have been increasing incidents of physical harassment and verbal bullying of youth for being gay, gender non-conforming, or perceived as either (Greytak, Kosciw, and Diaz 2009, Kosciw et al. 2010, Mayo 2010) sometimes resulting in violent death (Mayo 2010) or suicide. According to the Suicide Prevention Resource Center (2008), suicide is the primary reason for death among queer youth, with hanging as the primary means of death.

Learning Diversity through Children's Literature

Children's literature is engaging and informative. Well-written and relevant texts can facilitate establishing connections between the reader and the content. This is especially useful when teaching children about difference, introducing teachers to culturally responsive resources, and developing anti-bias mindsets (Escamilla and Nathenson-Mejia 2003). The International Reading Association (IRA) and the National Council of Teachers of English (NCTE) value these outcomes as reflected in their *Standards for the English Language Arts*. The first standard requires schoolchildren to read a wide range of print texts to develop an understanding of themselves and of cultures within and beyond the United States. A similar expectation is delineated in the Common Core State Standards Initiative (2010) adopted by 42 states. Further called for are texts that reflect gender diversity to foster readers' value of difference (IRA and NCTE 1996). Multicultural children's literature has long fostered appreciation for diversity. Whether defined as literature by and about diverse people or issues, or as narratives tacitly or expressly challenging bias, or affirming societal pluralism that ultimately move the reader toward an embracing stance (Bogum, Simpson, and Claudia 2010), children's texts about LGBTQ identities fit within the multicultural genre. Multicultural literature gives the reader access to unique perspectives and identities that may otherwise be inaccessible, illusive, or simply unknown (Brindley and Laframboise 2002, Singer and Smith 2003).

Children's picture books can help readers gain awareness of the circumstances and diversity of other people (Escamilla and Nathenson-Mejia 2003). Reading and critically examining the social construction of normalcy in storybook characters, families, gender roles, and relationships is one way to comprehend sexual diversity (Schall and Kauffmann 2003). Typically children's picture books are used to explore the dominant discourse of family diversity—usually fictional depictions of queer parents and caregivers, occasionally including caregivers of color, assisting with homework, coordinating extracurricular activities, and dispensing love or moral guidance (e.g., Snow 2004). In recent years, the narratives have begun to extend beyond the homogeneous, lesbian–gay binary to transgender identity and include racial and ethnic diversity—all of which can convey the physically and emotionally oppressive nature of homophobia (Swartz 2003) and "interrupt the cycles of inequity around [queer] issues in elementary education" (Hermann–Wilmarth 2010, 198)

Educators using children's literature to teach about the oppressive nature of heterosexism exists in a Seattle elementary school. *My Princess Boy* (Kilodavis and DeSimone 2010) is a biographical tale about a four-year-old boy of African descent, Dyson, and his preference for "traditional girl" things. Written by his mother, the story reveals Dyson's delight in wearing dresses, jewelry, and sparkly things. Wanting to quell the initial teasing directed toward Dyson because of his gender expression and also thwart school bullying incidents against other children, the vice-principal purchased copies of *My Princess Boy* to assist teachers in instructing about anti-bullying, acceptance, and tolerance (Fowler 2010). The real lives of children like Dyson, Keila, Jazz, Riley, Kyla, Brandon, Lilly, and Thomasina make queering children's literature a compelling undertaking.

Locating the Literature

A survey of children's picture books with prominent LGT characters, topics, and themes, was undertaken. Keyword and Boolean Internet searches were conducted using terms and phrases, such as: gay children's books/literature, gay and lesbian and multicultural children's books/literature, transgender children and books, transgender boys and literature/books, homosexuals and schoolchildren and books; LGBTQ and children's books/literature; and queer children's books. This search resulted in books and booklists classified gay-lesbian and rainbow on commercial, privately sponsored, public, and LGBTQ advocacy websites. Those same terms were then used to search local and nationwide university, community, and online library catalogues. Next, the terms gay, lesbian, LGBTQ, transgender, rainbow, and queer were used to search Amazon.com, WorldCat.org, and the Library of Congress for books ranked juvenile, children under ten, and elementary level. EBSCO databases for articles, reports, booklists, and book reviews pertinent to the topic were also searched.

This process yielded 109 children's picture and board books with explicit queer perspectives. The books were obtained via online purchasing, borrowing from local libraries, and through interlibrary loans, which supplied the bulk of the texts.

The goal for the immediate queering children's literature project was to locate children's books that would be personally meaningful, culturally appropriate, and racially/ethnically relevant to pubescent transgender females, gender non-conforming males, and gay school-age children. The increasing visibility of LGBTQ schoolchildren made the project focus sensible.

Queer Children's Literature

Based on the lives and deaths of actual and perceived queer youth, books are categorized as gender non-conformity (dress), gender non-conformity (behavior), race and ethnicity, transsexual, and gay. The hope is that the printed narratives will provide all readers, schoolchildren and educators, queer and straight, with meaningful resources that are encouraging and informing.

Gender Non-Conformity: Dress

Gender non-conformity in dress focuses on books featuring children born male with a penchant for making or wearing dresses and clothing usually associated with females. In *10,000 Dresses* (Ewert 2008), Bailey shares his dreams with his family about magical dresses only to be ridiculed when they tell him that he is a boy and should not be thinking about dresses. Bailey befriends Laurel, an older girl, who is inspired by Bailey's dreams. In friendship, they make dresses together, and Bailey finally becomes the girl he longed to become.

Another story about dreams and dresses is *Jesse's Dream Skirt* (Mack and Buchanan 1979). Jesse loves wearing skirts so much that he makes one to wear to daycare. Although supported by his mother, she warns him about possible teasing, which does happen and is addressed by the daycare teacher, Bruce. Another picture book featuring gender non-conformity in dress is the previously discussed *My Princess Boy* (Kilodavis and DeSimone 2010). These books would be useful in introducing gender non-conformity in dress. Boys who enjoy traditional girls' clothing or donning their mother's fashions might also relate to these storylines.

Gender Non-Conformity: Behavior

Gender non-conformity in behavior features books showing boys exemplifying behaviors typically associated with girls. *Tough Eddie* (Winthrop and Hoban 1985) is about a boy whose public persona is tough and boorish but at home enjoys the serenity of playing with his dollhouse. Dolls are also a theme in *William's Doll* (Zolotow and Du Bois 1972), a story about a young boy, William, who wants a doll. While his brother and a neighborhood boy tease him for being a sissy, and his father objects, William's grandmother buys him a doll, suggesting the toy will make William a great father.

The word "sissy" is expressly used in *Oliver Button is a Sissy* (DePaola 1979) and *The Sissy Duckling* (Fierstein and Cole 2002) to describe male characters who prefer culinary and the arts over sports. A similar theme exists in *Max, the Stubborn Little Wolf* (Judes, Bourre, and Robins 2001) about a young wolf named Max who wants to be a florist despite his dad's desire for Max to hunt. These texts would be useful in helping readers gain awareness of gender non-conforming behavior, particularly the perspective of young males who enjoy playful and social activities typically associated with girls. Furthermore, the literature offers gender-expressive males a resource with the potential for instilling confidence in and self-assurance of their identity.

Race and Ethnicity

The books in this section are classified as race and ethnicity. With some overlap, this is based on: primary character's ethnicity, reference to countries of colors, and dual languages.

First, at least one primary story character is of color. For example, *How My Family Came to Be: Daddy, Papa and Me* details the cross-racial adoption of an African American boy by a gay white couple (Aldrich and Motz 2003), and *While You Were Sleeping* tells of a similar adoption by a biracial lesbian couple (Burks 2004). International adoption is also discussed in *The White Swan Express: A Story about Adoption* (Okimoto, Aoki, and So 2002), which is an Asian-inspired narrative of four baby girls from a Chinese orphanage and the various families who adopt them, including a lesbian couple.

Second, in addition to characters' ethnicity, reference to countries associated with people of color encompasses the race and ethnicity classification. *Felicia's Favorite Story* features a young girl who enjoys hearing her favorite bedtime story of being adopted by her lesbian parents, one of whom is Guatemalan (Newman and Romo 2002). The reader learns Felicia means "happy" and sees colors and illustrations reflective of the Guatemalan landscape.

Third are books containing or referencing dual languages—primarily Spanish. *Best Best Colors* (Hoffman, Henriquez, and Vega 1999) is about a young Latino who uses the help of his two Latina mammas to choose his favorite color. The text offers mirrored English and Spanish on each page. A similar format is used in *Antonio's Card* (González and Alvarez 2005), which highlights a young boy who loves the power of words and their ability to express feelings such as love, pride, or hurt, but, on Mother's Day, he struggles to decide what words, particularly in Spanish, to express his love for his lesbian mother and her female partner.

Transsexual

As of this writing, *Carly: She's Still My Daddy* (Boenke and Dudley 2004) is the only published children's book addressing sexual reassignment. In it, young Tommy uses mature and appropriate language to tell of his father's transition from Carl to Carly. For example in describing how his "father is turning into a woman" (3) he states how a counselor "helped him (Tommy) figure out that he was transgendered—that's the word for people who look like boys, but know, inside, they are really girls, or the other way around" (5). Tommy further explains the meaning of people who are transitioning from female to male, intersex, cross-dressers, and those who live in the middle. The reactions of playmates, grandparents, and peers' parents are included. This book would be greatly informative in introducing young and adult readers to the general physiological dimensions of sexual transition. The narrative might be particularly reassuring to young gender dysphoric males hoping for sexual reassignment when they are older.

Gay

Another categorization of a singular text is *The Harvey Milk Story* (Krakow and Gardner 2001). Similar to most of the 109 children's books reviewed, including the 15 presented in this chapter, the storyline has biographical and historical elements. *The Harvey Milk Story* presents the life of a man who made history as the first elected city official who was openly gay in the United States of America. The text includes a message of angst felt by young Milk regarding the secrecy of being and struggle over coming out as gay:

> Harvey Milk knew he was gay by the time he was fourteen but he would keep that part of him a closely guarded secret for many years to come. Like

so many people of his time, he was afraid of what would happen to him if others knew he was gay.

(6)

The historical content makes the book educational to any reader. Several websites (e.g., http://milkfoundation.org/harvey-in-schools/using-the-harvey-milk-story-in-schools/) provide educators with curricular resources and ideas for teaching about bullying and abandonment, belonging, discrimination, hope, non-violent activism and homophobia. Pubescent males anguished about their gay identity might find this story reassuring.

Implications

There is value alone in knowing about the existence of children's picture and board books that challenge the heteronormativity inherent in children's literature and trouble the image of homosexual relationships as uncomplicated. However, these narratives yield other considerations: exposure to sexual diversity, academic development, and finding queer texts.

First, regardless of teachers' beliefs about the inclusion and use of queer texts, youngsters know about sexual diversity because they *are* sexually diverse. Schoolchildren are coming out at younger ages as gay, lesbian, expressing variant gender behaviors, or diagnosed as gender dysphoric. In addition, many youngsters have parents and caregivers who are LGBTQ. The same values of culturally responsive teaching regarding race and ethnicity extend to queer children's books and LGBTQ culture. "Culturally competent teachers understand ... the cultural diversity in their classrooms, including [the] sexual diversity" (Szalacha 2004, 68) of their students. A good education provides schoolchildren with the essentials necessary to be responsible and capable adults in the future (Hansel and Dubin 2010), and educators need to know and make sense of literature that is fully inclusive to develop schoolchildren's understanding of human diversity and uniqueness of their peers.

Second, educators are responsible for the academic development of every learner in their classroom. A responsible educator attends to the entire genre, which facilitates providing full access to knowledge and credible information (Swartz 2003). The IRA/NCTE, and many state curricula call for all schoolchildren to read myriad printed texts about diverse cultures, gender diversity, and family diversity. Queer children's literature is culturally relevant to many schoolchildren allowing them to make connections to texts, their themes, situations, and characters. In addition, the literature allows all readers—teachers and schoolchildren—an opportunity to view people and characters who are queer in a positive light. This is important to battle both willingly and unknowingly perpetuated hetero-normativity. The discovery and use of queer children's literature may be one way to initiate the shift beyond heteronormativity in elementary education.

Third, any educator intent on queering children's literature must commit to locating and obtaining the texts. While booklists, references, and bibliographies exist, they may not be found in expected places or through straightforward means. Although public libraries have long been perceived as community repositories for expansive topics, the reality of budget cuts, group opposition, and calls for censorship make it difficult to have immediate access to authentic, first-rate, well-written children's books about queer perspectives. Of the 16 texts presented in this chapter, some were independently published (Boenke and Dudley 2004), out of print, otherwise inaccessible (Mack and Buchanan 1979), or gained traction via mass media (Kilodavis and DeSimone 2010). Educators need to stay current and exercise multiple strategies to locate the books.

Educators would do well to build upon this list of children's LGBTQ titles. While books with traditional themes and storylines may be easier to access and implement, the truth is that many youth live knotty lives. Given this reality, educators should challenge themselves to locate—or even write—literature that is reflective of schoolchildren's authentic lives. The books delineated in this chapter are offered as a starting point.

Note

1   For this chapter, queer identity pertains to humans whose gender expression, sexuality, and intimate behaviors are non-conforming to societal expectations, normalcies, or ambiguous (Kumashiro 2002, Mayo 2010).

References

Aldrich, Andrew R., and M. Motz. 2003. *How My Family Came to Be: Daddy, Papa and Me*. Oakland, CA: New Family Press.

Asher, Nina. 2007. "Made in the (Multicultural) U.S.A.: Unpacking Tensions of Race, Culture, Gender, and Sexuality in Education." *Educational Researcher* no. 36 (2): 65–73. doi: 10.3102/0013189x07299188.

Bickmore, Kathy. 1999. "Why Discuss Sexuality in Elementary School?" In *Queering Elementary Education: Advancing the Dialogue about Sexualities and Schooling, Curriculum, Cultures, and (Homo)Sexualities*, edited by William J. Letts and James T. Sears, 15–25. Lanham, MD: Rowman & Littlefield.

Blanchard, Ray. 1988. "Nonhomosexual Gender Dysphoria." *Journal of Sex Research* no. 24 (1–4):188–193.

Boenke, Mary, and Delores Dudley. 2004. *Carly: She's Still My Daddy*. Washington, DC: Transgender Network of Parents, Families and Friends of Lesbians and Gays.

Bogum, Yoon, Anne Simpson, and Haag Claudia. 2010. "Assimilation Ideology: Critically Examining Underlying Messages in Multicultural Literature." *Journal of Adolescent & Adult Literacy* no. 54 (2): 109–118. doi: 10.1598/JAAL.54.2.3.

Brindley, Roger, and Kathryn L. Laframboise. 2002. "The Need to Do More: Promoting Multiple Perspectives in Preservice Teacher Education through Children's Literature."

Teaching and Teacher Education no. 18 (4): 405–420. doi: 10.1016/S0742–051X(02) 00006–9.

Bully Police USA. 2015. *Anti Bullying Lay Passage Calendar* [cited July 29 2015]. Available from http://www.bullypolice.org.

Burks, Stephanie. 2004. *While You Were Sleeping.* Victoria, BC: Trafford.

Clark, Caroline T., and Mollie V. Blackburn. 2009. "Reading LGBT-Themed Literature with Young People: What's Possible?" *English Journal* no. 98 (4): 25–32.

COLAGE. 2015. *Children of Lesbians and Gays Everywhere.* COLAGE [cited July 3 2015]. Available from http://www.colage.org.

DePaola, Tomie. 1979. *Oliver Button is a Sissy.* New York: Harcourt Brace Javanovich.

Endo, Hidehiro, Paul Chamness Reece-Miller, and Nicholas Santavicca. 2010. "Surviving in the Trenches: A Narrative Inquiry into Queer Teachers' Experiences and Identity." *Teaching and Teacher Education: An International Journal of Research and Studies* no. 26 (4): 1023–1030.

Escamilla, Kathy, and Sally Nathenson-Mejia. 2003. "Preparing Culturally Responsive Teachers: Using Latino Children's Literature in Teacher Education." *Equity & Excellence in Education* no. 36 (3): 238–248.

Ewert, Marcus. 2008. *10,000 Dresses.* Rex Ray, illustrator ed. New York: Seven Stories Press.

Fierstein, Harvey, and Henry Cole. 2002. *The Sissy Duckling.* New York: Simon & Schuster Books for Young Readers.

Fowler, J. 2010. "A Tale of Acceptance." *People* no. 74 (18): 71–72.

Fox, Robin K. 2007. "One of the Hidden Diversities in Schools: Families with Parents Who Are Lesbian or Gay." *Childhood Education* no. 83 (5): 277–281.

Fox, Robin K. 2008. "Where is Everybody? Adlerian Parenting Resources and the Exclusion of Parents Who are Lesbian, Gay, Bisexual, Transgender, Queer, or Questioning." *Journal of Individual Psychology* no. 64 (2): 252–259.

Goldberg, Alan, and Joneil Adriano. 2007. *'I'm a Girl'—Understanding Transgender Children: Parents of Transgender 6-Year-Old Girl Support Her Choice,* April 27 [cited July 29 2015]. Available from http://abcnews.go.com/print?id=3088298.

Goldstein, Tara, Vanessa Russell, and Andrea Daley. 2007. "Safe, Positive and Queering Moments in Teaching Education and Schooling: A Conceptual Framework." *Teaching Education* no. 18 (3): 183–199.

González, R., and C. C. Alvarez. 2005. *Antonio's Card.* San Francisco, CA: Children's Book Press.

Greytak, Emily A., Joseph G. Kosciw, and Elizabeth M. Diaz. 2009. *Harsh Realities: The Experiences of Transgender Youth in Our Nation's Schools.* New York: Gay, Lesbian and Straight Education Network (GLSEN).

Griffin, Pat, and Mathew Ouellett. 2003. "From Silence to Safety and Beyond: Historical Trends in Addressing Lesbian, Gay, Bisexual, Transgender Issues in K-12 Schools." *Equity & Excellence in Education* no. 36 (2): 106–114.

Han, Chong-suk. 2009. "Introduction to the Special Issue on GLBTQ of Color." *Journal of Gay & Lesbian Social Services: Issues in Practice, Policy & Research* no. 21 (2–3): 109–114. doi: 10.1080/10538720902771826.

Hansel, Lisa, and Jennifer Dubin. 2010. "Common Core Curriculum: An Idea Whose Time Has Come." *American Educator* no. 34 (4): 2.

Hermann-Wilmarth, Jill M. 2010. "More than Book Talks: Preservice Teacher Dialogue after Reading Gay and Lesbian Children's Literature." *Language Arts* no. 87 (3): 188–198.

Heroy, Emily. 2010. *Transgender Children* (Web log post), January 29 [cited July 29 2015]. Available from http://genderacrossborders.com/2010/01/29/transgender-children.

Hoffman, Eric, Celeste Henriquez, and E. Vega. 1999. *Best Best Colors.* St. Paul, MN: Redleaf Press.

Holmes, Sarah E., and Sean Cahill. 2004. "School Experiences of Gay, Lesbian, Bisexual and Transgender Youth." *Journal of Gay & Lesbian Issues In Education* no. 1 (3): 53–66.

Huegel, Kelly. 2003. *GLBTQ: The Survival Guide for Queer & Questioning Teens.* Minneapolis, MN: Free Spirit Pub.

IRA, and NCTE. 1996. *Standards for the English Language Arts.* Newark, DE: International Reading Association (IRA)/National Council of Teachers of English (NCTE).

Jennings, Kevin. 2008. "Understanding the 'Gayby Boom'." *Independent School* no. 68 (1): 90–93.

Judes, Marie-Odile, Martin Bourre, and J. Robins. 2001. *Max, the Stubborn Little Wolf.* New York: HarperCollins.

Keogh, Shauna. 2009. "Help & Support: Age 8 and Wanting a Sex Change." *Bodyshock* [TV series documentary].

Kilodavis, Cheryl, and Suzanne DeSimone. 2010. *My Princess Boy: A Mom's Story about a Young Boy Who Loves to Dress Up.* New York: Aladdin.

Kissen, Rita M. (ed.). 2002. *Getting Ready for Benjamin: Preparing Teachers for Sexual Diversity in the Classroom, Curriculum, Cultures, and (Homo)Sexualities Series.* Lanham, MD: Rowman & Littlefield.

Kosciw, Joseph G., and Elizabeth M. Diaz. 2008. *Involved, Invisible, Ignored: The Experiences of Lesbian, Gay, Bisexual and Transgender Parents and Their Children in Our Nation's K-12 Schools.* New York: Gay, Lesbian and Straight Education Network (GLSEN).

Kosciw, Joseph G., Emily A. Greytak, Elizabeth M. Diaz, and Mark J. Bartkiewicz. 2010. *The 2009 National School Climate Survey: The Experiences of Lesbian, Gay, Bisexual and Transgender Youth in Our Nation's Schools.* New York: Gay, Lesbian and Straight Education Network (GLSEN).

Krakow, Kari, and David Gardner. 2001. *The Harvey Milk Story.* Ridley Park, PA: Two Lives Publishing.

Kumashiro, Kevin K. 2001. *Troubling Intersections of Race and Sexuality: Queer Students of Color and Anti-oppressive Education, Curriculum, Cultures, and (Homo)sexualities:* Lanham, MD: Rowman & Littlefield.

Kumashiro, Kevin K. 2002. *Troubling Education: Queer Activism and Anti-oppressive Education.* New York: RoutledgeFalmer.

Letts, William J., and James T. Sears. 1999. *Queering Elementary Education: Advancing the Dialogue about Sexualities and Schooling, Curriculum, Cultures, and (Homo)Sexualities.* Lanham, MD: Rowman & Littlefield.

Lipkin, A. 2002. "The Challenges of Gay Topics in Teacher Education: Politics, Content, and Pedagogy." In *Getting Ready for Benjamin: Preparing Teachers for Sexual Diversity in the Classroom,* edited by Rita M. Kissen, 13–27. Lanham, MD: Rowman & Littlefield.

Loutzenheiser, Lisa W., and Lori B. MacIntosh. 2004. "Citizenships, Sexualities, and Education." *Theory Into Practice* no. 43 (2): 151–158.

Mack, Bruce, and M. Buchanan. 1979. *Jesse's Dream Skirt.* Chapel Hill, NC: Lillipop Power.

Mayo, Cris. 2010. "Queer Lessons: Sexual and Gender Minorities in Multicultural Education." In *Multicultural Eduction: Issues and Perspectives*, edited by J. A. Banks and C. A. M. Banks. Hoboken, NJ: Wiley.

Meyer, Elizabeth J. 2007. "'But I'm Not Gay': What Straight Teachers Need to Know about Queer Theory." In *Queering Straight Teachers: Discourse and Identity in Education*, edited by Nelson M. Rodriguez and William F. Pinar, 15–32. New York: Peter Lang.

Moje, Elizabeth B., and Mudhillun MuQaribu. 2003. "First Person Literacy and Sexual Identity." *Journal of Adolescent and Adult Literacy* no. 47: 204–257.

Morris, Marla. 2005. "Queer Life and School Culture: Troubling Genders." *Multicultural Education* no. 12 (3): 8–13.

Newman, Leslea, and Adriana Romo. 2002. *Felicia's Favorite Story*. Ridley Park, PA: Two Lives Publishing.

Okimoto, Jean, Elaine Aoki, and Meilo So. 2002. *The White Swan Express: A Story about Adoption*. New York: Clarion Books.

Pawelski, J. G., E. C. Perrin, J. M. Foy, C. E. Allen, J. E. Crawford, M. Del Monte, M. Kaufman, J. D. Klein, K. Smith, S. Springer, J. L. Tanner, and D. L. Vickers. 2006. "The Effects of Marriage, Civil Union, and Domestic Partnership Laws on the Health and Well-being of Children." *Pediatrics* no. 118 (1): 349–364.

Pinar, William F. 2007. "Introduction: A Queer Conversation, Toward Sustainability." In *Queering Straight Teachers: Discourse and Identity in Education. Complicated Conversation: A Book Series of Curriculum Studies*, edited by Nelson M. Rodriguez and William F. Pinar, 1–12. New York: Peter Lang.

Robinson, Kelly. 2002. "Making the Invisible Visible: Gay and Lesbian Issues in Early Childhood Education." *Contemporary Issues in Early Childhood* no. 3 (3): 415–434. doi: 10.2304/ciec.2002.3.3.8.

Robinson, Kerry H., and Tania Ferfolja. 2001. "'What are We Doing this For?' Dealing with Lesbian and Gay Issues in Teacher Education." *British Journal of Sociology of Education* no. 22 (1): 121–133. doi: 10.1080/01425690020030828.

Rosin, Hanna. 2008. "A Boy's Life." *Atlantic Monthly* no. 302 (4): 56–71.

Rowell, Elizabeth H. 2007. "Missing!: Picture Books Reflecting Gay and Lesbian Families." *Young Children* no. 62 (3): 24–26.

Ryan, Caitlin. 2002. *A Review of the Professional Literature and Research Needs for LGBT Youth of Color*. Washington, DC: National Youth Advocacy Coalition.

Ryan, Daniel, and April Martin. 2000. "Lesbian, Gay, Bisexual, and Transgender Parents in the School Systems." *School Psychology Review* no. 29 (2): 207–216.

Schall, Janine, and Gloria Kauffmann. 2003. "Exploring Literature with Gay and Lesbian Characters in the Elementary School." *Journal of Children's Literature* no. 29 (1): 36–45.

Sears, James T. 1999. "Teaching Queerly: Some Elementary Propositions." In *Queering Elementary Education: Advancing the Dialogue about Sexualities and Schooling*, edited by William J. Letts and James T. Sears, 3–14. Lanham, MD: Rowman & Littlefield.

Singer, Judith Y., and Sally A. Smith. 2003. "The Potential of Multicultural Literature: Changing Understanding of Self and Others." *Multicultural Perspectives* no. 5 (2): 17–23.

Snow, Judith E. 2004. *How It Feels to Have a Gay or Lesbian Parent: A Book by Kids for Kids of All Ages, Haworth Gay and Lesbian Studies*. New York: Harrington Park Press.

Suicide Prevention Resource Center (ed.). 2008. *Suicide Risk and Prevention for Lesbian, Gay, Bisexual, and Transgender Youth*. Newton, MA: Education Development Center.

Swartz, Patti Capel. 2003. "Bridging Multicultural Education: Bringing Sexual Orientation into the Children's and Young Adult Literature Classrooms." *Radical Teacher* no. 66: 11–16.

Szalacha, Laura A. 2004. "Educating Teachers on LGBTQ Issues: A Review of Research and Program Evaluations." *Journal of Gay & Lesbian Issues in Education* no. 1 (4): 67–79.

Tye, Marcus C. 2003. "Lesbian, Gay, Bisexual, and Transgender Parents: Special Considerations for the Custody and Adoption Evaluator." *Family Court Review* no. 41 (1): 92–103. doi: 10.1177/1531244502239355.

Winthrop, Elizabeth, and L. Hoban. 1985. *Tough Eddie.* New York: Dutton.

Zolotow, Charlotte, and Wiliam Pene Du Bois. 1972. *William's Doll.* New York: Harper & Row.

Interlude II

DO YOU NEED MY QUEERNESS TO DEFINE YOUR STRAIGHTNESS?

The Pedagogy of Queering-Deviance in the Academy

Anna V. Wilson

The format of this piece[1] is based on the format of the Babylonian Talmud first printed between 1484 and 1519 culminating in the complete edition of the Talmud produced by Daniel Bomberg (a Christian) in 1520–1530. These editions established the familiar format of placing the original text in square formal letters in the center of the page, surrounded by the commentaries of Rebbes Rashi and Tosafot, printed in a semi-cursive typeface. All subsequent editions of the Talmud until the present day have used the page divisions used in the Bomberg edition.

In the Talmudic method of text study, the starting point is the principle that any text deemed worthy of serious study must be assumed to have been written with such care and precision that every term, expression, generalization, or exception is significant, not so much for what it states as for what it implies. The contents of ideas as well as the diction and phraseology in which they are clothed are to enter into the reasoning.

Serious students themselves, accustomed to a rigid form of logical reasoning and to the usage of precise forms of expression, Talmudic-trained scholars attributed the same quality of precision and exactness to any authoritative work, be it of divine origin or the product of the human mind. Their attitude toward the written word of any kind is like that of the jurist toward the external phrasing of statutes and laws, and perhaps also, in some respect, like that of the latest kind of historical and literary criticism, which applies the method of psycho-analysis to the study of texts.

No limitation is set upon any subject; problems run into one another; they become intricate and inter-woven, one throwing light upon the other. There is a logic underlying this method of reasoning. It is the very same kind of logic underlying any sort of scientific research, and by which one is enabled to form hypotheses, to test them, and to formulate general laws. The Talmudic student approaches the study of texts in the same manner as the scientist approaches the study of nature. Just as the scientist proceeds on the assumption that there is a uniformity and continuity in nature so the Talmudic student proceeds on the assumption that there is a uniformity and continuity in human reasoning. Now this method of text interpretation is sometimes derogatorily referred to as Talmudic quibbling or pilpul. In truth, it is nothing but the application of the scientific method to the study of texts.

I deliberately choose to contextualize my work using the genre of Talmudic study that assumes the inter-connectedness of the rhetorical and theoretical question of the Queer Jew. Within this genre, I move from the traditional form of rigid logical reasoning and precise forms of expression to the criticality of the writer's identity and positionality in the research/writing process. As Butler (1990) contends that identities are relational, existing through mutually constitutive social relations, I find the Talmudic genre particularly facilitative of exploring the relational identities of Queer Jew.

Queer — what is queer? Who is queer? Is Queer a noun, a verb, an adjective? Is it a subject or an object , both or neither? Queering others, queering reading, queering thinking, queering being? Is Queering normal or not normal?

Who defines Queer? Are lesbians queer, gays queer, transgenders queer, all of the above or none of the above?

Queers are like Jews. Aren't they? Jakobsen contends these two categories are "overlapping – intertwined even – but not coextensive" (2003, p. 65). She then noted that in 1996, Supreme Court Justice A. Scalia portrayed "homosexuals, like Jews, as a small but overprivileged minority with both financial capital and political influence well in excess of either numbers or justified expectations" (p. 65). Justice Scalia's response was his dissent from the U. S. Supreme Court decision striking down Colorado's antigay amendment.

.

Jewish: what is a Jew? Who is a Jew? Is being Jewish a religious identity or is it a race? How can one be a Jew and Queer? Is it Jewish Queer or Queerish Jewish? Is one a Reform Jew, a Conservative Jew or an Orthodox Jew? Why is this important? Who really cares

The purpose of this paper is to interrogate the intersections of religion, sexual identity, race/ethnicity, and class through the hegemonic lens of heteronormativity privilege in the social construction of naming 'deviance' through the lens of a Queer Jew.

To interrogate this construction, we need to ask who and how, what else, who is Othered, who 'others' marginalizes, who carries privilege and how is it used.

This paper is not necessarily a 'research' paper in the strictest sense of the term. Rather it is a self-study, a reflective paper, a 'thinking' paper, questioning, deconstructing, challenging oneself in the framework of deviance, of privilege, of social justice.

Why, you might ask, is it important to 'unpack' or deconstruct the myriad ways of defining, labeling and conferring properties of deviance in higher education. I contend that in higher education, in our universities, in our classrooms, we, as professors, carry the responsibility of speaking through the silence of invisibility that exists for many of our students.

Deviant — What is deviant? Is it a person? Aren't people who do not obey the law deviants? Is the concept of deviance limited to individual acts and/or behaviors? Can communities be deviant?

Who defines the deviant and deviant behaviors? What is the relationship between/among the concepts of deviance, privilege, marginalization?

If I define/construct deviance, am I also at risk of being labeled by others as deviant? Whose voices do we listen to as we participate (or do we choose that participation) in the construction of naming deviance.

In this paper I hope to render visible the representational and ethical dilemmas of the vulnerable in self-studies of deviance in teacher education.

In the early 20th century, Durkheim raised an intriguing question: "Does it make sense to assert that deviant forms of behavior are a natural and even beneficial part of social life?" (1960, p. 102). Durkheim (1960) believed that even the most unusual behavior of a person may, in some cases, be considered 'normal'. Thus, Durkheim contended that not only crime but other forms of deviation actually "perform a needed service to society by drawing people together in a common posture of anger and indignation. The deviant individual violates rules of conduct which the rest of the community holds in high respect; and when these peopled come together to express their outrage over the offense and to bear witness against the offender, they develop a tighter bond of solidarity than existed earlier. The excitement generated by the crime, in other words, quickens the tempo of interaction in the group and creates a climate in which the private sentiments of many separate persons are fused together into a common sense of morality" (1960, p. 102)

Over a third (37.8%) of students experienced physical harassment at school on the basis of sexual orientation and more than a quarter (26.1%) on the basis of their gender expression.

Nearly one-fifth (17.6%) of students had been physically assaulted because of their sexual orientation and over a tenth (11.8%) because of their gender expression.

Last night, a student in my Diversity class shared her experience in 'coming out' to two of her high school students. Similar to most of us, if not all, she has not 'come out' at her school and, in fact, only came out to our class last week.

As she watched her two students struggle with their sexual identity, she shared quietly with them that they were 'not alone', she is there—in that space of Queerness, Deviance — with them, walking with them. As she shared her very powerful experience with our class, she looked at me and said "Now I understand why you 'come out' to us — so we don't walk alone and have the strength to share ourselves with our students."

Early May (2004) in North Carolina – I am working outside and my phone rings. When I answer the phone, Dean Don Cardinal asks if this is a good time to talk – I laughed and said "Yes, I'm just changing the spark plug and air filter in my lawn mower!" He also laughed and asked if that came with me and on a more serious note said he wanted to talk with me about the faculty position at Chapman. I took a deep breathe as I spoke these words prior to being offered a faculty position at this university. I could no longer remain in the closet of secretness, of deviance, of marginalization. After I 'came out' he again laughed said he and the faculty had hoped so but couldn't ask. I was stunned, relieved and excited beyond belief, as I currently lived in a state where being "out" cost people their jobs.

Why come out – and why now? I believe I have an obligation to make a difference in teacher educators' lives because I want to change how LGBT students are treated both in schools and higher education.

Our education students will have GLBT students in their classes – we have LGBT students in our university courses. As a teacher educator I have an ethical, moral responsibility to be honest with my students, despite the cultural resistance to discussions of sexual identity within the context of multicultural education and teacher preparation.

Risking to be Real

Before you offer me
the position,
I want you to know
I am a lesbian.

At the beginning of each class, I share my queerness, my Jewishness — my worldview, my lens. I do so thoughtfully and deliberately; yet with inward hesitation. I do not know what will be my students' reactions.

One night last spring, during my Diversity class, my phone rang. I had forgotten to turn it off and my partner called to leave me a message. My students laughed because my ringtone for her is Melissa Ethridge's "I want to stay here in this moment". Several said "If you hadn't shared with us you were 'gay', we would have known from that ringtone!." Stereotypes abound in our world!

Examining the privileges of heteronormativity within undergraduate and graduate classrooms unsettles the traditional narrative of difference. Combining further with the difference of religion – Jewish – challenges the dominant discourse of safety within the collective conscience of the dominant community (White, Christian, heterosexual, class privilege). This challenge, although couched in my revealing of my vulnerabilities, often evokes powerful resistance on the part of 'straights'. How do we then think about, contemplate the social construction of an inside/outside positionality? Namaste (1997, p. 201) raises the question if "a focus on this paradox – the simultaneous exclusion and presence of homosexuality – forces an examination of the manner in which heterosexuality achieves its legitimacy and apparent "naturalness"." In coming out do we then strengthen the positionality of heteronormativity? This is a conundrum with which we wrestle in this paper.

I must raise the question, was Weininger not only a Jew but a 'homosexual'; thus finding himself as effeminate and conflicted he escaped through suicide? Committing suicide for Jews is unacceptable — yet he had just written a book castigating Jews, women and effeminate men.

So who defines 'difference' or 'normal'? Why do you need my Queerness, my Jewishness? Why Must I be Responsible for your definition of 'Normal", of Straight, of Christian?

In 1903, Weininger's *Sex and Character* was published shortly after his suicide. Despite the fact that he was a Jew, Weininger equated Jews and women as the same "Those who have no soul can have no craving for immortality, and so it is with the woman and the Jew . . . as there is no real dignity in women, so what is meant by the word 'gentleman' does not exist amongst the Jews . . . the true conception of the State is foreign to the Jew, because he, like the woman, is wanting in personality; his failure to grasp the idea of true society is due to his lack of a free intelligible ego. Like women, Jews tend to adhere together"(1906, pp. 307-308)

Queer or Queerness is more than a word, it is about difference, about not being "normal". However, that is being defined and by whom, about exploding the very idea of "normal" with all its constraints. Queer or Queerness is about reading texts, people, and experiences more subtly, flexibly and creatively.

Am I "pursuing the vexed crossings of "woman" and "Jew"" as Garber (2003, p. 19) considers the disturbing overlay of sexual and racial stereotypes through the unpacking of *Yentle the Yeshiva Boy* by I.B. Singer.

So what is wrong with being Queer – being different – other than 'normal'? So difference is wrong? And if I am a Queer Jew, then what? Does that incrementally increase my difference, my deviance?

In Israel, most Jews do not wear the Star of David around their necks — they don't have to make the visible statement that they are Jews. I wore mine much of the time, but not always. I wear my Star of David here as a statement that I am a Jew — I also wear my Rainbow pendant with the Star to make the statement that I am a Queer Jew.

Our culture assumes the categories of homosexuality and heterosexuality have the status of assumed knowledge and that there exist distinct heterosexual and homosexual persons which from the centerpiece of the sexual wisdom of our society.

Historians have long documented the many ways Jews have been stigmatized such as "yellow circles made of cord at least an inch thick had to be worn on the chests of Venetian Jews by an order of 1430; Pisa a century earlier had required an 'O of red cloth'; and Rome insisted that male Jews wear red tabards and Jewish women red overskirts" (Hughes, 1986, pp. 17-18). Interestingly red or yellow clothing signs remained as an indicator of Jews throughout the Renaissance foregrounding the infamous yellow Star of David required by the Nazi regime.

Difference from what is usual or ordinary; Odd, Singular, Strange, Doubtful, Suspicious; Mentally unbalanced, Counterfeit, Not genuine.

Outing myself in higher education reveals my lived experience, makes visible the social injustices, the violations of rights of non-heterosexuals in a heteronormative world.

Identity is based on binaries – either one is heterosexual or one is homosexual, and this identity is fixed and irreversible.

Chinn (1994, p. 244) metaphorically links queer studies and minefields as she asks ". . . we can't help but recognize the temptations and pleasures of belonging to any institution, the safety of the office, the paycheck, the name in print. For me at least, the minefield of queer studies is strewn with fragrant flowers as well as shattering mortars, and it's impossible to intuit which I'll step on at any given juncture." She then thoughtfully queries "When we cross the minefield, do we leave it unchanged for those who follow us? Do we risk losing a limb, or dodge with our eyes closed, praying, or sprinkle more explosives behind us with the rationalization that the challenge of wading through bombs builds character? Do we drop the seeds for roses and hope they grow among the rubble, even as we leave them behind?"

Is fear framed by gender as well as sexual identity and religious difference? Does difference foreground fear — for everyone — or is just fear?

Why does the larger community define our conduct based on our sexual orientation as dangerous, embarrassing, or irritating. How does my Queerness affect your Straightness? And my Jewishness affect your religious identity? It doesn't —except that I hold different beliefs from you.

Munt (2007, p. 54) inquires "whether the institution of [lesbian] scholarship has led to a crushing poverty of representation for both students and faculty alike, as both struggle with the psychic inevitability of shame, hatred and envy that the presence of a few powerful women can provoke."

What is the face of your fear?

I know the face of my fear
As do my queer colleagues and students.
We know
The fear of contempt and censure
From family, friends, co-workers.

We know
The fear of being judged different,
Not normal,
We know the fear of recognition
– What will you do –
Do you see yourself in us?
We know the fear of challenge
– Why can't you/us change –
Why must we change
To fit your definitions of "normal".

We know the fear
Of violence,
Of losing our lives.

What if,

What if
Non-heterosexism
Was *normal?*

What if?

"Most minorities are condemned to a fantasy relationship with what is (wrongly) perceived to be the 'centre'; thus engendering projective identifications, whether longing or aggressive, toward those spectral powers" (Munt, 2007, p. 55)

Naming Others

The language
We use to describe people's
Identities and practices
Reflects
Who has the power,
The privilege
To
Name others.

How
Do you use
Your privilege
Of naming
Others?

The Power

Of naming, of defining
Heightens our sensitivity
To how language shapes
Our realities
Our imagination
Our possibilities
For living full and meaningful lives
Our risk
In contesting
The definition of
Queer as deviant,
Of us as deviant.

What If?

If you have the power, the privilege to 'name' others, to define others' behavior – my behavior - and if you represent the 'collective conscience' of the self-identified community to which you belong, you am co-constructing – with your community members – conduct that you consider as deviant.

I am not speaking of deviant as illegal but rather as conduct – behavior – identification that is outside the norms of the group/community to which you belong. But community to which a significant group of us do not belong – we do not belong on the basis of the 'community' to name us as deviant, as different – as implying danger, threat, etc.

As queer Jews, we must "challenge notions of margins and center, sameness and difference, normative and alternative, assimilation and separation by looking at the experiences of those who complicate these categories" Shneer and Aviv (2002, p. 4)

Thus as "queer and Jewish come to inform one another, queers Jews are not as compelled to seek out separate space, but instead create space within established institutions" (Shneer & Aviv, 2002, p. 5).

Alpert(1997) questions the assumption of the naturalness of heterosexuality through complicating the universality of the myth of heteronormativity which emanates from the book of Genesis and the story of creation. This story, which Alpert also names as myth, relates that G-d tells the woman that she shall have desire for her husband and that he shall rule over her. In addition, Adam is given the power to name his wife whom he calls Eve meaning mother of all living. Interestingly, Adam comes from adamah meaning the earth. The myth, according to Alpert (1977, p. 25) "assumes connections between sexuality, procreation, male dominance, and heterosexual desire."

Alpert (1997, p. 8) argues that the phenomena associated with lesbianism: "same-sex sexual desire and attraction; woman-identified romantic friendship and feminism; and gender nonconformity" are in fact the "key impediments that stand in the way of a lesbian transformation of Judaism." In other words, as lesbians we share the same stigma attached to gay men based on biblical prohibitions, as feminists we are wrapped in the cloak of invisibility shared by all women, and we defy the literal approach to gender roles in the traditional texts. She contends that the absence of a severe prohibition against female homosexuality does not make it permissible but rather renders it invisible, just as women are invisible in traditional Judaism, as in other patriarchal cultures. It is important to clarify that there is no universal Jewish lesbian perspective. No one lesbian speaks for all nor does one Jewish lesbian speak for all. Any view of Jewish life from a lesbian standpoint is always only partial, therefore my lens is partial – it is my lens and not others. However, it is through this lens that I examine experiences and ideas in what Patricia Hill Collins (1990, p. 21) names "a unique angle of vision."

As a Queer Jew, part of my lens is shaped by my Hebrew name "D'vorah" who was/is the only woman in the Torah/Bible not connected to a man – she was a judge and a prophetess who also led the Israelites in to battle and won.

However, problems complicate this story for feminists and for lesbians. The relationship of equality between man and woman is replaced by the relationship of dominance "and he shall rule over you" and further identifies the woman's primary identity as childbearer. The issue of dominance is somewhat less problematic for lesbians as we do not define ourselves within the group for whom "your desire shall be for your husband" applies.

Perhaps, as Alpert (1997) contends, "this is the most threatening aspect of lesbian existence, as it recognizes that there are women whose desires defy the assumption of the 'naturalness' of heterosexuality" (p. 25). In other words, Jewish lesbians (as well as all lesbians) challenge the notion of heteronormativity.

Alpert (1997) then questions the nature of the myth and whether it is prescriptive or descriptive. She contends that if the myth is descriptive "it is an effort to explain why men dominate women; when childbirth is both painful and dangerous, and yet women endure it anyway; and why heterosexuality is the norm." But, she states, if the myth is prescriptive, then "the author must have assumed that women's desire for their husbands must be made compulsory because women's desire is in fact diffuse and may be channeled in other directions" (p. 25). In other words, heterosexuality is not the norm, is not natural, and must be prescribed or "other-than-hetero-sexuality" Seidman, 1996, vii) will become/is the norm. Is it not interesting to think of other-than-heterosexuality as the norm?

Shneer and Aviv (2002, p. 24) argue that "to be a Jew is to have a history and to be a queer is to have another history just as to be a woman is to have yet another history."

Defining myself as a queer Jew means I open myself up to increasing multiplicity and innovation; thereby undermining the assumptions that my identity is determined solely via biology, it is transformative rather than assimilationist.

I would argue that I have another history as well, that of being adopted, raised in a secular Christian household, with interfaith birth parents – a Christian mother and a Jewish father. Despite my not being raised by my birth parents, internally I raise always raise the question of how much the inner voice of my Jewish heritage gives to my life choices. As an adult, after years of searching for a spiritual essence, I converted to Judaism. Being a Jew 'fit' for me and while I can remember 'not being a Jew' I seem to always have been a Jew – the multiplicity of my identity, or how very postmodern.

One could say I chose to be on the margins, but I have always been on the margins I just did not always acknowledge that marginality. Part of always being on the margins revolved around my sexual identity, that of being a lesbian in the closet, in denial, running away from that identity, running toward heteronormativity. But I never quite reached heteronormativity even when, from all appearances, I had achieved it. I knew internally that I was not heterosexual, I was lesbian – I was queer. Despite my being in the margins, I had White skin privilege. I passed - as white, Christian, straight, educated. I was part of the dominant discourse, the center, the place with privilege. Deliberating choosing to convert to Judaism and later to 'come out' as a lesbian immediately displaced me from the perceived dominant discourse. Interestingly, hanging out on the margins of queer and Jew, have paradoxically become a comfortable place for me. It is where I belong. I lost the sense of dis-ease I had when I 'passed'; I know where I belong and I am here. I have a community identity, I have a place. Within this place I work to dismantle the concept of normativity of Christian, White, Heterosexual that so pervades our discourse. Only through naming my identity as a Jewish, Feminist, lesbian, can I challenge the pathologizing inherent within the heteronormative discourse.

Identifying myself as a queer Jew affirms that I am making conscious, deliberate choices which interrogate classist, racist assumptions through the institutionalized structures. By the same token, I develop my collective identity based on my resistance to the dominant power by unpacking my own privilege with/in/out the heteronormativity of societal and Jewish institutions.

Our struggles will transform our traditions and our communities, as Cohen (2002, 173) contends "thinking that is alive and contemporary can allow for provisionality, uncertainty, and change." She continues "thinking with a sense of historic responsibility requires an unflinching willingness to consider the negative underside and discomforting implications of apparently positive developments to avoid naive surprises" (173). Cohen believes that incorporating an appreciation of irony, indeterminacy and paradox is helpful to a postmodern view of history. So what does it mean to have a postmodern view of queer and Jewish? Does taking a postmodern view of queer Jewish identity require documenting an "internal debate over the price of inclusion" while asking "difficult questions about sameness and difference" (Shneer & Aviv, 2002, 5). Consistent with Shneer and Aviv, I would argue that identifying as a queer Jew means having a moral responsibility to lead cultural change, pursue peace and seek justice – *tikkun olam*. It also resonates with the concept of being "twice blessed" – to have the dual task to lead rather than follow and to change rather than accept the status quo.

Who Am I?

In 11 states
My sexual identity can be
used legally to deny my
parental rights
In 17 states,
I am not protected by Hate
Crimes legislation

In 35 states
I am not legally protected
from discrimination based
on my sexual identity

In 42 states
School laws are non-
existent about issues re-
garding sexual orientation

Who Am I?

I can marry in nine coun-
tries
I have legal spousal rights
in seventeen countries

I Do Not have federal
rights in my country
My non-U.S. spouse can-
not become a full citizen
I cannot collect benefits
upon the death of my partner
Nor can s/he collect my
benefits
I cannot file jointly as a
married couple

Who Am I?

In one state, as a resident I
can marry
In three states I can have a
civil union
In five states I have domestic partner benefits
In two states I have limited
benefits

Who Am I?

I'm gay
I'm lesbian
I'm queer
I'm bisexual
I'm transgendered

Who Am I?

I'm White
I'm Black
I'm Indigenous
I'm Latino/a
I'm Asian
I'm Biracial
I'm Multiracial

Who Am I?

I'm short, I'm tall
I'm thin, I'm fat
I'm abled, I'm disabled
I'm dark, I'm light
I'm woman, I'm man

Who Am I?

I Am Speaking Out

I am no longer careless
I am no longer silent
I am changing
I am moving
I am waking up now
I am speaking out

Who Am I?

I'm your mother, your fa-
ther,
I'm your grandmother, your
grandfather,
I'm your aunt, your uncle
I'm your sister, your
brother,
I'm your daughter, your
son.

Who Am I?

I'm your teacher, your student,
I'm your police office, your
firefighter
I'm your neighbor, your
friend
I'm your co-worker, your
colleague
I'm your doctor, your nurse
I'm your professor, your
administrator

Who Am I?

I died in 9/11,
I was in the World Trade
Center
I was on Flight 93

I serve our country
I am injured
I died in Afghanistan
I died in Iraq
I'm in the Army, the Navy,
The Air Force, the Marines,
the Coast Guard

Who Am I?

You don't ask
And
I don't tell

Note

1 This chapter was originally presented at the *Journal of Curriculum Theory*'s Bergamo Conference, Dayton Ohio, October 2007.

References

Alpert, Rebecca. 1997. *Like Bread on the Seder Plate: Jewish Lesbians and the Transformation of Tradition*. Edited by Lillian Faderman and Larry Gross, *Between Men—Between Women: Lesbian and Gay Studies*. New York: Columbia University Press.

Butler, Judith. 1990. *Gender Trouble: Feminism and the Subversion of Identity*. New York: Routledge.

Chinn, Sarah. 1994. "Queering the Profession, or just Professionalizing Queers?" In *Titling the Tower: Lesbians/Teaching/Queer Subjects*, edited by Linda Garber, 243–250. London and New York: Routledge.

Cohen, Joanne. 2002. "Remembering the Stranger: Identity, Community, and Same-sex Marriage." In *Queer Jews*, edited by David Shneer and Caryn Aviv, 172–186. New York: Routledge.

Collins, Patricia Hill. 1990. *Black Feminist Thought: Knowledge, Consciousness, and the Politics of Empowerment*. Boston, MA: Unwin Hyman.

Durkheim, Emile. 1960. *The Division of Labor in Society*. Translated by George Simpson. Glencoe, IL: Free Press.

Garber, Marjorie. 2003. "Category Crises: The Way of the Cross and the Jewish Star." In *Queer Theory and the Jewish Question*, edited by Daniel Boyarin, Daniel Itzkovitz and Ann Pellegrini, 19–40. New York: Columbia University Press.

Hughes, Diane Owen. 1986. "Distinguishing Signs: Ear-Rings, Jews and Franciscan Rhetoric in the Italian Renaissance City." *Past and Present* no. 112 (August): 3–59.

Jakobsen, Janet R. 2003. "Queers Are Like Jews, Aren't they? Analogy and Alliance Politics." In *Queer Theory and the Jewish Question*, edited by Daniel Boyarin, Daniel Itzkovitz and Ann Pellegrini, 64–89. New York: Columbia University Press.

Munt, Sally R. 2007. "A Seat at the Table: Some Unpalatable Thoughts on Shame, Envy and Hate in Institutional Cultures." *Journal of Lesbian Studies* no. 11 (1/2): 53–67.

Namaste, Ki. 1996. "Genderbashing: Sexuality, Gender, and the Regulation of Public Space. Environment and Planning." *Society and Space* no. 14: 221–240.

Seidman, Steven. 1997. *Difference Troubles: Queering Social Theory and Sexual Politics*. Cambridge: Cambridge University Press.

Shneer, David, and Caryn Aviv. 2002. *Queer Jews*. New York: Routledge.

Weininger, Otto. 1906. *Sex and Character*. London: Heinemann.

SECTION III
Transformative Practices

Veronica E. Bloomfield and Marni E. Fisher

Naming the unnamed and daring to visit places beyond the edges of the map first brought us to trouble the waters of traditional responses to gender and sexuality in schools. The movements of our struggles and our willingness to begin the dance cause ripple effects that can reach system wide. The climate and culture of schools can be impacted by the actions of individual teachers, school-wide initiatives and student organizations. The changes to the climate and culture of schools bring us to this final section. As usual, when dealing with dragons, the question emerges: What are we transforming? Ourselves? Or the dragons? Yet, through facing the fire, we are transformed. Our worldviews, teaching practices, and interactions with others are changed as we are changed by the work we have committed to begin, sustain, and continue.

This section comes as a much-needed antidote to the attitudes of apathy and resistance that often accompany discussion about socially just educational practices, especially those that apply to LGBTQ youth. Consider these chapters a crash course in experience and a tonic for academic vitality and engagement!

Julia Heffernan and Tina Gutierez-Schmich chronicle how they used self-reflection, implementation of theory, and student feedback and reflections to revise a college course about multiculturalism and diversity. Inspired by the work of Kevin Kumashiro, they utilized specific strategies, print and media resources, and created lesson plans that queered the content and pedagogy of the class. All of these resources are provided throughout the chapter. Through this process they were able to create an educational experience which fostered empathy with "the Other."

Sean Robinson explores the intersection of LGBTQ issues and inclusive classroom practices with mass media. With the continuing rise in student access to online media, his chapter notes the ways media is helpful for LGBTQ students, and how to teach media assessment within the classroom.

J. Spencer Clark and James Brown encourage challenging dominant voices through dialogue and discussion. They see LGBTQ elements in teacher preparation programs as opportunities for future teachers to learn from the experiences of LGBTQ groups.

Finally, Marna Hauk's chapter explores a year in a school using both Gaian methods to build a community space and a Career Day activity to cross heteronormative assumptions. This chapter offers the richness of care for the planet, and a practical lesson for re-examining student assumptions about gender roles.

9

WE RECRUIT

A Queer Pedagogy for Teacher Education

Julia Heffernan and Tina Gutierez-Schmich

Considering a Creative Pedagogy for Anti-Oppressive Teacher Education

> I mean think about it, we wouldn't even exist as a species if people like him were just considered normal and allowed to do whatever they want with their bodies.
>
> An education foundation student defending his stance against allowing a transgender youth to identify as female

Julia

In the fall of 2008, my graduate teaching assignment was a freshman survey course entitled "Educational Issues and Problems." This was a 10-week course for college freshmen on race, citizenship, gender, sexuality, poverty, and disability in relation to education and the public school system. During the weekly course sessions, I was regularly fielding statements like: "Those kids [children with disabilities] shouldn't be put in a classroom with normal kids in the first place," and, "They [Native Americans] are walking around with that chip on their shoulder and playing the race card. They are being more racist toward whites than anything I've ever said or done to them."

Written responses for this course carried these arguments to another level, with students providing everything from pseudo-scientific genetic theories, to religious biases, to social Darwinism as a basis for educational stratification and discrimination. As one student explained in response to a reading about a transgender student:

> While he [the transgender student in the essay] claims to have the right to call himself a girl, I have the same right [as a teacher] to use his legal name Jason. The district cannot force me as a Christian to go against my faith and start acting like its okay for him to act like a girl and want to be treated like a girl. I have the same free speech rights Jason has and I would continue to call him that [Jason] and encourage him to stop pretending to be someone named Julia. I mean think about it, we wouldn't even exist as a species if people like him were just considered normal and allowed to do whatever they want to with their bodies.

The intent of this course was to introduce future educators to the concepts of social stratification, social reproduction, and structural inequality in schools. Yet, each week course time was derailed by hostility toward experiences of minorities and resistance to considering each social category as fully human and entitled to educational rights. It became clear this inability to relate to people living in marginalized social categories was central to student resistance of the course's educational goal of preparing future teachers to serve all of the students in their classroom.

Jump forward one year to the 2009–2010 academic year when I was to teach this course again, along with a more intensive course on schools and inequality. This time around, I not only would teach this large class of freshmen about the diverse issues and problems in education but also would teach seniors and graduate students the 10-week seminar, "Education and Homophobia."

From my earlier teaching experiences with these diverse topics and my personal experience as a researcher on LGBTQ issues in schools, I operated under the general assumption that both of these courses would be sites of significant discomfort and resistance on the part of student teachers, but the course on homophobia and LGBTQ issues would be the least relatable. As Kumashiro (2012) reiterates:

> "queers remain *arguably the most hated group of people in the United States*" (Unks, 1995, p. 3); because queer sexualities continue to incite wide public panic, anger and resistance, especially when discussed in the context of schools (Epstein & Johnson, 1998); [and] because educators do not feel the need to address homophobia and heterosexism in schools.
>
> (11, italics added)

Kumashiro's (2012) pedagogy of anti-oppressive education with a focus on queer issues offered equal opportunity curriculum capable of bringing students closer to the social categories addressed in the course. This included the desired outcome of students developing transformative ideas about schools as social organisms and about their identity as teachers in relation to creating more equitable and more humane classrooms and schools.

Tina

My path in recognizing the critical need for an anti-oppressive pedagogy that queers preservice teachers began in 1991 as I was coaching and mentoring early education teachers. Consistently invisible to teachers were issues and interactions that supported and privileged stereotypes of gender identity and gender roles in the classroom. Teachers were unconsciously guiding children into stereotypical play: boys to blocks and building and girls to housekeeping or art. Child behavior that fell outside of stereotyped roles was seen and addressed as problematic. Further, parents' stereotypes and fears surrounding their child's development were often reinforced. Most teachers did not have the knowledge, language, or skills to engage parents in a deeper conversation about their child's play and development. Ongoing attempts to teach, mentor, and coach toward issues of gender identity and gender roles met with discomfort and resistance.

By 2005, I was still working with early education teachers, but I had also begun work at the university in a role providing guidance and support for faculty in addressing classroom conflict, primarily related to diversity issues. Reports from marginalized university students highlighted their experiences of being the Other, the outsider, or invisible. Although faculty reported classroom interactions that included offensive comments, arguing, or exhibiting a general disregard for the experiences of marginalized students, efforts aimed at coaching toward implementing a more anti-oppressive pedagogy met with discomfort and resistance.

Finally, my research and interest in anti-oppressive pedagogy is fueled by my own experience as a queer student of color. My years as an undergraduate and graduate student include a plethora of examples of faculty exhibiting ignorance or silence surrounding issues of structural inequality and social reproduction. The intellectual and political barriers to knowledge of heteronormativity exist for future and current educators.

Theory

> The desire to learn only what is comfortable goes hand in hand with a resistance to learning what is discomforting, and this resistance often proves to be a formidable barrier to movements toward social justice.
>
> Kumashiro (2012, 4)

The central question in theorizing a new curriculum design for an equal opportunity course was how to develop a creative teaching praxis that could help future teachers experience "them" as individual humans, as part of the collective "us" of children within their classroom. The curriculum should help them consider how they would develop their own pluralistic curriculum rather than reproducing a violently dominant cultural model.

In considering how to expose a new cohort of future teachers to the violent oppression enacted upon queer youth, Julie was aware of the undercurrent of despair, if not disbelief, sympathetic students frequently registered at the magnitude of inequitable structures and practices within our society. Kumashiro's (2004) theory of social justice calls this learning through "crisis" where he defines the crisis as the educational space in which "we learn that our ways of making sense of the world are not only inaccurate, but also complicit with different forms of oppression, feelings of discomfort can intensify" (30). The homophobia course would need to address the crisis to move past denial and despair, finally arriving at some form of pragmatic educational activism. This type of change required a different discourse with students. Therefore, the theoretical framework for the course would come from pairing Kumashiro's four alternative discourses to challenge oppression and the elements of Birden's (2005) Out-sider praxis.

Discourses preparing teachers to challenge oppression could move beyond teachers as practitioners, researchers, and professionals (Kumashiro 2004). Although these more traditional discourses have a place in teacher education, historically they have not encouraged teacher education to challenge oppression. Kumashiro (2004) notes, "No practice is always anti-oppressive" (3), but as this course and curriculum highlights, there is a responsibility for teacher education programs to "explore the anti-oppressive changes made possible by alternative discourses on teaching" (3). The alternative discourses include preparing teachers for crisis, uncertainty, healing, and activism.

- Crisis refers to the "emotional discomfort and disorientation that calls on students to make some change" (30). Not all crisis in learning will lead preservice teachers to an anti-oppressive stance, but the types of crisis students experience and opportunities to move through the crisis are critical.
- Uncertainty is expected. As teachers, we never know what students are going to learn. "Depending on the ways students have already learned to make sense of and feel about themselves and their world influences what and how they learn the things taught at school" (39).
- A healing discourse within teacher education provides an avenue to address what knowledge we become attached to and the meaning we make of this knowledge. "People suffer because they attribute meaning and substance and value to knowledge, signs, and representations of reality rather than to reality itself" (47). A discourse on healing asks us to trouble and complicate knowledge and our relationship to knowledge, teaching, and learning.
- An activism discourse examines the process of changing what has been normalized. "How do we become uncomfortable and dissatisfied by the norms of society?" (53). Activism requires engaging outside what is traditional and comfortable and continually asking how our practices contribute to oppression.

In theorizing course curricular goals, there was a hope that, through the curriculum, the students would see the role of teacher as one *of a pragmatic educational activist*. The curriculum requires the educational praxis of the Outsider, in which the teacher is called to identify with the Out LGBTQ student and make "an educational commitment to generous dialogue across difference and to the abatement of heterosexism and anti-lesbian and gay prejudice, representing a retreat from compulsory heterosexuality" (Birden 2005, 25).

Curricular Goals

Crisis

1. Establish a shared knowledge base on power, privilege, and oppression in relation to education.
2. Establish a historical and contemporary understanding of the social implications of heteronormativity.
3. Examine the myriad experiences of oppression resulting from educational heteronormativity.

Uncertainty

4. Identify and highlight the hidden curriculum and encourage students to critically examine how they make meaning of these lessons.

Healing

5. Encourage students to examine current issues of homophobia in their schools, families, and social networks, consider how they make meaning of these experiences, and consider and plan how they might implement change.
6. Address the first crisis of social justice education through pragmatic exercises in interrupting heteronormativity.

Activism

7. Orchestrate opportunities to disrupt heteronormativity outside the classroom. Offering preservice teachers the opportunity to experience and identify with the Out-sider.
8. Address the experience of Out-sider status by offering pragmatic exercises for counter hegemonic teaching.

The question remained how to design a curriculum offering an Out-sider experience or identity to preservice teachers who did not identify as LGBTQ. There needed to be a means to carry students beyond a sympathetic experience of injustice toward the Other. We sought a curriculum design through which students could potentially experience the oppression of heteronormativity within a school context so we could return to the learning space to discuss, debrief, and strategize future moments of oppression.

The driving question was, what would bring to life the experience of a transgender child, a gay parent, or a lesbian teen? Were there expressive and artistic materials that would humanize the "Other" to students who generally lived outside of and unaware of this subject space? This is where the literary arts and creativity were embedded in the curriculum design.

Course Content

> The role-play scenarios were interesting to watch and to act out. I wish I could have acted out every part at least once, because I really got caught up in my character each time and it would have been good to get to know more experiences.
>
> Student reflection following role-play exercise, spring 2010

The course on homophobia made use of materials representing a diverse range of queer identities and experiences in relation to a series of themes within the framework of child development, schooling, and family experiences. While traditional sociological materials, statistics, and reports framed the larger patterns of inequality, the vast majority of curriculum materials were individual narratives, personal experiences of queer people within the educational context. Both the macro-analytic materials and the micro-level narratives were organized to highlight the themes for this course (Table 9.1).

TABLE 9.1 Organizing Themes

Understanding Discourse Theory: Words Matter
Homophobia in Relation to Heteronormativity
Gender Identity in Relation to Biologic Sex
Sexual Orientation
Queer Student Experiences
Children of Queer Parent Experiences
Queer Parent Experiences
Queer Teacher Experiences
Schools as Sites for Structural Homophobia
Sports and Embodiment and Homophobia
Intersectional Oppression: Race/Ethnicity, Sexual Orientation and Gender Identity
Intersectional Oppression: Religion, Sexual Orientation and Gender Identity
Homophobia and Interpersonal Violence
Heteronormativity and Institutional Silence
Queer Positive Curriculum Presently in School

These themes were arranged to build student knowledge of homophobia in a way that offered time for learning discomforting facts about structural inequality across society in and within school systems. Reflecting Kumashiro's (2012) notion of the crisis, uncertainty, healing, and activism and Birden's (2005) Outsider praxis, the themes for this curriculum were designed to offer a progressive knowledge base about structural and violent inequality of heteronormativity. Each theme was interspersed with narratives of hope, stories of possibility, and media examples of new outcomes which can be seen as working to establish more equitable classrooms and communities.

Instructional Methods

> I know homophobia exists and I really want to be working against it, but I find it difficult to picture how heterosexuality was privileged or even present in my elementary school.
>
> Student Field Journal, Week 1

Theorizing a course content within an "Equal Opportunity" sequence of courses included creativity and literary arts—spoken word, autobiography, documentary, and memoir—with a design connecting students to the unfamiliar social subjects of these courses. Thus, the primary instructional methods included field journals, anonymous teacher memos, traditional research writing, class presentations of research, viewing and discussing audio and video files, presenting this topic to the public in a film and speaker series, dramatic readings of autobiographical materials, role plays, and preparing simulated professional presentations on the topic.

Weekly field journals and teacher memos were the first two forums for students to connect to the materials. Field journals were both directed and open ended, offering a creative and imaginary space where students could write themselves into being as proactive Out-sider teachers. During this 10-week journaling, students' voices evolved from a distant hypothetical tone. Week one students journaled about their own experiences of privilege and difference as an elementary and high school student. By week five, students wrote from the perspective of a teacher attempting to enact equitable changes in their schools. Finally, by week 10, students wrote proposals they would present to parents, teachers, or school administrators to address heteronormativity in their school:

> The opening unit of families is a great diving board into topics of racism, classism, homophobia, and ablism. All of these topics are scattered through all lessons and not confined to Black history month and the study of Martin Luther King Jr. We feel it is necessary to reinforce these issues in all lessons for students to notice its impact on how people move through society. I know there may be some concerns about our goals for the year, but I urge

you to come and speak to me in person and I will help explain these topics in more detail. It is our wish that, again, everyone is treated humanely and that can't happen when we silence the voice of one group or another. Silencing an individual, a group, or allowing for derogatory comments signals to others it is okay to dehumanize others for their differences, when we should be embracing what makes us unique and special.

(Student Field Journal, Week 10)

This field journal process offered students the space to slowly consider, first, the ways in which homophobia is a pervasive discourse operating in schools, and second, a teacher's role in addressing this inequality.

Teacher memos written at the end of each class highlighted student concerns or tensions anonymously. It offered a pressure valve to address the crisis likely to occur within the first few weeks of this course. Memos were a space for students to highlight what they did not understand, what made them uncomfortable, and where they needed more time or materials to consider a topic. Once written, these memos were shared anonymously with the class in the next session. Student names were not tied to personal concerns, but, through this process, experiences of the emotional and intellectual crisis and uncertainty of social justice education could be named and supported by the collective group moving through developing awareness together.

For example, one anonymous memo brought up feelings of depression and a sense of overwhelming exhaustion after an early lecture on the material effects of homophobia. The group discussed and strategized what we (they and I) could bring to the next lessons to reduce this feeling of hopelessness. Students needed more examples of successful strategies in classrooms, and, in the next class, we considered lesson plans from Teaching Tolerance (2015), Welcoming Schools (HRC 2012), and the Gay, Lesbian and Straight Education Network (GLSEN) (2003–2015) as positive strategies to address homophobia. By four weeks into the term, students were no longer using the anonymous memo format, but stating aloud concerns they were having and how as a group we might address them.

Research writing and presentations took place throughout the term. At each class meeting one assigned student facilitated a group discussion of that day's assigned reading. The student facilitator composed focus questions and a handout—a "reading highlights" sheet—they shared with the group (Table 9.2). This student then took on the role of expert for a 15-minute discussion on key themes of that day's reading.

Audio and video files were shared both in the classroom and as a public forum on four different occasions (Table 9.3). The public film screenings of four films and discussions with community member panels were designed to engage the class in Birden's (2005) notion of praxis as well as teaching in the form of public pedagogy (Schey and Uppstrom 2010). Students were asked to promote attendance to the film screenings among their peers, arrive at screenings early, act

TABLE 9.2 Macro-social Texts for Education and Homophobia

Johnson, Allan (2001). *Privilege, Power, and Difference.* McGraw-Hill Higher Education.

Killoran, Isabel, and Jimez, Karleen Pendleton (2007). *Unleashing the Unpopular: Talking About Sexual Orientation and Gender Diversity in Education.* Association for Childhood Education Intl.

Kumashiro, Kevin (2012). *Troubling Education: Queer Activism and Antioppressive Pedagogy.* Routledge Falmer

Mayo, C. (2013). *LGBTQ Youth and Education: Policies and Practices.* Teachers College Press.

Pascoe, C. J. (2005). *"Dude, You're a Fag": Adolescent Masculinity and the Fag Discourse.* University of California.

TABLE 9.3 Media and Content

Media Format	Content Title	Course Themes
Short Documentary Films	*I'm Not a Boy* Media Matters	Gender Identity and Heteronormativity
	Homecoming Media Matters	School as a Primary Site for Homophobia
	All God's Children, De Colores, Straight from the Heart Unlearning Homophobia Series	Intersection of Race, Religion and Heteronormativity
Autobiographical Audio Files	*Beat It* This American Life	Sports and Homophobia
	I Like Guys This American Life	School as a Primary Site for Homophobia
	Tom Girls This American Life	Gender Identity and Heteronormativity
Full Length Documentary Films	*Training Rules*	Sports and Homophobia
	It's Still Elementary	Curriculum to Interrupt Heteronormativity
	Out in the Silence	School as a Primary Site for Homophobia
	Raising Cain (PBS)	School as a Primary Site for Heteronormativity
Education/Youth Documentary Films	*What Do You Know: Six-to-twelve-year-olds talk about Gays and Lesbians*	HRC Welcoming Schools LGBTQ Curriculum
	What Can We Do: Bias, Bullying and Bystanders	HRC Welcoming Schools Curriculum to Interrupt Heteronormativity
	Put This on the {Map}	Curriculum to Interrupt Heteronormativity

TABLE 9.3 continued

Media Format	Content Title	Course Themes
Sample Video Clips from Main Stream Media (MSM)	*The F Word* Southpark Episode 12, Season 13	Discourse Theory Language and Othering
	ABC What Would You Do? (May 19, 2010) Gay family refused restaurant service	Heteronormativity and Social Violence "Bullying"
	Bullycide In the Life	Heteronormativity and Social Violence "Bullying"
Poetry Slam Video Clip	*To All the Beautiful Femmes* Ivan Coyote	Gender Identity and Heteronormativity
	Slip of the Tongue Media Matters	Intersection of Race with Heteronormativity
Biographical/ Autobiographical Text	*Unleashing the Unpopular* Isabel Killoran and Karleen Pendleton Jimenez	Voices of the Other
	Queer 13: Lesbian and Gay Writers Recall Seventh Grade Clifford Chase	Voices of the Other
	One Teacher in Ten Karen Map	Voices of the Other
Role-play activities	*Confessions of a Closeted Queer Teacher Public Reading (anon.)*	Giving Voice and Embodying Other
	Theatre of the Oppressed Classroom simulations	Interrupting Heteronormativity

as hosts to the public, prepare to engage the panel in discussions, and finally to do a public performance of a dramatic reading at one of the screenings. One of the student performers reflected on this performance in her journal the following week:

> I was really proud last week when I got to read that poem, "Confessions of a Closeted Queer Teacher" at the movie last week. I could really feel people in the room connecting to what we were reading and I felt really powerful getting to stand in front of the room at the podium and say all those things teachers have to live with when they are closeted because they are afraid.

Dramatic readings of autobiographical materials allowed students to speak from the voice of oppression within a heteronormative discourse and they expressed powerful emotional responses to enacting this performance.

Making the group partially responsible for generating an audience for public performances also offered students the opportunity to engage in this topic outside of the classroom. Students took announcements to other classes and invited cooperating teachers and friends to the screenings of these new documentaries on homophobia and its effects on students in schools. Performing in this role as public educators, students expressed both pride and frustration at responses they received to this educational outreach. This practice in becoming activist educators offered a taste of the Out-sider experience for students in a relatively safe and controlled setting.

Role-play scenarios offered students a space to embody both the marginalized students and the dominant culture figures working to uphold heteronormativity against marginalized students. In the classroom, students were given role-play scenarios in which one student would portray the target of oppression while another would attempt to enforce gender and sexuality norms. The scenarios were taken directly from national news, research observations, and students' personal experiences. The role-play design with its focus on oppression and interrupting oppression came from the work of Augusto Boal's (1992) "Theatre of the Oppressed." Each scene was played out in an oppressive manner and then replayed repeatedly with different people trying on different roles and different improvisations to improve the outcome. Role plays became a favorite activity: "I would have liked to do more role-playing. Even though it is hard to do sometimes, it is the most beneficial when applying what we learned outside the classroom walls" (student's course evaluation).

Finally, students created professional presentations on some form of educational intervention to address pervasive homophobia in schools. Students created everything from lesson plans, to teaching units, to parent newsletters, to school council proposals. No one was required to enact their proposals, as not everyone had access to a professional setting; however, three students working in schools turned their class projects into real-world practices. One student played an online audio file, "Tom Girls," from *This American Life* (Kirchner and Glass 2009) for her tenth grade humanities class. Her students then created posters about the lives of these two transgender children. These posters were featured at our public screening of *It's Still Elementary* (Chasnoff and Symons 2007). Another student showed *Out in the Silence* (Wilson and Hamer 2009) to her tenth grade class and held a lively discussion about the relationship between sexism and homophobia. The third student took a comprehensive proposal for establishing a Gay–Straight Alliance (GSA) to her district leadership. She provided the administration with a written petition containing information on the at risk status of LGBTQ youth and a proposal for creating a GSA. Later her work was silently returned to her in her district mailbox with the word NO in red letters written across the words Gay–Straight Alliance. Later she was privately approached and told, "There are no gay students in our district."

These projects offered a practice space for public performances as an Out-sider teacher. While not all of the outcomes were affirming, the resistance experienced intensified their alliance with marginalized youth. As a student explained, "I just keep thinking, if it cuts me that deeply to be treated that way and have that big NO written on my work, what it must be like for a queer student or teacher who has this sort of thing happen all the time."

Student Experiences

> The media used in this class such as the films, documentaries, interviews, and radio excerpts gave the topic a very personal feel. With the opportunity to see and hear people that homophobia affects, I found that I was able to more accurately describe and articulate my arguments because I felt a personal connection to them all.
>
> Student end of term evaluation, spring 2010

At the end of the term, students reflected on the course. As demonstrated in one student's final journal task, students touched on each of the key areas of the course's theorized design:

> The videos were extremely useful because it increased my awareness of the severity to what is happening in school in the United States about these issues. Many schools are behind and it angered me to watch these schools do nothing about students who were being harassed on a daily basis. It has made me want to not ever allow this to happen in the school that I work at let alone tolerate any discrimination in my classroom. Some of the films also taught me how to bring up this topic in my classroom such as opening a dialogue by asking one simple question, "What does the word gay mean to you?" Watching a teacher teach this lesson in *It's Still Elementary* boosted my confidence with bringing this up in my own classroom. The kids loved the activity, responded well, and ended up being very great adults some who identified as LGBTQ themselves.

In this response, the student narrator shows she learned about homophobia through the crisis of examining injustice. The student also expresses forming her teacher identity as an Out-sider educator who will "not ever allow this to happen in the school that I work in." Finally, she illustrates how modeled lessons have offered her the pragmatic means to address this vast social problem on a singular educational scale.

Another student in this course arrived at a similar stance with regard to his professional role as a future teacher:

Teachers cannot simply erase all gender inequities or fix all of the problems created by traditional gender roles overnight, however they can attain considerable results by making a conscious effort to avoid gender inequalities in the classroom and encouraging other teachers to help illuminate the issue.

This student also arrived at a praxis for the Out-sider. And as Birden (2005) suggested, one does not need to personally identify as the Out-sider to engage in this praxis. Any educator can employ Out-sider praxis in interrupting and teaching against homophobia and heteronormativity, just as the male educator can employ Out-sider praxis in interrupting and teaching against gender privilege and androcentric educational norms.

A third student focused her course evaluation on the macro-social content presented for this course:

> I liked the Lipkin readings as well as Privilege, Power, and Difference. I think the GLSEN readings about school climate surveys should have been done more in class. We didn't go into enough depth with them.

The student's connection with these macro-social readings reflects the first two weeks of the course when we were framing in and defining homophobia and heteronormativity as well as documenting and exploring the material effects of these discourses on children and society. Her expressed concern with the lack of depth to these discussions highlights the tension time constraints held over this course the entire term. Meeting twice a week for 80 minutes, it was a consistent challenge to incorporate time for all course activities. At the beginning of the term, time was used to align everyone's understanding of the issues addressed through lecture and reading discussions. As the term progressed, less time was used to review and discuss the outside reading content and more time devoted to class activities and role plays.

Overall student reflections exhibited identification with and deeper under-standing of the Out-siders of heteronormative discourse, a professional sense of responsibility for addressing homophobia and heteronormativity in their teaching, and an ability to articulate ways in which they might address this issue in their classrooms and the professional school communities.

The final consensus of students was that all future teachers should be required to take this course. When we discussed this, all the students expressed anxiety about how they would be received as Out-siders by their professional peers. One student commented:

> You should have heard the silence when this topic came up in our other class! I mean there was [sic] just the few of us from this class and you could totally feel the tension when the professor told the group they would be expected to address homophobia in their classroom.

His classmates quickly confirmed they, too, felt they were "the only people in the room who knew how to talk about homophobia in schools."

This discussion closed by suggesting to this cohort that if, in fact, this lack of knowledge is true of their cohort, then they were the only people adept at talking about homophobia and heteronormativity in schools. Therefore, even as they felt the burden of this knowledge, they could recognize the power of it as well. Spending time exploring this topic and considering educational models to address this form of inequality had given these students power to speak, to name, to explain, and to address homophobia and heteronormativity in schools. While they would perhaps never again be working with a cohort of people who understood these issues to the degree that each of them will, their ability to articulate and lead will draw to them a coalition of outsiders and social justice-oriented educators who will listen, learn, and act with them in the future.

Questions for Consideration

In considering the future of this course, questions were posed to consider for planning and teaching this curriculum again.

What Would it Mean if Students Were Required to Take this Course?

This course was offered as one of five choices within an Equal Opportunity Seminar Series of courses. Students were required to take a minimum of two equal opportunity seminars and they were offered content focus areas including homophobia, poverty, gender inequality, environmental degradation, genocide, racism, and nationalism. While students were required to take courses on social inequality and education, they were allowed to opt into any of the five topics. While mandating the course properly elevates the topic as an abiding professional concern, the window of choice allowed for some self-selection on the part of students within this class.

On the one hand, we are compelled as advocates for marginalized populations to mandate that education students learn all of these structural inequalities in education. On the other hand, as an instructor, it seemed we were able to move more quickly and to a much deeper level of analysis because students self-selected into this course. During fall term, Julie taught on issues and problems in education as a course requirement for all education foundations students and, in that course, experienced more resistance and hostility toward the topics addressed in the syllabus. Therefore, there is not an easy answer to making this course an education requirement or mandating students to participate.

What Happens when Students are Experiencing Social and even Familial Loss over this Course Content?

It is important to note students experienced a variety of emotional and intellectual losses throughout this course. As students came to hold a deeper knowledge about inequality and bias, they expressed experiencing tensions within their family and peer relationships. One student shared he couldn't talk to his parents about everything he was learning, and his last visit home had been very upsetting. When he brought up this topic, he was silenced by his father's virulent homophobia. Another student found her supervisors became more adverse to her graduate studies after she brought in materials on LGBTQ bullying and advocated for the establishment of a GSA. As the course called for public pedagogy and pushed students to engage the world, Julie sought out means to support and advise these students as they opened doors only to have them slammed shut.

Conclusion

> It takes no compromising to give people their rights. It takes no money to respect the individual. It takes no survey to remove repression.
>
> Harvey Milk (1973)

The development of a creative curriculum for Equal Opportunity: Homophobia in Education has been a constant learning process for us. We would encourage more research on teacher education models for addressing minority concerns of marginalization and inequality within our public education system.

We continue to advance this form of teaching for social justice and modeling anti-oppressive pedagogy to students. We continue to collect journals, engage in dialogue, and observe as these future teachers enact this curriculum in the classroom.

References

Birden, Susan. 2005. *Rethinking Sexual Identity in Education*. Lanham, MD: Rowman and Littlefield.

Boal, Augusto. 1992. *Games for Actors and Non-actors*. Translated by Adrian Jackson. New York: Routledge.

Chasnoff, Debra, and Johnny Symons. 2007. *It's Still Elementary: Talking About Gay Issues in School*. San Francisco, CA: GroundSpark.

Epstein, Debbie, and Richard Johnson. 1998. *Schooling Sexualities*. Buckingham, UK: Open University Press.

GLSEN. 2003–2015. *Gay, Lesbian, and Straight Education Network (GLSEN)* [cited June 23 2015]. Available from http://glsen.customer.def6.com/participate/gsa/about-gsas.

HRC. 2012. *Welcoming Schools*. Human Rights Campaign [cited July 15 2015]. Available from http://www.welcomingschools.org.

Kirchner, Mary Beth, and Ira Glass. 2009. "Tom Girls," Somewhere Out There. In *This American Life*. Chicago: Public Radio International.

Kumashiro, Kevin K. 2004. *Against Common Sense: Teaching and Learning toward Social Justice*. New York: Routledge.

Kumashiro, Kevin K. 2012. *Troubling Education: "Queer" Activism and Anti-Oppressive Pedagogy*. New York: Routledge.

Milk, Harvey. 1973. Campaign speech for San Francisco Board of Supervisors.

Schey, Ryan, and Ariel Uppstrom. 2010. "Activist work as entry-year teachers: What we've learned. " In *Acting Out! Combating Homophobia through Teacher Activism*, edited by M. Blackburn, C. Clark, L. Kenney and J. Smith, 88–102. New York: Teachers College Press.

Teaching Tolerance. 2015. *Classroom Resources*. Teaching Tolerance [cited July 12 2015]. Available from http://www.tolerance.org.

10

OUT OF THE CLOSET AND INTO THE CLASSROOM

LGBTQ Issues and Inclusive Classroom Practice

Sean Robinson

The media system, like the educational system, is "one of society's key set of institutions, industries, and cultural practices" (Masterman 2001, 16). The media is often invoked to mean not only the mediums of communication, such as the radio, internet, film, print, music, and television, but also the products of these mediums—newspaper and magazine articles, film and television productions, websites, social media, and even video games. According to Couldry (2003), television, film, radio, and print are the "ways we imagine ourselves to be connected to the social world" (7); we can now add digital and hyperspaces, including the internet and venues such as Facebook and YouTube. Buckingham (2003) found that youth spend more time with media than any other institution, including schools; thus, it is axiomatic to say students and youth are growing up in a media-centric world. The implication of this is clear—media in all of its forms are now a central teaching tool for everyone.

Given the ubiquitous nature and forms of media present in our daily lives, the "informal" pedagogies of the popular culture and media appear to be quickly surpassing the "formal" educational pedagogies present in schools and universities. The images and information youth are exposed to every day are not just forms of entertainment; they serve both cultural and pedagogical functions as well. Media clearly assumes a more powerful role in teaching youth, and adults, about their world and culture, and the role they play in it. In light of how media representations shape one's definition of identity and social reality, the purpose of this chapter is to explore the intersection of the media and LGBTQ representations, highlight the underutilized role of media as an educational tool in addressing LGBTQ issues, and present a series of recommendations for teacher educators that results in culturally responsive classroom practices.

Mass Media and Sexuality

Historically, both film and television have served as the two predominant venues of mass media and critical cultural work. It is through television and film that many cultures and groups clarify their dominant values and beliefs, while subcultures and minority groups, including LGBTQ individuals, are often left to negotiate for their place at the table by scanning for positive media representations, or critically interrogating negative images and stereotypes. It is not just television and film, but also media—in all of its most central forms—that instructs, validates, and, in many instances, reifies cultural and social structures.

The media not only markets products, ideas, values, and attitudes, but also creates socially acceptable hegemonic behavior and attitudes for both adults and youth alike. Batchelor, Kitzinger, and Burtney (2004) demonstrated the heteronormative nature of media in our society. After examining a week's worth of general media, including nine teen magazines, 68 newspaper editions, and 88 hours of television, the researchers found that, in spite of limited high-profile representations in some contexts (e.g., *Queer as Folk* and *Buffy, the Vampire Slayer*), gay teens are not generally integrated into mainstream media formats. Additionally, in numerous instances male characters went so far as to disavow the inference they might be gay (e.g., in *The O.C.*). Overall, Batchelor and his colleagues found that for males being gay was most likely to be portrayed as a source for embarrassment or the target of teasing; furthermore, they found representations of lesbians were almost completely absent in the media they examined. Given these findings, we need to expose students to different media forms and teach students to engage with, and think critically about, the media they encounter. In order to teach critically, we as educators must first engage critically *with* and think critically *about* LGBTQ issues in various media.

Much of the scholarship and discourse around the visibility and representation of LGBTQ individuals has focused on television and film, posing questions such as: Do we see LGBTQ people in film and on TV? How often are LGBTQ people seen, and in what context or situation? Are these positive or negative images? What does it mean to have positive or negative images represented? Are these representations accurate and realistic? Mortiz (2003) maintains American television both reflects and creates cultural expressions as well as political, economic, and social realities. Reed (2005) echoes this sentiment, contending, "Television is a teacher, communicating how people need to act in social and cultural institutions such as school, church, and family" (24). Films, too, often limit the size and diversity of an audience, and thus limit the conversations around LGBTQ issues. Digital media, primarily found on the internet, offers a completely new world for expression and coalescence within the virtual public sphere. The internet, the world wide web, and new digital media offer a patchwork of new social worlds where identity, representation, production, consumption, and self-regulation take on new possibilities for LGBTQ people. The pervasiveness of these forms of media in the lives of youth underscores the crucial need to learn how to engage with such forms and decenter heterosexuality as the norm.

Several studies have shown the media has an important part to play in shaping the knowledge, discussions, and attitudes surrounding sexuality in general, and homosexuality in particular (Currie, Todd, and Thomson 1997, Davis and Harris 1982, Forrest 1997, Kehily 1999, Thomson and Scott 1991). Linné's (2003) narrative research study, involving an online discussion group aimed at explicating and negotiating meaning within certain media, found the dominant scripts of the media continue to represent negative portrayals of gays and lesbians that have circulated society for years. Nonetheless, while media remained limited in representations of LGBTQ individuals, the youth in his study were able to rewrite the media to create realistic self-images for themselves.

The role of media influence is complex and does not simply involve absorption or mimicry (Batchelor 2003, Kitzinger 1999). Scholars in the field of communication and mass media studies have suggested how individuals are portrayed is not necessarily a straight trajectory, nor is the path a linear one going from negative and harmful to positive and healthy (Berry 1998, Castiglia and Reed 2004, Clarke 1969). Such representations, whether related to race, religion, gender, class, or sexual orientation, influence not only how an outsider thinks about those group identities, but also how individuals think about themselves relative to those identities. Early research by Leifer, Gordon, and Graves (1974) demonstrated children's attitudes about people changed in relation to the television shows they watched. Yet, recent research by Simpson (2007) found that even when children were exposed to television programs including individuals of diverse backgrounds, they continued to maintain stereotypical, racist beliefs about minority groups unless the children's parents actively discussed those stereotypes and worked to negate them.

Of course, gender, race, and ethnicity, while at times the most visible aspects of stereotyping, are not the only dimensions serving to reinforce stereotypes. Heterosexuals form the dominant group in most societies, which defines, governs, and prescribes cultural norms, values and expectations, including those relating to relationships, sexuality, marriage, childrearing and parenthood, and family structures. Not surprising, then, that what the media portrays are often stereotypes about LGBTQ individuals, which tend to elicit, at best, neutral reactions, but more likely, negative reactions by both heterosexual and LGBTQ audiences. Most people, including LGBTQ individuals, learn almost everything they know about the LGBTQ world from popular media rather than from teachers, parents, or those who are in fact gay, lesbian, bisexual, transgendered, or queer (Croteau and Hoynes 1997). Croteau and Hoynes further suggest the passive acceptance of media as either innocent forms of entertainment or true expressions of culture and society ignores the fact that media is an extension of the individual who created it. In short, the producer cannot be separated from the larger context or cultural milieu in which he or she exists.

When LGBTQ adolescents and young adults are exposed to stereotyping or blatant invisibility in the media, they are bound to encounter problems as they develop their own identities. Many gays, lesbians, and bisexuals continue to remain in the closet if they perceive they do not "fit" the stereotypes portrayed in the media. Stereotypes create expectations about how people should behave. They may create self-fulfilling prophecies or influence one's interactions and experiences to conform to public expectations (Jussim 1991). In addition to watching current television programs with LGBTQ characters such as *Modern Family*, *Glee*, and *The Fosters*, among others, today's youth can create and read blogs, play video games, produce and watch videos on YouTube, and make connections and friends on Facebook, all in an effort to explore, compare, and understand their own identity and how they fit into the larger LGBTQ communities. Considering the manner in which identity development occurs, and the impact that media have on LGBTQ identity formation, creation, comparison, and acceptance or rejection, it is clear we as educators ought to pay attention to the what, how, when, and where of media consumption, creation, and dissemination.

Not all media showcase healthy LGBTQ individuals, or serve to disrupt stereotypes about LGBTQ people. In almost every episode of the popular cable shows *Queer as Folk* and *The L Word*, LGBTQ individuals are portrayed as living unrealistic lives revolving around alcohol, drugs, clubs, and casual sex. In contrast, Will and Jack, the two primary male characters in *Will and Grace*, embody the gay stereotypes common in most forms of media. Often we find both Will and Jack obsessed with fashion and sex, lusting after young well-built masculine men either in the gym or at a club. Both characters regularly demonstrate over-the-top emotional responses; giving the impression they are "drama queens." There is little or no discussion about gay relationships or romance. The two gay characters are friends, not lovers, and rarely shown in romantic situations. The primary relationships for both gay men are with the heterosexual female characters Grace and Karen. Gay sexuality was either portrayed as a joke, or erased altogether. Nonetheless, as Castiglia and Reed (2004) point out, Will and Grace offer a "rich resource of gay memory" (159). The character of Jack offers a glimpse into gay subculture as a pleasure, of being able to camp it up; Will offers viewers a more neutral gay man, who is often isolated and distant from gay subculture. In reality, many of us who identify as LGBTQ have experienced both sides of these characters, sometimes intentionally, other times not.

Television series such as *Queer as Folk*, *The L Word*, *Will & Grace*, *Modern Family*, and *Glee*, films such as *My Best Friend's Wedding*, *The Object of My Affection*, *Beautiful Life*, *Brokeback Mountain*, and *The Next Best Thing*, and reality television shows such as *Queer Eye for the Straight Guy*, limit exposure of LGBTQ individuals to predominately white, middle-class, attractive men and women who offer up stereotypical representations. The misrepresentation and portrayal of gay individuals in this light clearly demonstrates how a heterocentric media manipulates behaviors and attitudes of gays and lesbians, diminishing the depth and complexity of the characters, and silencing or marginalizing the experiences of those who are LGBTQ, all for the sake of popular entertainment. Even as younger generations' attitudes about LGBTQ individuals may be broadening in part because of representations in the media (Adelman, Segal, and Kilty 2006), the stereotypical representations still provide a static model of what it means to be LGBTQ. Youth and young adults who are still struggling with their sexual identities may harbor shame and fear as they internalize these distorted notions of what it means to be gay or lesbian.

Institutionalized Heterosexuality

Educators readily acknowledge the role the media plays in shaping attitudes, beliefs, worldviews and behaviors relating to race, ethnicity, gender, sex roles, and even religion. Yet, rarely will educators openly acknowledge the heterocentric position that the media occupies in shaping our daily lives relative to one's sexual orientation. The ways in which educational institutions normalize or perpetuate heterosexuality, much the same way as the popular media, is well researched (Davis 1993, Epstein, O'Flynn, and Telfor 2003, Mac an Ghaill 1995).

In recent research examining homophobia in schools, Adelman and Woods (2006) found that although many students wanted to do something about the homophobic behaviors they witnessed, they did not have the tools or resources to intervene when they witnessed such harassment. Even more problematic, students perceived teachers as not only failing to intervene, but also condoning or perpetuating homophobic behavior and harassment. Echoing these findings, Padva (2007) found most images of LGBTQ individuals on television and in film focus on themes of bullying, including harassment and violence. Padva's work clearly suggests we might be out, but we are still at risk, physically, emotionally, socially, and psychologically if we deviate too far from the expected heterocentric norms.

Within the educational arena, textbooks, discussions, films, papers, and most curricular activities communicate about sexuality as a heterosexually imagined future, with conversations and discourses almost exclusively framed within heterocentric norms and expectations, limiting how LGBTQ adolescents and young adults might imagine their own future identities and experiences (Epstein, O'Flynn, and Telfor 2003). The turmoil in accepting one's non-heterosexual identity is due in part to the heteronormative and heterocentric values, norms, and expectations portrayed in the media, and in part to the lived out daily routine of our educational institutions. Educators tolerate verbal attacks, slurs, and epithets hurled not only in the classroom and hallways, but also on the street, in stores, on buses, in theaters, in churches and synagogues, and the like. Although our culture does not tolerate racial slurs, it still ignores, allows, and even laughs at derogatory remarks aimed at LGBTQ individuals.

Negative societal attitudes can be life threatening for those who are LGBTQ. While 10 percent of the population is estimated to be gay or lesbian, studies on youth suicide report gay and lesbian youth are two to six times more likely to attempt suicide than other youth, and may account for close to 30 percent of completed suicides among adolescents (Remafedi 1974). Statistics from both the National Mental Health Association and the Sexual Information and Education Council reveal that over 87 percent of gay or lesbian youth report verbal or physical attacks at school, with 37 percent of those students hearing such slurs from teachers or staff. Kosciw and Diaz (2006) report 33 percent of students surveyed have been harassed because of actual or perceived sexual orientation at school, and nearly two-thirds of the students surveyed feel unsafe at school because of their sexual orientation. These numbers appear to be static. According to the most recent school climate report by the Gay, Lesbian and Straight Education Network (Kosciw et al. 2010), sexual orientation and gender identity ranked first (61.1%) and second (39.9%), respectively, as the most frequent reasons youth felt unsafe at schools. Among other startling statistics regarding sexual orientation:

- 88.9 percent heard "gay" used in a negative way;
- 84.6 percent were verbally harassed because of their sexual orientation;
- 40.1 percent were physically harassed at school because of sexual orientation;
- 18.8 percent were physically assaulted because of sexual orientation;
- 52.9 percent of LGBT students were the victims of cyberbullying.

A total of 62.4 percent of students who were harassed or assaulted in school did not report the incident, believing nothing would be done, or that the situation would become worse. Furthermore, 33.8 percent of those students who did report an incident said neither staff nor teachers did anything in response. These statistics implicate educators at all levels; it is the obligation of teachers and administrators alike to create safe environments for our youth, where they feel valued and respected. Yet, these data suggest such an environment does not occur. Teachers and educators must acknowledge LGBTQ youth are not simply victims of these homophobic remarks and attacks; they are also casualties of a heterocentric society, faced with a heterosexual media that perpetuates prejudice and bias against them from all sides. A heterocentric school curriculum that teaches heterocentric social norms, cultural values, and assists with the development of one's identity (including sexual identity) is bound to deny LGBTQ youth the capacity and the space to truly develop an authentic self. The presence of such a curriculum and pedagogy necessitates that LGBTQ youth resort to the popular media for information that is both distorted and biased.

This underscores the crucial importance of educators learning, practicing, and teaching for media literacy, so every one can lead lives of what Greene (1978) calls wide-awakeness. To approach our curriculum from a media literacy standpoint means we want students who critically evaluate the ways they see, interpret, produce, and respond to various forms of media. By teaching for media literacy, educators help their students to see and question the heterocentric and homophobic themes in our society, and the effects of these worldviews on heterosexual and non-heterosexual individuals alike. However, there are two issues that must be acknowledged in this pursuit. The first, and perhaps most formidable, challenge involves the reluctance of many teachers and teacher educators to broach the general topic of sexuality, much less to actively engage in discourse about LGBTQ issues. The second, more easily addressed challenge is training educators to use media literacy as a pedagogical strategy in the classroom.

Sexuality in the Classroom

Many schools operate along a narrow set of moral and religious beliefs that threaten teachers with dismissal for openly discussing controversial topics, such as homosexuality (Sears 1989). Prejudice, bias, and discrimination against LGBTQ people in schools and society stem largely from a lack of education about LGBTQ issues and identity development. Without informed knowledge, teachers are likely to conform to heterocentric norms and expectations, which are reflected in classroom pedagogy.

Regardless of the subject matter, and despite the systems around them, all educators must be encouraged and supported to engage in the type of teaching that allows all students, including gay, lesbian, bisexual, transgendered, queer, or questioning, to flourish and thrive. Many researchers (Au and Kawakami 1994, Darling-Hammond, French, and Garcia-Lopez 2002, Erickson 1987, Gay 2002, Jordan 1985, Ladson-Billings 1990) have challenged schools and educators to find creative ways to work with students from culturally diverse backgrounds. LGBTQ students, and even heterosexual students from same-sex families, should be among this group. As educators, we must be willing to address and expunge the biases and prejudices found in our curriculums and classrooms. We must be willing to challenge the assumptions and expectations of a heterocentric society. By acknowledging the existence and the sexual differences of LGBTQ individuals, educators can expose "that worldview in which the framework, points of reference, and assumptions are all heterosexual" (Stychin and Herman 2001, 260). By pointing out the heterocentric world in which we live and by confronting homophobia—the irrational fear or hatred of gays and lesbians—educators can begin to create positive experiences for LGBTQ students, or their families.

Yet, teachers are often likely to report a lack of preparation to engage in topics related to LGBTQ issues and concerns. When preservice teachers have received training, it has been either limited to the physiology of sex education, or it is a single lecture in a course on multicultural education (Alldred and David 2007, Howard-Barr et al. 2005, Price et al. 2003). Ferfolja and Robinson (2004) examined anti-homophobia in teacher education and found that dealing with

LGBTQ issues is often sidelined in multicultural education rhetoric and not included in textbooks or presented in most courses because LGBTQ issues are not legitimized as part of the multicultural repertoire. In addition, they found that teachers often feel confined and constricted by standards and objectives, as well as teaching for standardized testing, which does not place an emphasis on any form of diversity or multicultural education. In essence teachers were less inclined to believe that social justice issues were more important than the mechanics of writing or basic arithmetic. Ferfolja and Robinson also claim many teachers view sexuality as a private and moral issue that does not have any place in the classroom, especially teachers with conservative or religious views of homosexuality. A disturbing finding was some teachers believe students who display stereotypical gay behavior or mannerisms are just "asking for it," which pathologizes the student who is suffering or being harassed or bullied, and places the blame on the victim rather than addressing the real problems within heterocentric norms and beliefs.

The privileging of technical sex education over desires, feelings, and experiences of individuals is informed by what Rich (1983) has deemed compulsory heterosexuality. During their youth, LGBTQ individuals are confronted with heterosexist norms and rules regarding their assumed (and expected) sexual and gender identification, which can negatively impact psychosocial development as well as academics (Kosciw et al. 2010). Teacher educators and both in-service and preservice teachers "are likely to be legitimately anxious about the reactions of parents, and worse, the popular press if they stray into territory considered by some to be too risky (even risqué)" (Epstein, O'Flynn, and Telfor 2001, 136). Thoughtful teacher educators who write about their attempts to incorporate discussions related to sexual diversity and gender identification by countering the heterocentric nature of society have acknowledged the challenges while also questioning the impact and effectiveness of such efforts (e.g., Asher 2007, Gust 2007, MacIntosh 2007). Typically, this approach has involved "queering" the curriculum. Such an approach is not about reifying the rigid notions of sexuality along a simple dichotomy (heterosexual vs. homosexual), but rather seeks to deconstruct and decenter as normal heterosexuality. Thus, the purpose is to help all students examine how their own sexuality and gender identification has its origins in heterosexuality, and the problems this stance has on all young people. Even with the best of intentions in teacher education programs, it is naïve to think, though, that most teachers will go so far as to "queer" their curriculum or even their classrooms. Even if teachers have the knowledge and skills to deal with LGBTQ issues, or confront homophobia, an ever-present fear of "guilty by association" still permeates the halls of most schools. Robinson and Ferfolja (2002) found that when teachers addressed homophobic epithets in classrooms or hallways, they were accused of being gay. This causes consternation for both heterosexual teachers, and LGBTQ teachers who fear being outed.

Every day students and teachers face the prospect of walking into a school climate of intimidation with an undercurrent of homophobia and heterosexism that manifests in hate speech, bullying, harassment, and physical abuse. The degree to which teachers can and will confront this varies widely. Teaching from a media literacy standpoint is but one way teachers can use a set of teaching and learning strategies that do not place them at the center, and allows discussions about many issues and topics, including LGBTQ ones.

Media Literacy as Pedagogy

Good teaching comes from good teachers. The best teachers seek out continuing opportunities to explore new methods and expand their repertoire of strategies to *engage students in their own learning*. Teaching takes practice, and good teachers develop their skills by becoming lifelong learners themselves, and reflecting regularly with their peers on the effectiveness of their classroom praxis. Teachers who are also students are in the best position to understand the role and value of media literacy as a teaching and learning tool, but developing the skills needed to use media literacy in the classroom starts with effective teaching and role modeling on the part of teacher educators. The challenges to the dissemination of media literacy as an educational process in U.S. schools are numerous—a decentralized education system consisting of 16,000 autonomous school districts, little funding, a long tradition of content-based learning methods using printed texts, and a lack of knowledgeable and professional trainers and the infrastructure organizations to support them. In addition, U.S. educational systems are notorious for deep-seated resistance to technological innovations, such as computers, which enable student inquiry and independent learning that are the cornerstones of effective media literacy pedagogy.

Based on tenants from the National Association for Media Literacy Education, the following list of ideas can be used to help teacher educators and teachers explore and understand how media literacy is different from other literacies:

- Media "bashing" is not media literacy; however, media literacy sometimes involves *criticizing the media*.
- Simply producing media is not media literacy, although media literacy should include *media production*.
- Teaching with videos or other mediated content is not media literacy; one must also *teach about media*.
- Simply looking for political agendas, stereotypes or misrepresentations is not media literacy; there should also be an *exploration* of the systems making those representations appear normal.
- Looking at a media message or a mediated experience from just one perspective is not media literacy because media should be examined from *multiple positions*.

• Media literacy does not mean "don't watch"; it means *"watch carefully, think critically."*

Given these propositions, it is clear media literacy is primarily a process of *inquiry* about media culture. In addition to being able to help individuals *access, analyze,* and *evaluate* mediated messages and experiences, media literacy enables students to *express* and *communicate* their thoughts and views using all the creative tools available in today's multimedia culture.

The inquiry approach that best suits a critical media literacy classroom includes both analytical (deconstruction) skills as well as production (construction) skills. Teachers interested in media literacy need primarily to be skilled in *organizing and facilitating student-centered learning.* They do not necessarily require extensive knowledge of media theories or professional competency in journalism, video production or film-making, although such knowledge can certainly benefit students who desire to create their own forms of media.

Confronting and challenging students' beliefs, values, stereotypes, and judgments, and helping them to analyze their worldviews can be accomplished in a number of ways. A list of suggested questions can aid teachers and teacher educators become comfortable in helping students critically evaluate almost any form of media. As a starting point, to help students critically evaluate almost any form of media, teachers can consider both *messages* and *meanings*. This can then be followed by discussions and activities centered around *audience* and *authorship*: finally, teachers can have students consider *representations* and *reality* within the media (see Table 10.1).

The use of video segments from popular shows containing LGBTQ-identified characters can be used for exploration and discussion while challenging to critically deconstruct the images and messages seen or heard, and how those messages influence, exploit, or hurt LGBTQ individuals. Commercials and print advertising offer a rich repository for examining our heterocentric world. Students can evaluate and explore the values, attitudes, and behaviors mass advertising conveys and reinforces, which may ultimately lead to discrimination or bias against LGBTQ people. Teaching with newspapers provides another opportunity for educators to connect the lives of students to the world around them. Articles on topics such as hate crimes, material related to gay marriage bans, issues related to healthcare, and global gay rights offer a world of possibilities for discussions and debates, thus creating a more informed and empathic citizenry. Students can write, journal, or create their own forms of media about their lives, or the lives of gay, lesbian, bisexual, transgendered, or queer individuals. Using videos from the fall 2010 YouTube project *It Gets Better* as a starting place, teachers can ask students to imagine the world of an LGBTQ individual and why such videos and messages might be needed. Providing opportunities for students to enact those lives, or others, or to create their own videos can be a powerful tool for fostering critical shifts in attitudes and beliefs and has the potential to have a profound impact on the lives of all students.

TABLE 10.1 Critical Evaluation of Media

Messages and *Meanings*

What is this about (and what makes you think that)?
What ideas, values, information, and/or points of view are overt? Implied?
What is left out of this message that might be important to know?
What techniques are used to make or convey the message?
Why were those techniques used?
How do they communicate the message?
How might different people understand this message differently?
What is my interpretation of this and what do I learn about myself from my reaction or interpretation?

Audience and *Authorship*

Who made this message?
Why was this made?
Who is the target audience (and how do you know)?
Who paid for this?
Who might benefit from this message?
Who might be harmed by it?
Who was included in the message? Why?
Who was left out of the message? Why?
Why might this message matter to me?
What kinds of actions might I take in response to this message?
What kind of actions might others take in response to this message?

Representations and *Reality*

When was this made?
Where or how was it shared with the public?
Is this fact, opinion, or something else?
How credible is this (and what makes you think that)?
What are the sources of the information, ideas, or assertions?

Conclusion

Introducing media literacy into the classroom, thereby exposing negative LGBTQ stereotypes present in popular media, is but one starting point for exploring these issues in any educational setting. The mass media provide a rich array of material and experiences for critically evaluating and examining the implicit and explicit ways in which our society perpetuates heteronormative attitudes and behaviors as the standard by which we should all live. Utilizing media education and teaching media literacy in the classroom allows educators and students the chance to critique society, the world, and each other. Furthermore, as teachers, we must accept our youth can and do have a very real impact on our culture and environment. They interact with one another, are influenced by pop culture and mass media, and, in turn, create their own forms of media. By teaching for media literacy in our classrooms, we can engage all of our students in the process of critical engagement and empowerment.

The use of mass media as a teaching tool encourages students not only to understand what a stereotype is, but also to question the ways in which such stereotypes about individuals who are LGBTQ truly reflect, and impact, the lives of such individuals. More importantly, such conversations can be used as a springboard to analyze the manner in which all stereotypes dehumanize others or may have very harmful consequences. Using media for critical discussion requires a constructivist and generative classroom (Kornfeld and Goodman 1998). Teachers who strive for open, constructivist, and generative classrooms are constantly asking students to think for themselves, to voice opinions and ideas, to challenge others' opinions, and to examine the way in which topics, and in this case, media, connect to their own lives. Connecting media to the lives of youth situates it in their everyday existence, and helps them to understand its relevancy. Lewis and Jhally (1998) suggest "media literacy should be about helping people to become sophisticated citizens rather than sophisticated consumers" (109). This requires that teachers forgo their neutral role as conveyors of information, and instead adopt a role of critical facilitator, empowering students to change the rules of engagement in their world.

Teaching for media literacy and the use of formal instructional activities related to the use of popular media can have a profound impact on helping students make sense of their world as they encounter an ever-present media blitz. Using books, newspapers, music, films, magazines, ads, television, and web-based material as vehicles, teachers can begin to create healthy dialogues around LGBTQ issues. The exploration of media can provide a means for understanding the forces that shape who we are or who we desire to be. In addition, such an exploration can expose the harmful effects of the media in maintaining unhealthy stereotypes, bias, prejudice, or discrimination for many individuals, not just those who are LGBTQ.

References

Adelman, Madelaine, Elizabeth A. Segal, and Keith M. Kilty. 2006. "Introduction: Transforming LGBTQ Inequalities in the Twenty-First Century." *Journal of Poverty* no. 10 (2): 1–4. doi: 10.1300/J134v10n0201.

Adelman, Madelaine, and Katheryn Woods. 2006. "Identification without Intervention: Transforming Anti-LGBTQ School Climate." *Journal of Poverty* no. 10: 5–26.

Alldred, Pam, and Miriam E. David. 2007. *Get Real about Sex: The Politics and Practice of Sex Education, Educating Boys, Learning Gender.* Maidenhead, UK: Open University Press.

Asher, Nina. 2007. "Made in the (Multicultural) U.S.A.: Unpacking Tensions of Race, Culture, Gender, and Sexuality in Education." *Educational Researcher* no. 36 (2): 65–73.

Au, Kathryn, and Alice Kawakami. 1994. "Cultural Congruence in Instructiom." In *Teaching Diverse Populations: Formulating a Knowledge Base*, edited by Etta R. Hollins, Joyce Elaine King and Warren C. Hayman, 5–24. Albany: State University of New York Press.

Batchelor, S. 2003. "Teenage Sexuality in the Media: Too Much Too Young?" In *Young People and Sexual Health: Social, Political, and Individual Contexts*, edited by E. Burtney and M. Duffy, 2–17. London: Palgrave.

Batchelor, S. A., J. Kitzinger, and E. Burtney. 2004. "Representing Young People's Sexuality in the 'Youth' Media." *Health Education Research* no. 19 (6): 669–676.

Berry, Gordon L. 1998. "Black Family Life on Television and the Socialization of the African American Child: Images of Marginality." *Journal of Comparative Family Studies* no. 29 (2): 233–242.

Buckingham, David. 2003. "Media Education and the End of the Critical Consumer." *Harvard Educational Review* no. 73 (3): 309–327.

Castiglia, Christopher, and Christopher Reed. 2004. "'Ah, Yes, I Remember It Well': Memory and Queer Culture in 'Will and Grace'." *Cultural Critique* no. 56: 158–188. doi: 10.2307/1354720.

Clarke, Cedric. 1969. "Television and Social Controls: Some Observations on the Portrayals of Ethnic Minorities." *Television Quarterly* no. 8 (2): 18–22.

Couldry, Nick. 2003. *Media Rituals: A Critical Approach*. London: Routledge.

Croteau, David, and William Hoynes. 1997. *Media/Society: Industries, Images, and Audiences*. Thousand Oaks, CA: Pine Forge Press.

Currie, C., J. Todd, and C. Thomson. 1997. *Sex Education, Personal Relationships, Sexual Behaviours, Health Behaviours of Scottish School Children*. Edinburgh: HEBS and RUHBS.

Darling-Hammond, Linda, Jennifer French, and Silvia Paloma Garcia-Lopez. 2002. *Learning to Teach Social Justice*, Multicultural Education series. New York: Teachers College Press.

Davis, Brownwyn. 1993. *Shards of Glass: Children Reading and Writing Beyond Gendered Indentities*. St. Leonards, NSW: Allen & Unwin.

Davis, Sally M., and M. B. Harris. 1982. "Sexual Knowledge, Sexual Interests, and Sources of Sexual Information of Rural and Urban Adolescents from Three Cultures." *Adolescence* no. 17: 471–492.

Epstein, Debbie, Sarah O'Flynn, and David Telfor. 2001. "'Othering' Education: Sexualities, Silences, and Schooling." In *Review of Research in Education*, edited by Walter G. Secada, 127–180. Washington, DC: American Educational Research Association.

Epstein, Debbie, Sarah O'Flynn, and David Telfor. 2003. *Silenced Sexualities in Schools and Universities*. Stoke on Trent: Trentham Books.

Erickson, Frederick. 1987. "Transformation and School Success: The Politics and Culture of Educational Achievement." *Anthropology & Education Quarterly* no. 18 (4): 335–356. doi: 10.2307/3216661.

Ferfolja, Tania, and Kerry H. Robinson. 2004. "Why Anti-Homophobia Education in Teacher Education? Perspectives from Australian Teacher Educators." *Teaching Education* no. 15 (1): 9–25.

Forrest, S. 1997. "Confessions of a Middle Shelf Magazine Shopper." *Journal of Contemporary Health* no. 5: 10–13.

Gay, Geneva. 2002. "Preparing for Culturally Responsive Teaching." *Journal of Teacher Education* no. 53 (2): 106–116.

Greene, Maxine. 1978. *Landscapes of Learning*. New York: Teachers College Press.

Gust, Scott William. 2007. "'Look Out for the Football Players and the Frat Boys': Autoethnographic Reflections of a Gay Teacher in a Gay Curricular Experience." *Educational Studies* no. 41 (1): 43–60. doi: 10.1080/00131940701308999.

Howard-Barr, E. M., B. A. Rienzo, R. M. Pigg, Jr., and D. James. 2005. "Teacher Beliefs, Professional Preparation, and Practices Regarding Exceptional Students and Sexuality Education." *Journal of School Health* no. 75 (3): 99–105. doi: 10.1111/j.1746–1561.2005.tb06649.x10.1111/j.1746–1561.2005.00004.x.

Jordan, Cathie. 1985. "Translating Culture: From Ethnographic Information to Educational Program." *Anthropology & Education Quarterly* no. 16 (2): 105–123.

Jussim, Lee. 1991. "Social Perception and Social Reality: A Reflection-Construction Model." *Psychological Review* no. 98 (1): 54–73. doi: 10.1037/0033–295X.98.1.54.

Kehily, Mary Jane. 1999. "More Sugar? Teenage Magazines, Gender Displays and Sexual Learning." *Sex Education Matters* no. 9: 7–8.

Kitzinger, J. 1999. "Some Key Issues in Audience Reception Research." In *Message Received: Glasgow Media Group Research, 1993–1998*, edited by Greg Philo, 2–20. Harlow, UK: Longman.

Kornfeld, J., and J. Goodman. 1998. "Melting the Glaze: Exploring Student Responses to Liberatory Social Studies." *Theory Into Practice* no. 37 (4): 306–313.

Kosciw, Joseph G., and Elizabeth M. Diaz. 2006. *The 2005 National School Climate Survey: The Experiences of Lesbian, Gay, Bisexual and Transgendered Youth in Our Schools*. New York: Gay, Lesbian and Straight Education Network (GLSEN).

Kosciw, Joseph G., Emily A. Greytak, Elizabeth M. Diaz, and Mark J. Bartkiewicz. 2010. *The 2009 National School Climate Survey: The Experiences of Lesbian, Gay, Bisexual and Transgender Youth in Our Nation's Schools*. New York. Gay, Lesbian and Straight Education Network (GLSEN).

Ladson-Billings, Gloria. 1990. "Culturally Relevant Teaching: Effective Instruction for Black Students." *College Board Review* no. 7 (155): 20–25.

Leifer, Aimee Dorr, Neal J. Gordon, and Sherryl Browne Graves. 1974. "Children's Television More than Mere Entertainment." *Harvard Educational Review* no. 44 (2): 213–245.

Lewis, J., and S. Jhally. 1998. "The Struggle Over Media Literacy." *Journal of Communication* no. 48 (1): 109–120.

Linné, Robert. 2003. "Alternative Textualities: Media Culture and the Proto-queer." *International Journal of Qualitative Studies in Education (QSE)* no. 16 (5): 669–689. doi: 10.1080/0951839032000142940.

Mac an Ghaill, Máirtín. 1995. *The Making of Men: Masculinities, Sexualities and Schooling*. Buckingham, UK: Open University Press.

MacIntosh, Lori. 2007. "Does Anyone Have a Band-Aid? Anti-Homophobia Discourses and Pedagogical Impossibilities." *Educational Studies* no. 41 (1): 33–43. doi: 10.1080/00131940701308874.

Masterman, L. 2001. "A Rationale for Media Education." In *Media Literacy in the Information Age: Current Perspectives*, edited by R. W. Kubey, 15–68. New Brunswick, NJ: Transaction Publishers.

Mortiz, Marguerite. 2003. "Recapturing the Archetype: An Inclusive Vision of Sexuality and Gender." In *Images that Injure: Pictorial Stereotypes in the Media*, edited by Paul Martin Lester and Susan Dente Ross, 197–206. Westport, CT: Praeger.

Padva, Gilad. 2007. "Media and Popular Culture Representations of LGBT Bullying." *Journal of Gay & Lesbian Social Services* no. 19 (3–4): 105–118.

Price, James H., Joseph A. Dake, Gregg Kirchofer, and Susan K. Telljohann. 2003. "Elementary School Teachers' Techniques of Responding to Student Questions Regarding Sexuality Issues." *The Journal of School Health* no. 73 (1): 9–14.

Reed, Jennifer. 2005. "Ellen DeGeneres: Public Lesbian Number One." *Feminist Media Studies* no. 5 (1): 23–36.

Remafedi, Gary. 1974. *Death by Denial: Studies of Suicide in Gay and Lesbian Teenagers.* Boston, MA: Allyson.

Rich, Adrienne. 1983. "Compulsory Heterosexuality and Lesbian Existence." In *The Signs Reader: Women, Gender, & Scholarship*, edited by Elizabeth Abel and Emily K. Abel, 139–168. Chicago: University of Chicago Press.

Robinson, Kerry H., and Tania Ferfolja. 2002. "A Reflection of Resistance: Discourses of Heterosexism and Homophobia in Teacher Training Classrooms." *Journal of Gay & Lesbian Social Services* no. 14 (2): 55–64.

Sears, James T. 1989. "Personal Feelings and Professional Attitudes of Prospective Teachers toward Homosexuality and Homosexual Students: Research Findings and Curriculum Recommendations." In *Annual Meeting of the American Eductional Research Association (AERA).* San Francisco, CA: AERA.

Simpson, Birgitte Vittrup. 2007. *Exploring the Influences of Educational Television and Parent-child Discussions on Improving Children's Racial Attitudes.* Austin: University of Texas.

Stychin, Carl F., and Didi Herman. 2001. *Law and Sexuality: The Global Arena.* Minneapolis: University of Minnesota Press.

Thomson, Rachel, and Sue Scott. 1991. *Learning about Sex: Young Women and the Social Construction of Sexual Identity, WRAP paper: 4.* London: Tufnell Press.

11

DEVELOPING CRITICAL DIALOGUE

J. Spencer Clark and James S. Brown

As educators we are constantly seeking ways to better cultivate dialogue among students of different cultures in our classrooms. This work is driven by optimism that dialogue can promote a more equitable and socially just society. Central to this optimism, educational settings have long been charged with the responsibility of providing a space to allow marginalized voices to fairly challenge dominant voices (Boler 2004). This charge starts with teacher education. Through dialogue, teacher educators attempt to challenge the dominant notions and cultural stereotypes[1] of historically marginalized groups, which preservice teachers have developed from their experiences in schools and society. Panel discussions provide one method of representing marginalized voices in the classroom. As teacher educators for the past nine years, we have used panel discussions for a variety of topics and critical issues in education, including Lesbian, Gay, Bisexual, Transgender, and Questioning (LGBTQ) issues. This chapter will provide some insights, based on our own critical reflections, on the use of panel discussions to transform preservice teachers' understanding of LGBTQ issues in schools.

Dialogue is essential to developing understanding among members of a historically marginalized group and members of the dominant culture. Ideally in a democratic classroom, individuals who do not typically speak are given the opportunity to be heard, because, as educators, we want to "'hear the voices' of those who have previously been silent" (Jones 2004, 58). However,

> democratic dialogue is far more than an opportunity for the exchange of ideas, or gathering interesting information about other people's lives. It is an explicitly political event because it attempts to shift the usual flow of power in order to un-marginalize the marginalized. Voices that are usually

marginalized—which is to say silenced—are to be centered and therefore empowered.

(Jones 2004, 59)

While difficult, we take every opportunity to model and promote respectful dialogue, especially dialogue across difference, in our teacher education classrooms. In the appropriate context, "dialogue between diverse groups dispels ignorance about others, increases understanding, and thus potentially decreases oppression, separation, violence, and fear" (Jones 2004, 57). As educators, we are always searching for this ideal form of dialogue in action, to answer the charge given to schools. The increasingly diverse school settings provide plenty of opportunity for educators to facilitate cross-cultural dialogue in the hope of bridging difference among their students. If new teachers are to engage their students in cross-cultural dialogue, they need experience with this dialogue, regardless of cultural background.

As authors, our work centers on developing curriculum that attempts to cultivate authentic dialogue among students and teachers of different ethnicities in a variety of countries. The individuals often differ in culture, language, and/or religion, which are differences often carrying socioeconomic implications. While we initiate dialogue, we question whether the dominant group members "hear" the members of the marginalized group, and if the marginalized culture wants to be "heard." We also critically question ourselves as Western white males, and ask if we actually "hear" either culture.

As teacher educators, we are concerned with cultivating dialogue with our own students and hope to challenge them to facilitate cross-cultural dialogue in their future classrooms, to openly confront issues of oppression and discrimination. Most of our students are from the dominant culture, and they may engage in dialogue with members of historically marginalized groups in their teacher education courses, but do they engage in productive or transformative ways? This question sparked our inquiry and critical reflection on each panel discussion we conducted, which led to the insights contained in this chapter. The intention of our critical reflection was to develop our panel discussions on LGBTQ issues into transformative practices for preparing our preservice teachers for their diverse classrooms and for developing dialogue across difference in their classrooms.

Panel Dialogues

Panel discussions, which have been used for a variety of educational purposes, provide one method of cultivating dialogue on a specific topic, and are used frequently in higher education settings (Cotten-Huston and Waite 1999, Green, Dixon, and Gold-Neil 1993, Reyes 2001). To be effective, a panel involves members of a historically marginalized group so notions held by the dominant or mainstream culture are challenged and "heard" by the members of the dominant culture. Jones (2004) identifies this relationship as potentially problematic because in a Western higher educational setting, the dominant culture feels it is their privilege to hear marginalized voices. This privilege "calls for access to the other, and to the knowledge and experiences of the other" (63). However, to prevent this access from merely becoming a cultural show-and-tell, the members of the historically marginalized group need to feel empowered to use their "own language" and have the dominant culture "hear" their challenges in the group's "own language."

Panel discussions can not only privilege the dominant culture, but also have mixed results. Green, Dixon, and Gold-Neil (1993) examined a panel discussion involving Gay, Lesbian, and persons with AIDS panelists and an audience of college students. The purpose of the panel was to positively change the attitudes of college students regarding Gays, Lesbians, and persons with AIDS. Pre-tests and post-tests determined that the panel discussion positively changed female student attitudes with only minor positive changes to male student attitudes. Cotten-Huston and Waite (1999) similarly looked at the use of a panel discussion as a means of disrupting "anti-homosexual" attitudes in college students. The panel discussion had little or no effect on attitudes, and they concluded a smaller audience or seminar setting, "which tend to stimulate participation and focus on getting to know the panelists as people, human beings, that is, not just gay men or lesbians," would be more effective (128). In these studies, the panel discussions had similar purposes to the panel discussions we use in our teacher education classrooms, and similarly faced challenges in sparking transformative or critical dialogue between the panelists and audiences.

Reyes (2001) examined a panel of teenage Asian American students who discussed their culture and identity with an audience of mostly teachers, administrators, and advisors from their school district. Reyes (2001) found the audience's questions positioned the students in ways which challenged their cultural identification. Essentially, the audience failed to recognize the students' identification with their respective Asian cultures and was more concerned with the students' assimilative identifications with mainstream American culture. This study represents a panel discussion using dialogue rooted in the dominant or mainstream culture, despite the proposed effort to hear historically marginalized voices intended to inform dominant or mainstream perspectives. The tension in this study also represents a similar challenge we faced initially in our panel discussions on LGBTQ issues with preservice teachers.

Our experience, and the literature, demonstrate a panel discussion may appear to be informal discussion; however, specific communicative behaviors take shape as students interact within the social dynamic of a panel discussion. These communicative behaviors can ultimately contribute to the success or failure of the panel discussion as a learning activity. For the purpose of this chapter, our panel discussions were intended to provide a format for students to enter into dialogue with individuals of a different culture and sexual orientation. However, in our early panel discussions, and similar to the Reyes (2001) study, the audience of preservice teachers shifted the discussion from its intended transformative purpose, by only using and recognizing certain stereotypical LGBTQ identifications that were part of the dominant mainstream culture. We realized from these early panel discussions that we needed to help our preservice teachers better understand their role and purpose in the panel discussion.

Discussion practiced in classrooms is a good exercise in civic skills, implementing "public voice" (Levine 2008). In an ideal setting, students exercise their public voice, discussing freely the issues at hand, enriching their public voice by engaging with the public voice of others. "One important motivator is that one can reach other people: an audience" (Levine 2008, 129), and the panel discussion provides this other audience, apart from their classmates and teachers. In this instance, the role of audience is that of the preservice teachers themselves, yet their public voice is demonstrated through comments and questions given to both the panel and their classmates. Students in panel discussions are forced to negotiate the public discourse space of *two* audiences. The consideration of these two audiences creates a space of complex interaction with constant identification, negotiation, and positioning among participants. In the public sphere, the public speaker assumes the duties of an ethical and rational legislator, addressing an assembly of peers on matters of public concern (Gutman and Thompson 1996, Levine 2008).

As public speakers, each participant in the panel discussion considers their audiences (i.e., panelists and classmates), and positions themselves inline with any number of economic, political, and social identifications to maintain or modify the discourse of the session. In using their public voice to address multiple audiences, a pattern of position taking may also emerge between both the panelists and the audience of students, and between the panelists themselves. "Positions may emerge 'naturally' out of the conversational and social context. But sometimes an initial seizure of the dominant role in a conversation will force the other speaker into speaking positions they would not have occupied voluntarily so to say" (VanLagenhove and Harre 1995, 363). The act of positioning takes place in many, if not most, social interactions. Social positioning is the discursive construction of personal stories that make a person's actions intelligible and relatively determinate as social acts. Scholars (Burr 1995, Davies and Harre 1990, Shotter 1989) have examined such social discourse in light of post-structural notions of identity construction, and have noted that persons can comprise multiple selves by which they define their identities, and, as these selves, are the products of social interactions with many possible constructions. In the context of panel discussions, students operate as active developers of their identities, and can have multiple modes of positioning through discursive practice.

Panel discussions, in this sense, characterize the larger society through replicating the representation of the groups involved, by their assigned roles in the session, along with the cultural stereotypes that are a basis of discussion and understanding of the "other" group. Cultural stereotypes often affect how individuals identify within their social context, and thus how they interact with others. Cultural stereotypes were used throughout the interaction of early panel discussions, often as a basis for mutual understanding in the discussion: "Stereotypes can only be understood when placed in their conversational context … the bulk of the available social psychological research on (cultural) stereotypes has focused on the 'reconstruction' aspect of stereotypes while neglecting its 'positioning' aspect" (VanLagenhove and Harre 1995, 364). Commonly trafficked cultural stereotypes— both mainstream and LGBTQ—used throughout early panel discussions are signified by panelists utilizing their own experiences that fit a storyline the audience understands and accepts, and even reciprocates to sustain the discussion. Our goal has been to move preservice teachers away from dialogue utilizing cultural stereotypes to dialogue that is more transformative and action oriented.

Ideally in a panel discussion on LGBTQ issues, the audience simply asks "individuals and groups how they want to describe themselves, listen carefully to their responses, explore collaboratively the institutional factors that obstruct such self-determination, and interrupt our own demands for others to fit some predetermined, restrictive category of acceptability" (North 2010, 382). However, it is also a choice for the panelists to either engage or not engage with the audience in dialogue. The panelists may even choose to remain "silent" or be uncritical in their dialogue. This may be troubling to educators, who view it as problematic to the intended outcomes of promoting dialogue. Yet, being uncritical may be purposeful, or as Jones (2004) notes, "Silence may be a rational response to their (dominant) peers' lack of ability to hear and understand" (60). The panelists' perception of the audience, as the dominant group, can heavily influence the outcome of the dialogue: "A recognizable interaction coheres as the speakers and audience are positioned in socially meaningful ways … and depend on each other for their meaningfulness" (Reyes 2001, 70). We want to prepare our preservice teachers to "hear" in panel discussions and to promote meaningful and transformative dialogue from which the panelists do not disengage.

As suggested, educators' "calls for dialogue may be in danger of reproducing the very power relations they seek to critique" (Jones 2004, 64). For example, panel discussions may marginalize the panelists when all participants use cultural stereotypes as a common language for the panel dialogue. As we saw in early panel discussions on LGBTQ issues, when marginalizing dialogue happens early in the discussion, it suppresses any challenges to mainstream notions of LGBTQ culture, deferring critical dialogue. By "critical dialogue," we mean questions intended to help better understand how LGBTQ identities take shape in schools, as well as questions addressing the tension between LGBTQ culture and mainstream culture that ask how oppressive societal attitudes have affected the panelists' identity and interaction in mainstream culture. When marginalizing dialogue was used early in the discussion, we found that even if the preservice teachers tried to engage in critical dialogue later in the discussion, often the panelists responded by using cultural stereotypes to avoid engaging in critical dialogue, and signifying their choice to not be "heard" by the audience. This further highlights the importance of preparing preservice teachers for critical and transformative dialogue in the panel discussion.

Implications for Teacher Education

There are several ways we have made panel discussions on LGBTQ issues more consistently engaging, critical, and transformative practices. We have broken this down into three types of practices: preparing for the panel discussion, during the panel discussion, after the panel discussion.

Preparing for the Panel Discussion

Jones (2004) suggests, "Dialogue requires particular pedagogical work from the subordinate group" (64) to provide access to their experiences and views. Dialogue also requires work on the part of the audience, "the work of hearing" (64). Bringing in representative voices is only the starting point for the particular pedagogical work Jones suggests, and "what is ultimately most significant to dialogue is not the talking by the marginalized, but the hearing by the dominant group" (65). This requires disruption of notions they previously held and developed from society, avoiding more typical dialogue, which is considered to be "a repetition that does not disrupt the common wisdom" (Berlak 2004, 142). While the focus of a panel discussion is dialogue and the voices of the marginalized, the audience plays a subtle, but important role in the orchestration of a session. What the audience hears ultimately influences the direction of the session, as they interact with the panelists and ask questions accordingly with what they hear. In the course of these interactions, a common language is established to maintain the expected interaction, providing an opportunity for patterns of interaction to emerge. These patterns provide comfort in setting the limits and potential of the dialogue. To prepare our preservice teachers to "hear" the LGBTQ panelists, we have developed some practices to prepare them for the panel discussion and shape the common language they use.

In preparation, we focus on the development of questions as one aspect that will guide the discussion to be more critical or transformative. Some have suggested having questions scripted to specifically explore institutional factors that obstruct self-determination, and interrupt our own demands for others to fit some predetermined, restrictive category of acceptability (North 2010). Scripting questions beforehand allows the preservice teachers access to a framework and vocabulary to discuss LGBTQ issues before the panel discussion. Yet, we like the questions to be as authentic as possible. Therefore, we take some class time to guide the students in developing questions related to concepts we have discussed in our class to balance the prescription and authenticity in questions.

Related to developing questions, a predominant issue we found in our early panel discussions was that preservice teachers focused their questions more on examples from their own schooling, which were predominately stereotypical, uncritical, and not focused on current issues regarding LGBTQ students. Therefore, we ask our students to avoid framing questions or introducing questions with personal or antidotal experiences—unless of course they are directly related to a pertinent school issue. We also want to allow for the construction of exploratory questions, which probe the very foundation of the cultural stereotypes related to the panelists' culture and the panel discussion, in part because these questions also highlight common misconceptions among the dominant culture about LGBTQ culture. These types of questions can simultaneously serve to prepare both the teacher educator and the audience to "hear" the panelists in the discussion, and more importantly allows the class to properly frame these exploratory questions. Such preparation can also limit the potential for "settling" into the comfortable positions of the panelists and audience, thus further disrupting their common language and providing the teacher educator and moderator opportunities for rich patterns of interaction.

Another method we have used to prepare students for a panel discussion on LGBTQ issues in schools is to discuss the concept of "coming out" in LGBTQ culture. We have found this is important in addressing generalizations or misconceptions about "coming out." Also, a preparatory discussion of "coming out" prepares preservice teachers better to discuss how to handle their future students "coming out" in schools and ask more precise questions of the panelists. From early panel discussions, we found that our preservice teachers commonly thought of "coming out" as a one-time event for individuals who identify as LGBTQ. When they learned from the panelists that it is not a one-time event, and is, instead, an ongoing process, the discussion became focused on comparing how many times the panelists have "come out." Therefore, a discussion of "coming out" as an ongoing process, due to normative structures in society and schools, significantly helps frame the central LGBTQ issues in schools, as well as why we are having a panel discussion in our course.

During the Panel Discussion

In many ways, while there are clear benefits in fostering discussions of diversity in a teacher education classroom, there can also be repercussions in furthering the Otherization of social groups. North (2010) asserts, "Pedagogies aimed at addressing human difference in the classroom benefit from caution, humility, and consideration of the potential reverberations of our instructional choices on the marginalized social groups represented in our curricula before we dive in" (376). As teacher educators, it is precisely this humility and caution that should factor into our preservice teaching courses, to discuss both purposefully and respectfully.

During the panel discussion, there are a few practices we have found to be helpful in maintaining the purpose and respect of the session, which also build upon the preservice teachers' preparation for the panel discussion.

One of our overall goals of the panel discussion is to break down the binary of dominant and marginalized cultures. We have found that starting the panel discussion in small groups, with one panelist per group, aids in breaking down this binary. When we start in a more personal and intimate setting of a small group, it makes the discussion more comfortable, but most importantly it does not encourage the positioning between panelists and audience for the discussion. We have also found that in the course of the panel discussion it is important for each panelist to provide insights to each question. This helps provide multiple perspectives on each question, and aids in dispelling any generalizations or stereotypes that our students may have about LGBTQ culture, by understanding that there are multiple experiences within the culture. Lastly, we would like to remind the instructors that while you may want to allow the discussion to be as student-generated as possible, it is important to manage the discussion to make sure the limited time you have for a panel discussion is focused on the pertinent LGBTQ issues.

After the Panel Discussion

In order to achieve the disruption of generalizations and misconceptions, it is vital to consider the reverberations of the discussion itself, and to plan for a semi-structured activity after the panel discussion to provide opportunities for applying what preservice teachers learned in the panel discussion. There are a few activities that we have found help the preservice teacher debrief the panel discussion and apply what they "heard" from the LGBTQ panelists. The goal for each of the activities we engage in with preservice teachers after the panel discussion is focused on reflection for action. Ideally, all aspects of preparing for and engaging in the panel discussion would be to transform and shape our preservice teachers' future actions. Therefore, we debrief what they learned and focus on how it will inform their future practices. For example some common questions we ask are:

- What did the panelists want you to know or take away from the discussion?
- What did you learn? How will you use what you learned as a teacher?
- What is your role as a teacher in negotiating LGBTQ issues and the normative structures of schools and society?
- From the panel discussion, what would you share with current teachers, your cooperating teachers, or your future colleagues who are less informed about LGBTQ issues in schools?
- What else would you like to know, or was there anything you felt was missing from the discussion?

Lastly, we have found that assigning an inquiry assignment or project is vital to really helping the preservice teachers understand how to apply what they have learned in the panel discussion. We ask students to research the LGBTQ-related issues (Gay–Straight Alliances, discrimination policies, bullying policies, etc.) at schools or districts they would potentially want to work at. We ask them to then assess the way the school or district is addressing the issues, which includes looking at other schools' handling of similar issues and thinking about the panel discussion. Then, as a product of their inquiry, we ask them to create an action plan to address one of the issues, and improve policies or awareness regarding the issue. The goal is to have them apply what they learned from the panel discussion to update or improve school policies.

Conclusion

There is a delicate nature in the format of discussing critical issues that can be improved for the benefit of the students, panelists, and teachers. Developing the skills necessary to carry on meaningful and deliberate discussions should always be a focal point for teacher education programs, and as a method, it must be completed in a humble, cautionary manner, examining the potential ramifications of culturally insensitive or stereotype-perpetuating discussions (North 2010). We, as educators, should strive for discussions focusing on critical and democratic dialogue, to give those who are often unheard the chance to speak, and those who fail to listen the chance to hear.

Note

1 This study identifies "An act of personal stereotyping can be defined as a speech act that is (a) part of a specific storyline, (b) used in order to position both speaker and the object of the stereotyping and (c) draws upon social representations of the stereotyped objects (the cultural stereotypes) which are available in certain moral orders" (VanLagenhove and Harre 1995, 366–367).

References

Berlak, Ann C. 2004. "Confrontations and Pedagogy: Cultural Secrets, Trauma, and Emotion in Anti-Oppressive Pedagogies." In *Democratic Dialogue in Education: Troubling Speech, Disturbing Silence*, edited by Megan Boler, 123–144. New York: Peter Lang.

Boler, Megan. 2004. "All Speech is Not Free: The Ethics of 'Affirmative Action Pedagogy'." In *Democratic Dialogue in Education: Troubling Speech, Disturbing Silence*, edited by M. Boler, 3–14. New York: Peter Lang.

Burr, Vivien. 1995. *An Introduction in Social Constructionism*. London: Routledge.

Cotten-Huston, Annie L., and Bradley M. Waite. 1999. "Anti-Homosexual Attitudes in College Students." *Journal of Homosexuality* no. 38 (3): 117–133. doi: 10.1300/J082v38n03_07.

Davies, Brownwyn, and Rom Harre. 1990. "Positioning: The Discursive Production of Selves." *Journal for the Theory of Social Behavior* no. 20 (1): 43–63.

Green, S., P. Dixon, and V. Gold-Neil. 1993. "The Effects of a Gay/Lesbian Panel Discussion on College Attitudes toward Gay Men, Lesbians and Persons with AIDS." *Journal of Sex Education and Therapy* no. 19: 47–63.

Gutman, Amy, and Dennie Thompson. 1996. *Democracy and Disagreement.* Cambridge, MA: Harvard University Press.

Jones, Amanda. 2004. "Talking Cure: The Desire for Dialogue." In *Democratic Dialogue in Education: Troubling Speech, Disturbing Silence*, edited by M. Boler, 57–68. New York: Peter Lang.

Levine, Peter. 2008. "A Public Voice for Youth: The Audience Problem in Digital Media and Civic Education." In *Civic Life Online: Learning How Digital Media Can Engage Youth*, 119–138. Cambridge, MA: MIT Press.

North, Connie E. 2010. "Threading Stitches to Approach Gender Identity, Sexual Identity, and Difference." *Equity & Excellence in Education* no. 43 (3): 375–387. doi: 10.1080/10665684.2010.491415.

Reyes, Angela. 2001. "Culture, Identity, and Asian American Teens: A School Disctrict Conference Panel Discussion." *Working Papers in Educational Linguistics* no. 17 (1–2): 65–81.

Shotter, John. 1989. "Social Accountability and the Social Construction of 'You'." In *Texts of Identity*, edited by J. Shotter and K. J. Gergen, 133–151. London: Sage.

VanLagenhove, Luk, and Rom Harre. 1995. "Cultural Stereotypes and Positioning Theory." *Journal for the Theory of Social Behavior* no. 24 (4): 359–372.

12

QUEER EARTH

Troubling Dirt, Humanness, Gender Assumptions, and Binaries to Nurture Bioculturally Responsive Curricula

Marna Hauk

> Land is the place where lessons are taught, where Wisdom abides; where we learn lessons about life and death from the seed broken open in darkness, dying in order to come to life in a different form, and from the compost which teaches us that decay is needed for life's richness. Land is the place where we are healed when no words can comfort or explain. It is the place where we are taught about and find community; where everything is connected to everything else, and nothing exists independently; the place where everything feeds on and depends on the other.
>
> Jeanne Clark (2012)

Queer-ness is not just an intellectual category, and unlearning homophobia is not just a passing fad. In the 1990s, I lived in womyn's land community for two years, then in a feminist intentional community for another two, before I apprenticed in another womyn's natural land community. In Oregon, the seizures of the conservative right to actively promote discrimination against LGBTQ communities were producing violent outcomes. Two lesbians had just been murdered in southern Oregon, so a friend sponsored me taking a self-defense class before the move to increase my safety. I had been menaced, chased, and harassed while living on queer intentional community outside of Portland during the time of great activity of the Oregon Citizen's Alliance.

For some of us, our lives depend on the learnings of queer-ness, the unlearning of homophobia, and cultural shifts. Certainly, given the high levels of bullying and epidemic of queer teen suicide (e.g., Honig 2012), the questions are as relevant today as they were two decades ago.

It was my background in natural building, particularly in an ancient practice[1] of mixing dirt, sand, and straw with water (called "cob"), and in permaculture ecological design that brought my invitation to the school. Ultimately, it was the queer, feminist context of my learning and the transgressions of being into dirt, troubling gender as a queer in construction that brought many levels of success and deep learning to the project.

Queer Land/Queer Earth

The current industrial-growth cultural matrix positions the land and the Earth as dangerous, queer, and subversive. Queer land and queer earth are used here to convey this reclaimed space at the intersection of literal and virtual "queerness" and land-based spaces and earth/eco-education practices. Queer/querying extends the position of queer peoples and the culturally liberating practices of bending, questioning, and fluidizing of industrial growth culture's rigidity, conformity, and oppression. Inspired by feminist theory, queer theory offers "a resistance to orthodoxy – expounding, elaborating, and promoting alternative ways of being, knowing, and narrating experience – through scholarship, through embodied being, through social and political interventions in 'regimes of the normal'" (Alexander 2008, 108). Queering should include polyvocal voices and the experiences of differently positioned queers and avoid erasing difference (Alexander 2008, Anzaldúa 1987). This impulse includes Sykes's (2011) exploration of how "queer curriculum studies involves listening for ways I am implicated and complicit with White supremacy on theoretical, political and personal levels" (29–30). Thus, queer earth and queer dirt theorizing also involves the evocation of the term "queer" to "spin the term outward along dimensions that can't be subsumed under gender and sexuality at all: the ways that race, ethnicity, postcolonial nationality criss-cross with these and other identity-constituting, identity-fracturing discourses" (Sedgewick 1993, 9).

Literature in critical pedagogy lacks queer voices (Warniment and Longhurst 2012). Outside of educational research, some theoreticians have detailed the complex intersection of queer and ecology (see Mortimer-Sandilands 2010), including troubling the cultural dialectic "that pits the perverse, polluted, and the degenerate against the fit, the healthy, and the natural" (3).

Some such literature, however, misses the importance of the long herstory of actual queer and lesbian land communities, which have been an ongoing source of educational experimentation in direct, immersive, experiential, and biocultural learning. This tradition subverts or queers the traditional association of wilderness with heteromasculinity (Mortimer-Sandilands 2010, 14). These queer land experiments, along with the subversive nature of dirt (embodiment/power) in industrial culture and education contexts, indicate how the practices of reclaiming and reconceiving the margins and marginalization as the fertile edges and ecotones of queer earth and human/nature fusion can support vitalizing educational praxis.

Ecologies of Place in Education

Queering land and dirt intersects with critical pedagogies of place and sustainability educational theorizing that find in ecopedagogies opportunities to pursue the twinned goals of decolonization and reinhabitation in the wild nature of urban *and* rural contexts. David Gruenewald (2003, now Greenwood) synthesizes Freire (1970/2005) and Bowers (2011) in a critical pedagogy of place in which both reinhabitation and decolonization are active means of meaningfully embodying engagement with(in) place. Andrea Olsen's (2002) *Body and Earth: An Experiential Guide* offers one of the most practical, creative curriculum books for exploring the personal and embodied connections between dirt, body, and earth: decolonizing and reinhabitating at the scale of the body. Grace Lee Boggs, a Detroit feminist eco-organizer pointed out:

> At a time when we desperately need to heal the Earth and build durable economies and healthy communities, too many of our schools and universities are stuck in the processes and practices used to industrialize the Earth in the nineteenth and twentieth centuries.
>
> (Boggs and Kurashige 2011, 149)

She succeeded in innovating inner-city Detroit programs that attend to sustainability and social justice built on community-based pedagogies of liberation, creativity, empowerment, and presence:

> We need to create a much more intimate connection between intellectual development and practical activity, to root students and faculty in their communities and natural habitats, and to engage them in the kind of real problem solving in their localities that nurtures a love of place and provides practice in creating … sustainable economies, equality, and community.
>
> (157)

Boggs was successful at organizing exactly these intersections that "root students and faculty" while nurturing ecological and economic viability.

Bioculturally Responsive Curricula and Gaian Methods

Dirt (earth) subverts: it queers gender, disrupts binaries around civilization and wilderness, and emplaces rural islands of queer empowerment safe from heteronormative urbanity/hegemony. Scholarship and theorizing at the "edge" or intersection of dirt touches on the grounding theories of deep ecology and radical biocentrism (Mathews 2008), place (Gruenewald and Smith 2008), and ecojustice informed pedagogies (Bowers 2011, Martusewicz, Edmundson, and Lupinacci 2011) as well as educational approaches informed by people–nature fusions such as indigenous ecological knowledges (e.g., Cajete 2000, 2008), biocultural diversity (Maffi and Woodley 2010), and ecopsychology (e.g., Buzzell and Chalquist 2009, Clinebell 1996), which represent a spectrum of strategies to include the more-than-human in solidarity with social justice in anti-hegemonic pedagogies.

Queer earth helps inspire us to extend culturally responsive curriculum approaches to be *bioculturally responsive* (Hauk 2014). Gaian methodologies are a large container of these methods and reflect this movement to radically decenter humans from agency in educational design and research. This move includes the (queer/transgressive) practice of accessing, honoring, and including the ecocentric presence of place and the planetary as independent voices in polyvocal classroom practice. The work includes the pivot of focusing on spaces of common intention for engaged solidarity and action (Mohanty 2003). Particularly, "as the Western notion of 'progress' continues to devour life-sustaining ecosystems, it is vital that indigenous peoples and their allies, including critical scholars, struggle for political, economic, and educational reforms that recognize the inherent connection between the cultural and ecological crises" (Grande 2004, 80).

Places of greatest biological diversity also reflect the greatest linguistic thus cultural diversity (Maffi 2004). This combination of biological, ecological, and cultural diversity is called biocultural diversity. Research in

> ethnobiology and ethnoecology … is bringing about an increasingly rigorous understanding of the human–environment relationships … projects … seek to cross the natural–social science divide by adopting a biocultural perspective and acknowledges such research requires inter- and transdisciplinary training and approaches as well as inclusion of indigenous local scientists and knowledge holders.
>
> (22–23)

Bioculturally responsive curriculum can include education that actively decolonizes the practices of erasure of long time, highly skilled and sustainable plant use and cultivation by which indigenous knowledge holders, cultures, and practitioner-scientists continue to live in biocultural symbiotic thriving with complex ecologies (Deur and Turner 2005) and thus complicate notions of "pristine wilderness" and trouble the continuing assaults on first nations' sovereignty and access perpetrated now in the name of conservation. Bioculturally responsive curriculum draws in place and communities as well as ecological justice to the terrain of curriculum consideration, queering human-centric bias that would otherwise prevail.

This biocultural diversity approach is important in addressing the human-centrism of the movement regarding culturally responsive curriculum. Bioculturally responsive curriculum weaves also in a biocultural, human/ecology, ecotonal perspective that queers the boundaries between bios and culture. Thus, biocultural diversity requires an understanding of human cultures that includes an earthy grounding and attention to place affiliation, land, earth, dirt, ecology, sustainability, and embodiment. Approaches to bioculturally responsive curriculum include situating curriculum in place, emplaced identity, embodied relationality with the more-than-human within which we are collaborating to thrive, and cultivating and honoring human-place sustainable biocultural practices. Bioculturally responsive curriculum invites us to get down and dirty in appropriate and non-appropriating modes with such practices as natural building, organic gardening, wildcrafting medicinals, cultivating permacultural practices, honoring indigenous histories and practices of thriving in particular places, while decolonizing the curriculum and undermining human-supremacist curricular approaches along with racism, classism, gender constructions, ableism, colonizing, dominating, and cultural supremacist assumptions. Bioculturally responsive curriculum cultivates in students precious awareness of and connection with the subtle, evident, tangible possibilities of biocultural embedment and thriving, access to an enlarged socioecological intelligence, and skills in collaboration (with both human and non-human), as well as the intellectual skills of transdisciplinarity.

Queering binaries draws down the false conflicts between nature/nurture and nature/culture. For example, Watkins and Shulman (2008) use ecological restoration and landscape regeneration as a central model for psychologies of liberation. Human/non-human binaries dissolve with Gaian education methods and bioculturally responsive curricula offer more robust, post-anthropocentric, earth–human fusion of truly queer pedagogies. Future vistas include dismantling career day itself; the more important question, along the lines of *Thinking Like a Mountain* (Seed et al. 1988) becomes, not what human-identified function we will fulfill within capitalist production; rather, what species (plural) will we be/support/become?

Careers and Gender Stereotype Liberation

Social Cognitive Career Theory (SCCT) explores how "social forces may influence women's career development and create gender segregation in different types of occupations" (Williams 2010, iii). This includes questioning social forces shaping core cognitive variables, including outcome expectations and self-efficacy (Williams 2010). Recent meta-analysis for social cognitive career theory, particularly self-efficacy, showed significant correlations for self-efficacy with self-esteem, vocational identity, peer support, vocational outcome expectation, and career indecision variables and deemed gender and career choice as having a pervading, multifaceted influence, by shaping learning opportunities and experiences (Choi et al. 2012, see 446).

A great deal of the educational literature clarifies the distinction between gender and biological sex (e.g., Carl 2012, HRC 2011–2015, Killerman 2015) with its known complexities at the transgendered intersections. Holding beliefs about biological gender theory was linked to self-stereotyping, with harmful consequences for women: "biological gender theory was linked to stronger gender self-stereotyping tendency (as reflected by greater endorsements of negative feminine traits and slower reaction time in denying stereotypic feminine traits)" (Coleman and Hong 2008, 34). Additionally, North (2010) confirms:

> pushing students and ourselves to assume responsibility for our readings of texts and the world can effectively challenge harmful beliefs toward human difference. Due to the performative and, thus, unpredictable nature of anti-oppressive education, 1 argue that this responsibility includes undertaking ongoing, critical investigations of our teaching practices so that we do not inadvertently reinforce harmful beliefs and practices.
>
> (375)

English (2003) discusses strategies for "moments in which our learning about specific and historical identities also involves unlearning identities as fixed, ahistorical certainties" (5).

Some research has found that avoiding referencing the frame of gendered occupations can avoid further disempowering women. Rudman and Phelan (2010) found that exposure to traditional gender role priming reinforced stereotypes and "reduced interest in masculine occupations" for women (192). Surprisingly, they also found exposure to non-traditional role priming also created discouraging effects:

> exposure to nontraditional roles (e.g., a female surgeon and a male nurse) decreased women's leadership self-concept and lowered their interest in masculine occupations, suggesting that female vanguards (i.e., successful women in male-dominated careers) can provoke upward comparison threat, rather than inspire self-empowerment … priming either traditional or nontraditional gender roles can threaten progress toward gender equality, albeit through different mechanisms (stereotypes or self-concept, respectively).
>
> (192)

Other research found emergent effects at the group level reinforcing social dominance orientations from patriarchy by self-stereotyping (Schmitt and Wirth 2009). These research insights would argue, beyond simply switching traditional gender stereotypes in relation to occupation to subvert them, a strategy of liberating learners from gender stereotypes altogether would be a more effective strategy.

Related literatures include how feminist discourse and gender theory can empower performance artists, break down gender socialization limitations, and enhance performance and collaboration (Chaffin, Crawford, and Imreh 2002).

Also, queer discourses (including male to female discourses) provide sufficient disruptions to gender-sex fixities that they offer other models; for example, "a chronotopic model, by which the body is conceptualized as a process existing in both time and space, [as] more useful in counter-hegemonic theory" (Wilton 2000, 237). Identities emerge and flow out from experience and action informed by social and personal contexts; identities are more fluid and emergent rather than fixed facts (Wetherell 2009).

Through the Window

As a queer, feminist educator with European farming ancestors and a background in intentional feminist, land-based, queer communities, I came to the middle school classroom through the window; beyond the "Art and Ecology" classroom window was a flat grass courtyard for the entire middle school. The innovative seventh grade teacher, Mr. Klockee,[2] wanted to turn the featureless courtyard into a creative learning space.

There were several transgressive elements to the earthen bench-building experience. One of them related to gender and dirt. I had an assumption it would be the middle school young women students who would be more averse to getting dirty mixing the cob. For our mammoth learning bench, we mixed dirt and sand with water, then straw, to conjure our building materials. Mixing the cob is not for the faint of heart, it involves getting barefoot, rolling up cuffs, and plunging up to the ankles in a wet, muddy, stiff mix of clay subsoil and sand, and tromp-dancing.

I was worried the girls would not want to get dirty. I grew up in southern California "behind the Orange Curtain" where (gender) appearance compliance and spotless grooming were requisite to avoid bullying. I was surprised to discover that, in this teaching context, it was some of the boys/young men who didn't want to get dirty. Some eventually brought smocks or garden shirts to protect their teenage gear.

Earth can be the great subversive. Collaborative mixing, making something out of dirt dug from the foundation, and for some the science of mixing the "perfect" batch of cob were so engaging that it was an invitation to break out of suburban gender rules of all varieties. Dirt undermines domestication and reconnects with wilderness. It cultivates category transgression along multiple dimensions: queer/straight; muddy/clean; urban/rural; domesticated-civilized/wild. These students were shoveling and turning compost on a daily basis (still sometimes squealing, "Gross!") and planting native plants in hillocks of dirt. They were building out of dirt: hands in mud, feet in mud. Something larger often came into play on the building site. The booming school garden initiatives are similarly connecting with the subversive and liberatory power of dirt (e.g., Williams and Brown 2012). These types of affirmative, hands-on projects for middle schoolers help prevent the introduction at too early a developmental stage of overpowering statistics regarding earth destruction, the latter of which can actually backfire and create ecophobia in young learners (Sobel 1996).

Career Day

Some time into the project, Mr. Klockee invited me to speak to his class for career day. I brought Jessica,[3] my Americorps volunteer who had been active on the bench-building project. We started out at the front of the classroom, me with my crew cut and dirt-rubbed clothes, and Jessica, a cherry-cheeked, healthy-hiker straight girl, nearly twenty, committed to the earth. We were speaking about being "women in construction," a category that I rarely considered and had no relevance to me unless someone was praising my pickup truck or because of how it allowed me to teach at the Oregon Tradeswomen Network Fair; yet, that category transgression of being "women in construction" opened the door to a very different learning that day.

I had survived high school by being labeled "gender neutral," survived teaching in Portland Public Schools by leveraging students' questions about "What are you, Marna, a boy or a girl?" This was the inevitable question of each class, and I used it as a natural teaching opportunity by answering with other questions and a conversation that was intuitively metacognitive for my 5–8-year-old students: "Why is that an important question?" "What is your guess and why?" "What difference will knowing the answer make?"

This middle school was in a suburban/rural town on the conservative outskirts of a larger metropolitan area, a town of 20,000, over 90 percent white, 1 percent African American, 1 percent Native American, 2.5 percent Asian American, 3 percent Hispanic/Latino, and a small percentage Pacific Islander or mixed race-identified. In particular, I was an anomaly, possibly the first outwardly non-gender conforming queer the students had ever met. The students were curious about how Jessica and I could be women in construction. We defied their reality just by existing. Then the opening happened. Someone asked, "Are there lots of women in construction?"

I took the opportunity to spontaneously re-organize the experience and engage the students. First, I asked for their help thinking through this question of why it was a strange feeling to speak of women in construction. We brainstormed a gender and then what job would be surprising or unusual for that gender. Students generated a list with few surprises: women-fire fighter, men-nurses, women-computer scientist, men-hair stylist, women-nuclear physicist, men-florist or childcare provider. In the literature we might call this surfacing biased assumptions (Denissen 2010). The first step toward gender queering, similar to troubling other dominating categories of structural violence, involves becoming self-aware of (metacognitive with) our own assumptions. The students became excited, even riveted by this discussion. What Bache (2008) calls "a living classroom" experience emerged, one in which the classroom "takes on a life of its own," a living learning arises, a kind of static/ecstatic/resonant process.

Second, I asked those who had offered ideas to line up as "women" or "men," regardless of their own gender, to represent the gender-work category transgression pairing they had proposed. "Women" (stereotypes[4]) lined up on the right of the classroom and "Men" (stereotypes) on the left side, where students "performed" (not the word I used) the gender stereotypes. Some students (regardless of genders) hammed it up. "Women" tip-toed in stiletto heels, swished, and put on lipstick. Some "Men" flexed their muscles. In some instances, the student performing "Male Florist" swished and assumed a "gay" stereotypical affect or the "Female Scientist" began "butching." The students were all engaged, while we constructed the exercise (see Figure 12.1).

Third, I asked students what it felt like in their roles. "I feel like I am on display. I am uncomfortable." "I feel really closed off, like I need to look at the floor." "I feel fabulous" (swish swish)—some were more able to self-reflect than others.

Fourth, I asked them to cross to the other side of the room, switching gender while staying in the same work category role, and then they "strutted" or "bulldogged" their way across before performing their work category in their new gender. I asked again, somatically, what it felt like being in that other gender (see Figure 12.2).

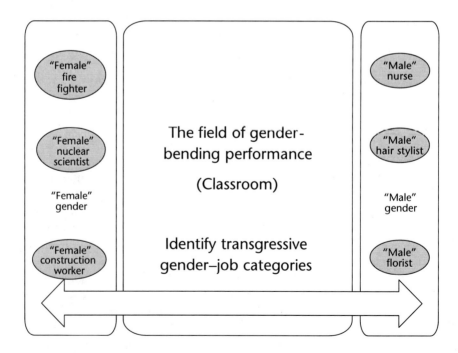

FIGURE 12.1 Identify Transgressive Gender–Job Categories

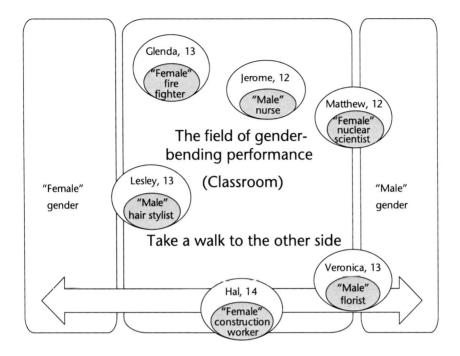

FIGURE 12.2 Take a Walk to the Other Side

Finally, I thanked the contributors and we sat down and debriefed the experience. Many students were thoughtful and/or surprised. They shared feeling energized to talk about this. We discussed why there might be these notions of genders being better at certain jobs or forbidden to do others. Students made the connection regarding anti-category gender behavior and queerness. We discussed examples of how they had seen or experienced different genders actually competently serve in different professions, then reflected on the idea of stereotypes and assumptions (see more discussion below on assumptions), and how they might keep people from being free.

The students were given language about differentiating between biased behavior (to focus on the ___ist behavior rather than thinking of another person as an ___ist),[5] and to offer the difference between discrimination, which has the force of societal structures of enforced inequity behind it, and prejudice. Additionally included were distinctions between gender identity, gender expression, and biological sex (see Killerman 2015).

Mr. Klockee thought this a valuable experience and scheduled Jessica and me to present in five more classes that day, meeting with almost the entire school of seventh and eighth graders on queering gender assumptions, taking "Career Day" to a whole new level of awareness. As one eighth grader, who had not initially seemed to participate as much, stated: "This was the best day of middle school!"

Career Day Findings and Conclusions

Whereas the original example of gender fluid career performances emerged as a spontaneous teaching intervention, it can serve as a case study or demonstration of many lineages of effective pedagogy and reflects extensive research findings in both feminist pedagogy, pedagogy of place, and research on gender and career. Likewise, the mentioned interventions of binary-busting and earth-connecting building with dirt, and queer land research affirm findings in the literature and offer meaningful classroom approaches for what we might term bioculturally responsive curricula.

Significance

This work has important repercussions not only for liberating students from stereotypes regarding gender identity and gender expression—liberating them from what in the current cultural tempo is referred to as "gender jail"—but also for interrupting oppression regarding sexual orientation. Further, this work can catalyze and amplify disrupting cultural stereotyping and supporting student critical thinking and metacognition across unconscious couplings inherent in many oppressive stereotypes. These liberatory habits of mind include self-disruption of internalized hegemonic lenses that extend to include racism, classism, and human domination of natural systems.

This concept applies in the classrooms across dimensions. First, in our explicit curriculum, are we offering a truly diverse, accurate rendering of the talents and capabilities and possibilities of all peoples (and beings)?[6] Second, in our implicit (or performed) curriculum, are we embodying open-mindedness and diverse approaches, honoring the multiple, divergent, and the suppressed? Are we liberating place- and earth-immersion to cultivate contexts of biocultural thriving?

Open-Mindedness

Several key pedagogical concepts apply here, to both the explicit and the implicit curricula, including open-mindedness to avoid dogmatism. Open-mindedness includes, according to the Critical Thinking Foundation (2013),

> the intellectual virtue that involves a willingness to take relevant evidence and argument into account in forming or revising our beliefs and values, especially when there is some reason why we might resist such evidence and argument … It means being critically receptive to alternative possibilities, being willing to think again despite having formed an opinion, and sincerely trying to avoid those conditions and offset those factors which constrain and distort our reflections.
>
> (para. 17)

The willingness to reflect and revise is the hallmark of open-mindedness, which is a core competency in critical thinking. Judy Grahn (2012) advocates for a reflective process favoring adaptive empathy when obversity (extreme or oppositional emotional reactions to cultural difference) might otherwise lead to closed mindedness and conflict.

Dogmatism

Hand in hand with cultivating open-mindedness, including willingness and skills in revising our own thinking, is avoiding dogmatism. Dogmatism is the end-run of closed-mindedness, when we are completely unwilling to self-reflect. We become insistent on sometimes unreflected beliefs. The danger of dogmatism is its insularity, its recursive consistency in a closed system. In complex adaptive systems terms, this means the system has become closed instead of open, and there is an incapability of receiving feedback loops from outside the system. Ambrose (2012) finds that "problems arise when individuals or groups become trapped within a single world view and suffer from thought confinement" also known as "'dogmatic insularity'" (12). This cultivation of adaptive and resilient critical open-mindedness and the release of gender, colonial, human-centric, and other dogmatisms are the site of great promise for bioculturally responsive curriculum including queer dirt encounters and queer earth pedagogy.

Postscript: Ten Years Later

Ten years after the Earth Day school pageant that marked the triumphant completion of the earthen bench-building project in Mama Bear Meadow at the middle school, I ran into Mr. Klockee in town. He told me this traumatizing news: the principal signed a slip of paper, not realizing what it was. During the summer, the grounds crew leveled the entire site: all the design, the intricate tessellation tiles from the math students, the carefully sculpted brown bear snout looking over Mama Bear Meadow. The earthen bench has been leveled.

Never be mistaken, Queer Dirt, our efforts are still tentative and subject to erasure. The dominant paradigm, straight lines, wilderness flattened and dirt erased, will attempt to reassert itself. My solace is the change in the learners themselves, the wild queerness and spaces that have blossomed within them. The life-changing encounters with transformative dirt and the living earth systems—that is a fierce wilderness of possibility that even large machinery cannot flatten. Many of the earthen community spaces I worked on are leveled within five to ten years.

Perhaps we were ahead of our time, but the earth, ever subversive, is never contained. It continues to contest. And when submerged, never doubt, the ground swells and, with the help of bioculturally responsive curriculum, the earth (in/with humans) returns. The promise of subverting gender expression constrictions and refiguring "careers" as climate resilient and bioculturally embedded wise thriving persists. Alexis Pauline Gumbs (2010) offers an ecological approach to polyphonic feminism that imagines this long-arc'd reinhabitation and "intergenerationally accountable" earthly thriving resurgence moving in and through us:

> ***An ecological approach is long-term.*** The intentional practice of growing a vision for a lovingly transformational way of life in an economic system that seeks to make our lives and love unthinkable feels ambitious and risky. It is actually as simple as remembering who we are, what life is, and acting accordingly, for the rest of our lives … and with an intergenerationally accountable relationship to the future with us always.
>
> (4)

Notes

1 Arising multiple times in human invention, including in Wales, Afghanistan, Mesoamerica, parts of Africa, and many other cites globally.
2 Name anonymized.
3 Name anonymized.
4 Throughout this, I never used the word "stereotype."
5 See, for example, a discussion of this strategy in M. K. Kaye/Kantrowitz (2002, 287).
6 Just to avoid anthropocentric approaches, I include "all beings" here to indicate the more than human world and the ways in which systems of domination objectify and narrow the possibilities of animals, geographies, landscapes, and the living system of the planet as well as creating polarity and discrimination in human realms.

References

Alexander, Bryant Keith. 2008. "Queer(y)ing the Postcolonial through the West(ern)." In *Handbook of Critical and Indigenous Methodologies*, edited by Norman K. Denzin, Yvonna S. Lincoln and Linda Tuhiwai Smith, 101–133. Thousand Oaks, CA: Sage.

Ambrose, Don. 2012. "Finding Dogmatic Insularity in the Territory of Various Academic Disciplines." In *How Dogmatic Beliefs Harm Creativity and Higher-Level Thinking*, edited by Don Ambrose and Robert J. Sternberg, 9–25. New York: Routledge.

Anzaldúa, Gloria. 1987. *Borderlands/La Frontera: The New Mestiza*. San Francisco, CA: Spinsters/Aunt Lute.

Bache, Christopher M. 2008. *The Living Classroom: Teaching and Collective Consciousness, SUNY Series in Transpersonal and Humanistic Psychology*. Albany: State University of New York Press.

Boggs, Grace Lee, and Scott Kurashige. 2011. *The Next American Revolution: Sustainable Activism for the Twenty-first Century*. Berkeley, CA: University of California Press.

Bowers, Chet A. 2011. *Perspectives on the Ideas of Gregory Bateson Ecological Intelligence, and Educational Reforms*. Eugene, OR: Ecojustice Press.

Buzzell, Linda, and Craig Chalquist. 2009. *Ecotherapy: Healing with Nature in Mind*. San Francisco, CA: Sierra Club Books.

Cajete, Gregory. 2000. *Native Science: Natural Laws of Interdependence*. Santa Fe, NM: Clear Light.

Cajete, Gregory. 2008. "Seven Orientation for the Development of Indigenous Science Education." In *Handbook of Critical and Indigenous Methodologies*, edited by Norman K. Denzin, Yvonna S. Lincoln and Linda Tuhiwai Smith, 487–496. Los Angeles, CA: Sage.

Carl, John D. 2012. "Gender vs. Sex: What's the Difference?" *Montessori Life: A Publication of the American Montessori Society* no. 24 (1): 26–30.

Chaffin, Roger, Mary Crawford, and Gabriela Imreh. 2002. "VII. Performing Gender." *Feminism & Psychology* no. 12 (2): 182–189.

Choi, Bo Young, Heerak Park, Eunjoo Yang, Seul Ki Lee, Yedana Lee, and Sang Min Lee. 2012. "Understanding Career Decision Self-Efficacy: A Meta-Analytic Approach." *Journal of Career Development* no. 39 (5): 443–460.

Clark, Jeanne. 2012. *The Land*. Garden Digest [cited July 23 2015]. Available from http://www.gardendigest.com/earth.htm.

Clinebell, Howard John. 1996. *Ecotherapy: Healing Ourselves, Healing the Earth: A Guide to Ecologically Grounded Personality Theory, Spirituality, Therapy, and Education*. Minneapolis, MN: Fortress Press.

Coleman, Jill M., and Ying-Yi Hong. 2008. "Beyond Nature and Nurture: The Influence of Lay Gender Theories on Self-Stereotyping." *Self & Identity* no. 7 (1): 34–53. doi: 10.1080/15298860600980185.

Critical Thinking Foundation. 2013. *Open Minded Inquiry* [cited July 23 2015]. Available from http://www.criticalthinking.org/pages/open-minded-inquiry/579.

Denissen, Amy. 2010. "The Right Tools for the Job: Constructing Gender Meanings and Identities in the Male-Dominated Building Trades." *Human Relations* no. 63 (7): 1051–1069.

Deur, Douglas, and Nancy J. Turner. 2005. *Keeping it Living: Traditions of Plant Use and Cultivation on the Northwest Coast of North America*. Seatle: University of Washington Press.

English, Hugh. 2003. "Learning and Unlearning Historical Sexual Identities." *Radical Teacher* (66): 5–9.

Freire, Paulo. 1970/2005. *Pedagogy of the Oppressed*. Translated by M. B. Ramos. 30th Anniversary ed. New York: Continuum. Original edition, 1970. Reprint, 30th Aniversary.

Grahn, Judy. 2012. "An Obverse Approach to Diversity. " In *Association for the Study of Women and Myth*. San Francisco, CA.

Grande, Sandy. 2004. *Red Pedagogy: Native American Social and Political Thought*. Lanham, MD: Rowman & Littlefield.

Gruenewald, David A. 2003. "The Best of Both Worlds: A Critical Pedagogy of Place." *Educational Researcher* (4): 3–12. doi: 10.2307/3700002.

Gruenewald, David A., and Gregory A. Smith. 2008. *Place-Based Education in the Global Age: Local Diversity*. New York: Lawrence Erlbaum.

Gumbs, Alexis Pauline. 2010. "This is What It Sounds Like (An Ecological Approach)." *The Scholar & Feminist Online—Polyphonic Feminisms: Acting in Concert* no. 8 (3).

Hauk, Marna. 2014. "Gaia E/mergent: Earth Regenerative Education Catalyzing Empathy, Creativity, and Wisdom. " Doctoral dissertation, Prescott College, Arizona.

Honig, Megan. 2012. "Speaking Out." *School Library Journal* no. 58 (6): 40.

HRC. 2011–2015. *Sexual Orientation and Gender Identity: Terminology and Definitions*. Human Rights Campaign [cited July 23 2015]. Available from http://www.hrc.org/resources/entry/sexual-orientation-and-gender-identity-terminology-and-definitions.

Kaye/Kantrowitz, Melanie. 2002. "Representation, Entitlement, and Voyeurism: Teaching Across Difference." In *Twenty-first Century Feminist Classrooms: Pedagogies of Identity and Difference*, edited by A. M. Macdonald and S. Sanchez-Casal, 281–298. New York: Palgrave Macmillan.

Killerman, Sam. 2015. *The Genderbread Person v.3.0 [Web log post and edugraphic]* [cited July 26 2015]. Available from http://itspronouncedmetrosexual.com/2015/03/the-genderbread-person-v3/.

Maffi, Luisa. 2004. "Maintaining and Restoring Biocultural Diversity: The Evolution of a Role for Ethnobiology." In *Ethnobotany and Conservation of Biocultural Diversity*, edited by T. J. S. Carlson and L. Maffi, 9–35. New York: The New York Botanical Garden Press.

Maffi, Luisa, and Ellen Woodley. 2010. *Biocultural Diversity Conservation: A Global Sourcebook*. London and Washington, DC: Earthscan.

Martusewicz, Rebecca, Jeff Edmundson, and John Lupinacci. 2011. *Ecojustice Education: Toward Diverse, Democratic and Sustainable Communities*. New York: Routledge.

Mathews, Freya. 2008. "Thinking from within the Calyx of Nature." *Environmental Values* no. 17 (1): 41–65.

Mohanty, Chandra Talpade. 2003. *Feminism without Borders: Decolonizing Theory, Practicing Solidarity*. Durham and London: Duke University Press.

Mortimer-Sandilands, Catriona. 2010. "A Geneology of Queer Ecologies." In *Queer Ecologies: Sex, Nature, Politics, Desire*, edited by C. Mortimer-Sandilands and B. Erickson, 1–48. Bloomington: Indiana University Press.

North, Connie E. 2010. "Threading Stitches to Approach Gender Identity, Sexual Identity, and Difference." *Equity & Excellence in Education* no. 43 (3): 373–387.

Olsen, Andrea. 2002. *Body and Earth: An Experiential Guide*. Foreword by John Elder, Middlebury Bicentennial Series in Environmental Studies. Hanover: Middlebury College Press; University Press of New England.

Rudman, Laurie A., and Julie E. Phelan. 2010. "The Effect of Priming Gender Roles on Women's Implicit Gender Beliefs and Career Aspirations." *Social Psychology* no. 41: 192–202. doi: 10.1027/1864–9335/a000027.

Schmitt, Michael T., and James H. Wirth. 2009. "Evidence that Gender Differences in Social Dominance Orientation Result from Gendered Self-Stereotyping and Group-Interested Responses to Patriarchy." *Psychology of Women Quarterly* no. 33 (4): 429–436.

Sedgewick, Eve K. 1993. *Tendencies*. Durham, NC: Duke University Press.

Seed, John, Joanna Macy, Pat Fleming, and Arne Naess. 1988. *Thinking Like a Mountain: Towards a Council of All Beings*. Santa Cruz, CA: New Society.

Sobel, David. 1996. *Beyond Ecophobia: Reclaiming the Heart in Nature Education*. Great Barrington, MA: Orion Society.

Sykes, Heather. 2011. "Queering Curriculum Studies." *Journal of Curriculum and Pedagogy* no. 8 (1): 29–31.

Warniment, Gwen P., and Jesse M. Longhurst. 2012. "Promise and Pitfalls: Place-based Education and Marginalized Students." In *American Educational Research Association*. Vancouver, BC: AERA.

Watkins, Mary, and Helene Shulman. 2008. *Toward Psychologies of Liberation, Critical Theory and Practice in Psychology and the Human Sciences*. New York: Palgrave Macmillan.

Wetherell, Margaret. 2009. *Theorizing Identities and Social Action, Identity Studies in the Social Sciences*. New York: Palgrave Macmillan.

Williams, Christine Marie. 2010. "Gender in the Development of Career Related Learning Experiences." Dissertation/Thesis, University of Akron, Ann Arbor, OH.

Williams, Dilafruz R., and Jonathan D. Brown. 2012. *Learning Gardens and Sustainability Education: Bringing Life to Schools and Schools to Life*. New York: Routledge.

Wilton, Tamsin. 2000. "Out/performing Our Selves: Sex, Gender and Cartesian Dualism." *Sexualities* no. 3 (2): 237–254. doi: 10.1177/136346000003002008.

DÉNOUEMENT

Speaking Up

Marni E. Fisher and Veronica E. Bloomfield

As the finale of our book, we decided to engage in a dialogue of concluding thoughts reflecting our journey throughout the creation of this book. Thus, this final chapter wears the non-traditional molds of our interludes and engages in mapping through rhizomatic dialogue inspired by Bakhtin (1981) and Deleuze and Guattari (1987) while mimicking the dialogic forms of hooks (1994) and SooHoo et al. (2004).

VERONICA: Speaking up and taking action is a very personal choice. How we speak up, when we speak up, and to whom we do the speaking will vary from person to person, moment to moment. Taking action can start with small steps. We might start with reading a book, initiating a conversation, being a listener, or becoming a trusted friend. Taking action can happen quietly, by putting a pink triangle or rainbow sticker on your door. It can mean having a reputation, by word of mouth, that you are someone students can trust. Or taking action may mean joining PFLAG, starting a club, getting out your bullhorn, being loud and proud and publicly unwavering in your commitment for social justice and safe schools. The way that you take action must be something that you feel comfortable with; it must be something that you can live with, and stand by, and feel proud.

MARNI: Speaking up is also about listening. It can be about looking for silenced voices, and about creating spaces of safety, spaces where voices can be heard. In education today, both teachers and students have been silenced by standardization, marketing practices (Apple 2006) and scripted lessons (Ede 2006) adhering to an efficiency model of education where children are treated as products. As educators, we need to see children as unique and diverse, embrace all forms of diversity within the classroom, and recognize hegemonic and heternormative patterns. Instead of allowing the majority to define diversity and diverse groups as Other, "we need to develop our understanding of difference by creating a situation in which hitherto marginalized groups can name themselves, speak for themselves, and participate in defining the terms of interaction, a situation in which we can construct an understanding of the world that is sensitive to difference" (Hartsock 1987/2013, 375).

VERONICA: I remember at the onset of this book project, Dr. Wilson said to me, "Because you are working on a book like this, you may get pigeonholed as a scholar. Some people will assume you are a lesbian because your name is on the book."

MARNI: She didn't warn me. (Laughing.) She just invited me on board. I dislike the idea of labeling, especially external labeling. Status "is constructed through social processes in which categories of people are (1) named, (2) aggregated and disaggregated, (3) dichotomized and stigmatized, and (4) denied the attributes valued in the culture" (Gordon and Rosenblum 2001, 6). One of the strengths of the term "LGBTQ" is you can choose your own label, if desired.

VERONICA: This brings to mind the privilege of passing. Individuals who can pass as straight, middle class, and/or white, for example, garner more social privileges than those who cannot. Claiming a label and risking the loss of privilege, status, safety, and employment, among other losses, are things I have never had to grapple with as a straight, middle class "white" woman.

MARNI: I refuse to identify myself in terms of heteronormativity and/or LGBTQ. This is a conscious choice. I have recently been forced to identify my (dis) ability over and over. While my hearing loss affects how I teach, how I work, it does not, ultimately, reduce my performance as a teacher. The directionality of my sexual orientation is none of your business, nor does it affect how I perform my job, what I research, or how I write. It does not change my passion for creating alternative spaces in education for all student and teacher voices—multicultural, (dis)abled, LGBTQ, or otherwise.

VERONICA: Your choice to rebuke labels, despite any privilege you may have been able to acquire by conforming to heteronormative standards, seems like an act of solidarity with individuals who suffer at the hands of gay bashing, gender bias, and bullying. I know you mentioned that it is none of anyone's business how you express and identify yourself, yet I am curious as to what further implications this has beyond a personal level. Have you intentionally decided to trouble the entire idea of sexual expression and sexual identification via un-labeling?

MARNI: I suspect my choice of "un-labeling" has more to do with my long study of silencing, of the things said without words, and of voice … not to mention my love of intersections, liminalities, and fuzzy spaces.

VERONICA: Typically, people feel safer when categorization can take place, and when someone intentionally occupies a fuzzy space and/or refuses to be categorized, it can make me question my own space. If I cannot place you, then I may feel displaced. In purposefully un-identifying, you inhabit those fuzzy spaces, shining a light on how other categories and labels are shakier than we think. My category may be fuzzier than I think it is, or I may realize the category itself is completely illusory.

MARNI: Then again, by occupying a fuzzy space, it is also safer to stay silent. It becomes harder to speak up when others categorize me, even if I do not internalize that categorization. Or maybe I have just been schooled in silence. Perhaps that is why I am always searching for what is unseen, unheard, and unspoken—all of which exist as ignored fuzzy spaces.

VERONICA: I adhere to a more conventional gender performance. I have attempted to use my position of privilege as a heterosexual person, living in a heterodominant culture, as a means to promote equity and tolerance through personal and professional relationships. As an educator, I have used my position as a member of the dominant culture in ways that allow for and encourage a multiplicity of gender expressions and sexual identities in the classroom. I think each of our positionalities indicates there are many different ways to address the social construction of gender and sexuality, both personally and within academia.

MARNI: Talking about gender is never a simple discussion about male and female. Gender is a complicated conversation, and the amorphous dance between concept and form and the need for "subjective and social reconstruction"[1] of concepts could—and should—be applicable to the intricate dance between gender, expression, sexuality, and identity (Killerman 2015, Stiffler 2014).

VERONICA: This brings to mind the unending and ever-evolving nature of learning. Knowledge is not static; it is a dynamic and progressive endeavor that invites the learner to continue to grow, examine, and revise what we thought we knew (or didn't know).

MARNI: Arborescent[2] (and hegemonic) discussions are always dangerous. Applying this type of thinking to the male/female and gay/straight conversation is both dichotomous and false. Reproductive equipment aside, the discussion that ensues needs to include the wide differences in expression, identity, and attraction, which may be entirely separate from biological sex (Killerman 2015, Stiffler 2014). Additionally, the assumption that LGBTQ is only about sexuality and sexual orientation allows different groups to denounce sexuality while allowing for the continued gendering of male roles into the gender straitjacket (Pollack 1999), bullying based on heteronormative pressure, sexualization and objectification of women, and promotion of the rape culture.

VERONICA: What this experience has taught me is that many of the terms I continue to use about LGBTQ issues are outdated. For example, I had not heard the terms "cisgender" or "intersex." Even as an ally, my understandings and conceptualizations needed updating and expanding.

MARNI: As a theorist, I have enjoyed how this book has expanded my knowledge base and study into queer theory, which bucks conventional thinking and taught how gendering patterns and heteronormativity affect so many other areas. The more I study, the more I find that the world is interconnected…

It is here that we leave you—one conversation ending as another begins. The dance continues as we learn new steps, find our own rhythms, and embrace the challenges and accomplishments that accompany us on our way.

We, your co-editors, conclude the book on much the same note. This conversation is not finished, the dialogue goes on. Here we invoke Freire's (2000) concept of "unfinishedness":

> The real roots of the political nature of education are to be found in the educability of the human person. This educability, in turn, is grounded in the radical unfinishedness of the human condition and in our consciousness of this unfinished state.

(58)

The ending is unfinished, our learning is unfinished, and the work of advocacy for LGBTQ students, colleagues, and families remains—unfinished, and ongoing. Dance on!

Notes

1 Pinar (2012), in discussing curriculum theory, refers to the need for complicated conversation that is "variable in theme and form," portending to "subjective and social reconstruction" (227).
2 Deleuze and Guattari (1987) use the term "arborescent" to describe reoccurring patterns within Western thinking: the "creation" of "new" thoughts/ideas are really based upon duplicating previously established patterns.

References

Apple, Michael W. 2006. *Educating the "Right" Way: Markets, Standards, God, and Inequality.* 2nd ed. New York: Routledge.

Bakhtin, Mikail M. 1981. *The Dialogic Imagination: Four Essays by M. M. Bakhtin.* Translated by Michael Holquist and C. Emmerson. Austin, TX: University of Minnesota Press.

Deleuze, Gilles, and Feliz Guattari. 1987. *A Thousand Plateaus: Capitalism and Schizophrenia.* Minneapolis: University of Minnesota Press.

Ede, Anita. 2006. "Scripted Curriculum: Is It a Prescription for Success?" *Childhood Education* no. 83 (1): 29–32.

Freire, Paulo. 2000. *Pedagogy of the Oppressed*. 30th anniversary ed. New York: Continuum.

Gordon, Beth O., and Karen E. Rosenblum. 2001. "Bringing Disability into the Sociological Frame: A Comparison of Disability with Race, Sex, and Sexual Orientation Statuses." *Disability & Society* no. 16 (1): 5–19. doi: 10.1080/09687590020020831.

Hartsock, Nancy. 1987/2013. "A Theory of Power for Women?" In *Social Theory: The Multicultural, Global, and Classic Readings*, edited by Charles Lemert, 375–378. Philedelphia, PA: Westview Press.

hooks, bell. 1994. *Teaching to Transgress: Education as the Practice of Freedom*. New York: Routledge.

Killerman, Sam. 2015. *The Genderbread Person v.3.0 [Web log post and edugraphic]* [cited July 26 2015]. Available from http://itspronouncedmetrosexual.com/2015/03/the-genderbread-person-v3/.

Pinar, William. 2012. *What is Curriculum Theory?* 2nd ed., Studies in Curriculum Theory. New York and London: Routledge.

Pollack, William S. 1999. *Real Boys: Rescuing Our Sons from the Myths of Boyhood*. New York: Henry Holt.

SooHoo, Suzanne, Penny Bryan, Don Cardinal, Delores Gaunty Porter, Jan Osborn, Jeff Sapp, Susie Westin, Tom Wilson, and Chapman University Social Justice Consortium. 2004. *Essays on Urban Education: Critical Consciousness, Collaboration, and the Self*. Creskill, NJ: Hampton Press.

Stiffler, A. 2014. 5 Things You Should Know About Your Agender Acquaintance. *Everyday Feminism Magazine* [cited November 16 2015]. Available at: http://everydayfeminism.com/2014/07/5-things-about-agender/.

CONTRIBUTORS

Markus Bidell, Ph.D., is an Associate Professor at Hunter College in the Educational Foundations and Counseling Department. He trains mental health and school counselors and works with teacher educators on supporting the psychosocial health and academic success of students. Markus is a certified school counselor and licensed mental health counselor in New York State. His research focuses on LGBT psychosocial, education, and mental health disparities among youth and adults.

Veronica E. Bloomfield, Ph.D., is an adjunct instructor at Chapman University and California State University, Los Angeles. She holds Master's degrees in Cultural Studies and Education from Claremont Graduate University. Veronica earned her doctorate in Education from Chapman University in 2013. Her recent publications include "A Homegrown Methodology: Cultural Intuition and Connected Knowing" in *Culturally Responsive and Socially Responsible Research Methodology*, edited by Suzanne SooHoo, Mere Berryman, and Ann Nevins; and, with Anna V. Wilson "But What about Me: Listening to the Silenced Voices of Children," in book one of the trilogy *The Hope for Audacity: From Cynicism to Hope in Educational Leadership and Policy*, edited by Lilia Monzo and Ann Mertz. She has worked in the field of education as a classroom teacher, site-based literacy coach, county-wide literacy specialist, and educational consultant on equity, diversity, and advocacy for English Learners. She is a multicultural educator whose research focuses on culture, identity, curriculum theory, feminist methodologies, and disrupting "whiteness."

Cynthia H. Brock, Ph.D., is Lecturer in Literacy at the University of South Australia and a Wyoming Excellence in Higher Education Endowed Chair in

Literacy Education. Her primary teaching interests include literacy instruction for children in the middle and upper-elementary grades, literacy and diversity, and qualitative methods. She studies the literacy learning of upper-elementary children from diverse cultural and linguistic backgrounds. Her current work focuses on disciplinary literacy teaching and learning in the elementary grades. She also explores how to work with preservice and in-service teachers to foster literacy learning for upper-elementary children from diverse backgrounds.

James S. Brown, M.Ed., is a doctoral candidate in Curriculum Studies at Indiana University, defending his dissertation in 2015. His research focuses on social studies and international education. He works on civic education initiatives at the Center for International Education, Development & Research at Indiana University.

J. Spencer Clark, Ph.D., is an Assistant Professor at Utah State University. His research focuses on the concept of agency in civic or social education, experiential education, and teacher education. He develops curriculum and leads professional developments that focus on deliberation and discussion of controversial public issues.

Danné E. Davis, Ph.D., is an Associate Professor of Elementary Education at Montclair State University (MSU) and recipient of numerous awards including the National Association for Multicultural Education 2011 G. Pritchy Smith Multicultural Educator of the Year and MSU 2013 Faculty/Staff LGBTQ Ally of the Year. She has published and presented various papers about diversity in teacher education. Currently, she is examining LGBTQ children's literature and teacher candidates' awareness of and responsiveness to the narratives.

Kris De Pedro, Ph.D., is Assistant Professor of Educational Leadership at Chapman University. His scholarly interests are educational reform, LGBTQ youth, and military-connected students. Before his research career, he was a special education teacher in Los Angeles and New York City.

Marni E. Fisher, Ph.D., teaches Education courses at Chapman University and English Composition at Saddleback College. Her background includes a doctorate in education with a culture and curriculum studies emphasis, Master's degrees in Educational Leadership and English with a teaching emphasis, an MFA in creative writing, 15 years of studying studio arts, 12 years of K–8 teaching in all subjects, and five years in administration. She was junior editor for *Issues in Teacher Education* Journal 2014–2015, and she has presented over 20 times at conferences. Her current research interests revolve around developing prism theory as a new theoretical framework for studying education and testing prismatic inquiry as an educational research methodology across topics such as social justice, leadership, democratic education, curriculum, subjectivity, engaged pedagogy, active engagement, and educational theory.

Tina Gutierez-Schmich, M.S., has taught, supported, and coached teachers in early education, K–12, and higher education for the past 25 years. She is currently the Equity Coordinator for a school district, and doctoral candidate in education studies at the University of Oregon. Her primary research interests are teacher knowledge and preparation through the lens of post-structuralism, feminist pragmatism, and queer theory. Her research examines public and conflict pedagogy as strategies in teacher education. In 2010 Tina and Julia Heffernan developed UOTeachOUT, an annual education studies conference on gender identity and sexual orientation issues in education (http://uoteachout.com/).

Marna Hauk, Ph.D. in Sustainability Education 2014, serves on the faculty of Prescott College. She directs the Institute for Earth Regenerative Studies (www.earthregenerative.org) in Portland, Oregon with programs at the intersection of creativity, ecological restoration, and the living wisdom traditions. Her methods include Gaian methods, complexity research design, arts-based research, and mixed methods. Her research areas include queer climate resilience action, earth empathy, geometries of liberation, wisdom school design, and ecosocial regenerative creativity. She is committed to education and action for Gaian flourishing.

Julia Heffernan, Ph.D., taught middle and high school social studies and language arts for eight years and was an education administrator for another eight years before beginning an academic career in Education Studies at the University of Oregon. She has been teaching future teachers about the social context of schooling for six years. Her primary research interests are in gender and sexuality studies in education through the lens of post-structural feminist theory and queer theory. Her research considers sexual orientation and gender identity in classrooms and other educational settings. In 2010 Julie and Tina Gutierez-Schmich developed UOTeachOUT (http://uoteachout.com/). Entering its sixth year, this conference is an extension of the course Equality of Opportunity: Education as Homophobia.

Eric Nava is a veteran illustrator/artist of the computer game industry, working as a 2D/UI Artist for over 20 years. His work can be seen on various genres and platforms via—PlayStation, PC, Xbox, Gameboy Advance, Mobile (pre-iPhone), iPod, and iPhone. He has a background in Illustration from the Academy of Art University in San Francisco and studied Commercial Art at Chabot College. His soft skills include leading projects, mentoring, troubleshooting, and building team moral. Over the years, Eric has shown and won numerous awards for his exceptional traditional work in pencil and oils. In the spring of 2014, he was showcased as a Featured Artist in Style magazine.

Elise Paradis, Ph.D., is an Assistant Professor in the Leslie Dan Faculty of Pharmacy at the University of Toronto. She is also a Scientist at the Wilson Centre. She is a versatile researcher who combines qualitative and quantitative methodologies to the study of collaboration and the health professions. Before coming to Toronto, Elise was Assistant Professor at the University of California, San Francisco. She received her Ph.D. in Sociology of Education from Stanford University in 2011.

Elizabethe Payne, Ph.D., is Founding Director of QuERI—The Queering Education Research Institute©, a research and policy initiative dedicated to bridging the gap between research and practice to create more LGBTQ affirming school environments. She is also Visiting Associate Professor and Interim Director of the LGBT Social Science and Public Policy Center at Hunter College's Roosevelt House (CUNY). As a sociologist of education, she specializes in qualitative research methodology, critical theory, youth culture, queer girlhoods, bullying, and LGBTQ issues in education. QuERI will be located in Hunter College's LGBT Social Science and Public Policy Center at Roosevelt House through summer 2016. www.queeringeducation.org.

Julie L. Pennington, Ph.D., is a Professor of Literacy Studies in the College of Education at the University of Nevada, Reno. Her research and teaching focus on how literacy teachers' knowledge and dispositions related to diversity connect to their teaching practices.

Sean Robinson, Ph.D., is an Associate Professor of Higher Education and Student Affairs at Morgan State University, in Baltimore. He has over 20 years' experience in a multitude of educational settings at all levels. His primary teaching and research areas include leadership and teaching for social justice, student identity development, organizational behavior, and research methods.

Michael Sadowski, Ph.D., is the author of *In a Queer Voice: Journeys of Resilience from Adolescence to Adulthood* and *Portraits of Promise: Voices of Successful Immigrant Students*, both published in 2013. He also is the editor of the Youth Development and Education book series for Harvard Education Press and Director of the Bard Early College-Hudson Initiative.

Stacy E. Schupmann, M.S., hails from Southern California where she longboards, stays strong as one of the couples married before Prop 8, and hangs out with her wife, brand new daughter, and West Highland white terriers. She spends her time working on college campuses and writing her blog (babyschup. wordpress.com). She is fully committed to the efforts of positivity, LGBTQA inclusiveness in all aspects of society, and challenging the status quo in the nicest way possible. After her mildly subversive behavior is over, Stacy enjoys the time outside of work where she serves as the resident beer expert among family and friends.

Melissa J. Smith, Ph.D., is Assistant Professor and Director of English Education at University of Central Arkansas, and Assistant Director of Research at QuERI–The Queering Education Research Institute©, a research and policy initiative dedicated to bridging the gap between research and practice to create more LGBTQ affirming school environments. Her primary research focus is on heterosexual, cisgender teachers who self-identify as Allies for LGBTQ students. She specializes in integrating LGBTQ content into teacher education and professional development and is currently developing professional development programming about integrating LGBTQ content into English/Language Arts curriculum in public schools.

Kevin Stockbridge, M.A., M.Div., is currently a doctoral candidate in education at Chapman University. He has been religious minister, a teacher of theology, Coordinator of Christian Service for an urban Catholic high school, and a caseworker at a group home for teenagers on probation. His experience includes 11 years of teaching at the middle and high school levels of Catholic schools and adult education. Kevin holds a Master of Arts in theology and a Master of Divinity with emphasis on ecumenical and inter-religious dialogue. Devoted to socially just education of both mind and spirit, Kevin's research interests include the experience of LGBTQI students in Catholic education and queer spiritual pedagogies.

Lynda R. Wiest, Ph.D., is a Professor at the University of Nevada, Reno. Her areas of scholarly interest include mathematics education, educational equity, and teacher education. She is also a Faculty Associate with the Gender, Race, and Identity program, an interdisciplinary program based in the College of Liberal Arts.

Anna V. Wilson, Ph.D., now retired and happily married to her wife, holds doctorates in criminology and education. She taught for over 35 years, wrote over 100 scholarly articles, made numerous conference presentations, and contributed to university life in a variety of ways. Along her academic journey, she underwent a personal transformation when she came out as a lesbian. This affected her scholarship, her theorizing, and the courses she both taught and developed along the way. She has long been established as an LGBTQ activist and scholar. Currently, her work has emerged into her second love—ArtEscapes—viewing the world and life through paintings.

INDEX

Note: Page numbers in **bold** are for figures, those in *italics* are for tables.